HAWAI'I
JOINS THE WORLD

HAWAI'I

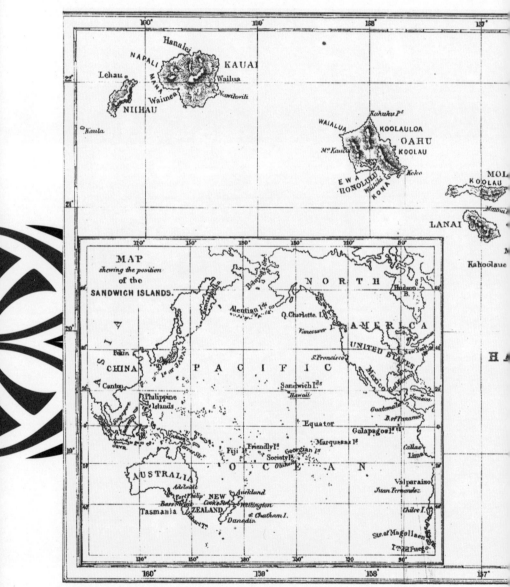

(Cummings, C.F. Gordon. Fire Fountains... London: William Blackwood & Sons, 1883.)

JOINS THE WORLD

Walter F. Judd

Mutual Publishing
Honolulu Hawaii

Cover art. The Hawaiian flag on Honolulu Fort, 1853. (From Paul Emmert's oil painting of Honolulu Fort in the Hawaiian Historical Society). King Ka-mehameha I began to fly the Hawaiian flag at the time of the War of 1812 between Great Britain and the United States. It indicated friendship with both warring nations. The United States was recognized by the eight white, red and blue stripes in the field, representing the old American Grand Union flag, and also the eight islands of the Hawaiian group. Great Britain was recognized by the Red Cross of St. George and the White Cross of St. Andrew joined on a blue union – the British Union Jack.

Library of Congress Catalog Card Number 98-68054

Design by Mark Abramson

First Printing, March 1999
1 2 3 4 5 6 7 8 9

Softcover ISBN 1-56647-227-x
Casebound ISBN 1-56647-233-4

Mutual Publishing
1215 Center Street, Suite 210
Honolulu, Hawaii 96816
Telephone: (808) 732-1709
Fax: (808) 734-4094
E-mail: mutual@lava.net
Url: http://www.pete.com/mutual

Printed in Taiwan

to
Jenifer and Elisabeth

PREFACE

Hawai'i Joins the World IS A NARRATIVE OF the rich part of our past during which the long-isolated Hawaiians progressed from Polynesian feudalism to become part of the world. Most of this evolution took place from Captain Cook's discovery of the islands for the western world in 1778 to the mid-1800s.

During this time the Hawaiian horizon was drastically lifted. The inevitable transformation was not easily achieved.

Among the overwhelming pressures were: startling new ideas acquired from contacts with strange and exciting people who had different perspectives, values and material goods; Christian ethics changed the Hawaiian way of life; literacy gave their world new dimensions; support for visiting vessels and the sale of sandalwood began economies which caused many commoners who lived under serf-like conditions to become free laborers; confirming the chiefs' inheritance of lands led to fee simple ownership; the feudal control of leaders evolved to a constitutional monarchy; "gunboat diplomacy" and the eventual recognition of sovereignty by the major powers led to further changes.

The most significant convulsion was made early on – purely and solely by Hawaiian leaders – when they abolished, as false, their traditional religion and intertwined kapu (forbidden) system of government.

While viewing the strivings of the islanders to evolve to a modified and different society, it is worth noting that the Hawaiian islands were the only significant Pacific group not taken possession of by one of the major powers during this era.

History is made by people. One should evaluate from the view-point of "who-did-what" during preceding events – rather than using today's hindsight. The following account tells of important and lesser figures whose efforts, pro and con, were part of this matrix.

What is known about a minor chief named Ke-ku-anao'a (1794-1868) is traced throughout the unfolding changes. He provides us with basic information about a Hawaiian chief's way of life and social norms. The narrative arbitrarily begins with yesteryear's ramifications of Ke-ku-anao'a's 1794 birth and informs about his younger years under the system of kapu.

Ke-ku-anao'a's career in secondary kingdom roles is tracked during the ensuing course of events until he became the important governor of the island of O'ahu, charged with day-to-day dealings with white men at Honolulu. Ke-ku-anao'a married a high lineage chiefess and became father of Kings Ka-mehameha IV and V.

The recounting of this period of history ends with the death of King Ka-mehameha III in December 1854, for by that time Hawaiians were well on their way to western-style civilization.

Significant reference material quoted or referred to is indicated by – bibliography source number : page number.

TABLE OF
CONTENTS

LIST OF ILLUSTRATIONS

LIST OF
ILLUSTRATIONS

PROLOGUE

A SOMEWHAT DETAILED DESCRIPTION OF Ke-ku-anaoʻa and his background are worth examining for several reasons. He not only straddled two worlds, he did it successfully. This was unusual among Hawaiians of his time. He also came to a rare understanding of white men and the western way of life.

Mataio Ke-ku-anaoʻa was born January 9, 1794 in Hilo, Hawaiʻi. He was an aliʻi (chief class) and named for the tall masts of British Naval Captain George Vancouver's ship then visiting just offshore.[14:352]

His mother was Inaina, daughter of Pupuka, a prominent Oʻahu chief.[43:223n] His father is accepted to have been Nahiolea, whose own father was a cousin of Ke-kau-like, ruler of Maui, and whose mother came from the powerful aliʻi family I of Hilo, Hawaiʻi.[43:223n] It has been handed down that Inaina had two husbands at the time of Ke-ku-anaoʻa's birth, the second one a Hawaiʻi chief named Kiʻi-lawe-au.[*][58:146] As it may be, Hawaiian genealogists considered that lineage from the mother was superior proof, and accepted current mate as father.

Ke-ku-anaoʻa's father, Nahiolea, had two important half-brothers. Kaʻi-ana, descended on his father's side from Keawe, ruler of Hawaiʻi; and Na-makehaʻ, related to the ruler of Maui.[43:222 70:153, 173]

These three chiefs were noted and turbulent warriors who changed allegiances frequently. When the Maui ruler Ka-hekili successfully attacked Oʻahu in 1783, they were among the leaders. Then the three defected to aid some family-connected Oʻahu chiefs who were revolting against Ka-hekili, were defeated, and fled to Kauaʻi.[43:222] Nahiolea and Na-makehaʻ wended their way back to

---

* Not to be confused with Kiʻi-lawe-au (w), mother of Hawaiʻi island chief Ke-kua-o-ka-lani.[70:209]

Hawai'i. Ka'i-ana went with Captain John Meares to the Orient and Northwest for three years, 1787–1790, before returning to the island of Hawai'i. There he became a powerful war leader and almost rival of Ka-mehameha, ruler of that island.

Ka'i-ana and Nahiolea were with Ka-mehameha when he invaded Maui and O'ahu after Ka-hekili died in 1794. They defected en route to aid the Maui warriors then defending O'ahu. Both were slain at the Battle of Nu'uanu April–May 1795.[43:348 58:146]

The remaining half-brother, Na-makeha', did not respond to Ka-mehameha's call for forces to invade Kaua'i, and began a rebellion among the people of Hilo, Puna and Kau. He was defeated, and sacrificed in January 1797.[43:222n 70:174 84:16]

Ke-ku-anao'a's father, Nahiolea, was killed at the Battle of Nu'uanu by two Hawai'i island chiefs who were "older/senior cousins."[58:146] His wife, Inaina, was with him but no mention was made of her fate. Normally the family of a traitor would be also killed, or sacrificed. Strangely enough, Nahiolea's bones were deposited in the Hale-o-Keawe heiau on Hawai'i as a mark of respect.[58:139] Customs and practices in a case like this are not understood today – although perhaps a clue is the fact that these Hawai'i and Maui ali'i were closely related. Somehow the one-year-old Ke-ku-anao'a survived.

The old Hawaiian society had a great impact on the first third of his life. Thereafter the Hawaiians evolved toward westernization on their own initiative and modified values.

Ancient Hawaiian society was similar to feudalism with a small, rigid upper class of chiefs and chiefesses (ali'i). Learned and professional people were in a small "middle" class (kahuna), with the bulk of the population being commoners (maka'ainana) who lived under serf-like conditions. There was no upward mobility for them. Downgrading from an upper level occurred if one did not know his ali'i lineage and could not convince learned genealogists.

There were apparently 11 degrees of chiefs[71:4] descended from a god-like figure or early ruler. A chief of the highest rank would have the purest bloodline by mating brother and sister (ni'aupi'o), and the lowest degree (ali'i maka'ainana) would be the offspring of a chief and a commoner.

It appears that, although of good Maui–O'ahu lineage, Ke-ku-anao'a belonged to the ninth degree, that of kaukau ali'i. This came to light after forces from the island of Hawai'i conquered the others.[72:207]

So when the various genealogists considered ali'i stature, forebears and power and location came into consideration. A complicated matter… Suffice it to say that Ke-ku-anao'a was of low ali'i caste.

The only way one could hope to raise one's status was by marriage or hanai (adoption) into a higher rank.

Adoption, usually at birth, was a customary practice of the ali'i. It bound one's family with another of equal or higher caste. Aside from raising one's bloodline, adoption endeavored to concentrate ancestry, prestige and power. There may have been finite differences between "hanai" (adoption), "kahu" (guardian) or "kahu hanai" (foster parent), but the end result was being raised in another's household with character formation by others than one's natural parents.

Lucy Thurston, wife of Rev. Asa Thurston, recorded her western opinion in 1825:[133:89] "They dispose of their children without one idea of building up a family of brothers and sisters. Indeed, parents are tacked together very loosely. They come together and separate as convenience and inclination dictate. One man will have several wives, or one woman will have several husbands. Here is a mass of humanity in a chaotic state."

Research has not discovered any evidence that Ke-ku-anao'a was adopted at birth, but it would have been most unusual if he had not been. It was customary, and there is no valid reason why this should not have occurred (only the higher-born sometimes felt they could not improve their bloodline). It is hypothesized that Ke-ku-anao'a was hanai because:

1 He probably survived his father's fate – killed for being a traitor – by being hanai, a member of another's family.
2 In an instance of "like seeks out like," one of his father's Maui ali'i cousins could have become his kahu hanai.
3 Ke-ku-anao'a soon served in the ruler's court. This may very well be attributed to the influence of Ka-'ahu-manu, Ka-mehameha's favorite queen, and Ka-lani-moku, then Ka-mehameha's chief administrative officer, both of whom had been brought up together on Maui. The fact that Ke-ku-anao'a was later in the retinue of Liholiho (Ka-mehameha II) on his 1823 trip to Great Britain is also significant.
4 One can't help but be struck by the similar careers of Ka-lani-moku and Ke-ku-anao'a. Both were lower grade ali'i who rose to great stature through their loyalty, integrity and accomplishments. As a general statement, the ruggedly independent ali'i of the time

were not noted for these characteristics. It is also possible that Ka-lani-moku became mentor of Ke-ku-anao'a. During the reign of Ka-mehameha II Ke-ku-anao'a performed administrative duties under Ka-lani-moku's younger brother Boki, then governor of the island of O'ahu.

Clans used poetic license in describing the relationships of their extended families. For example, Ke-ku-anao'a at one time referred to himself as "younger brother of Boki," and Ka-'ahu-manu was "aunt-in-law." [70:291] [58:141] This raises the question about another tantalizing unknown, "Kapoo, elder sister," who willed property to Ke-ku-anao'a in 1834. [14:347-48] Was she his natural sister, in-law sister, sister in an adopted family, or clan sister? There was also a Chief Kapoo who reared Ka-'ahu-manu and Ka-lani-moku. [58:141]

There is one clue as to who may have adopted Ke-ku-anao'a – he was willed several pieces of property by Chief Kinopu, who died in 1840. [14:348-50] Their association went back to at least 1819. Research finds only two small references to Kinopu – in both he was praised as a chief who was trusted and useful to Ka-mehameha. [14:348] [58:51] Alas, no hanai proof…

2

EARLY YEARS

To be a baby boy chief in a chief's compound was bliss. Hawaiians had a love of children, and Ke-ku-anao'a did not want for comforting arms and attendant wet nurses in the chiefess' retinue. Based on his adult health and achievements, his early years can be imagined as follows: the infant grew quickly and soon began to crawl and scramble around with chortles of glee. Recognition of whose arms were comforting was soon followed by determined efforts to attempt walking and talking. He was introduced to the sea and could paddle about almost as soon as he could walk. How much fun the ocean was with its constant motion and waves. He learned early on that sea water wasn't for drinking.

When Ke-ku-anao'a was weaned from mother's milk, he would have been taken to the hale mua (men's eating house) to be raised by men. Like all Hawaiians he was now under the eating kapu (forbidden) and no longer allowed to take food with women.[83:87]

The ability to communicate increased day by day and was a delightful accomplishment. Vocabulary and comprehension blossomed. Schooling began.

A boy was first taught survival necessities. If he ever heard "kapu moe" (prostrate yourself), he was to immediately fall to the ground in a prone position and remove any other clothing than his malo (loin cloth). Kapu moe meant the coming of a chief of the highest caste, or his garments or possessions. Not to honor him meant death. Death was also the penalty for casting one's shadow on a high chief, wearing a high chief's garments, entering his presence other than crawling, and obeying many other laws. Lesser forms of respect were due to chiefs of lower caste. Ke-ku-anao'a, being an ali'i, had far fewer requirement for respect than the maka'ainana (commoners).

There were many kapu, most established by the ali'i to preserve their superior beings and authority over the maka'ainana. They had a powerful sense of their own sacredness or divinity.[54:36]

A number of kapu directed the way of life for Hawaiians and assured a disciplined society. Death or mutilation was the usual penalty for infraction. To transgress was a psychic sin – and those who were not apprehended usually withered away and died. Kapu were also intertwined with the Polynesian religion.

The Hawaiians strove to make the unknown, the future, and the present their allies through strong spiritual beliefs and practices. Major Polynesian gods were Kane, deity of life, sunlight and fresh water; Lono, deity of peaceful pursuits, fertility and the harvest; and Ku, special deity of the ali'i, warriors and warfare. The latter was offered human sacrifices. A host of lesser akua (gods) were the spiritual guardians of professions, occupations, families, locations, etc. Religious structures (heiau) were constructed to venerate the gods and they were represented by stone and wooden images.

A supreme god, Io or Oi-e, creator of all things, was known only to the high priests and ali'i.[54:43]

Ke-ku-anao'a must have avidly listened to and memorized many myths and stories of the past. It was necessary to be thoroughly drilled and recite his entire genealogy in order to prove his ali'i ancestry.

He would have naturally played with other boy chiefs, including some vigorous games which brought suppressed tears. Elementary boxing, wrestling and use of weapons provided great fun for this husky youngster who had the promise of fulfilling the stature of his warrior ancestors.

Circumcision was part of the religious rite that installed Ke-ku-anao'a into the manhood of the hale mua. Family and friends gathered as a pig was cooked and offered to the gods. Four men held him fast while a priest performed his important task with a sharp piece of bamboo.[83:93-94] One may be sure that Ke-ku-anao'a did all he could to be stoic…

At about this time, important changes were occurring in Hawaiian society as a whole. Ka-mehameha, conqueror of the islands, had moved his court to Honolulu to better control the recently conquered island and participate directly in trade with westerners who came to that harbor. He also took his court on frequent visits to the other islands.

It was customary for the ruler to have a number of young ali'i boys as his personal attendants. One may be sure that selection was avidly vied for as the boys would be directly under their ruler's eyes. These attendants had to be highly disciplined, as carelessness could easily violate a kapu and mean death.[58:59] They crawled and scurried around very carefully.

Somehow there was enough influence brought to bear that Ke-ku-anao'a was selected. He probably started helping take care of or move the ruler's garments and possessions, then later progressed to such court duties as using a small kahili or coconut rib fan to chase away flies. The senior task was the most trusted and honored – custody of and providing the ruler's spittoon when needed. The spittoon-bearer was responsible for none of the spittle getting into the hands of a sorcerer with evil intent who might use it to pray the ruler to death.[18:13]

Ke-ku-anao'a was 10 years old in the spring of 1804. There was great excitement as Ka-mehameha was poised to launch an invasion of Kaua'i, the only island in the group not under his control. It had taken five years to prepare and assemble some 7,000 warriors, 800 Peleleu canoes (large single canoes lashed together to form double canoes, rigged with mainsail and jib) and 21 schooners. Now they had to cross the difficult 61-mile Ka-'ie'ie Waena channel between O'ahu and Kaua'i.

But...the gods were adverse. An epidemic called mai okuu (perhaps cholera or bubonic plague) suddenly began to spread. It was thought to have arrived from China on a sandalwood trading vessel. Thousands died throughout the islands. Ka-mehameha himself was very ill, but managed to overcome it. The pestilence took its toll for three months, and the invasion was bitterly called off.[77:49] [125:95-97] [70:187-90]

After this, Ke-ku-anao'a was sent to the retinue of Ka-mehameha's highest born son, Liholiho. Liholiho was the eldest son of Keopu-o-lani, who had the highest ali'i caste of ni'aupi'o. In 1801, when the boy was five, Ka-mehameha had designated Liholiho as head of the worship of the gods.[70:187-88] Ke-ku-anao'a was only three years older than Liholiho, and became more of a punahele (companion) rather than attendant.

Ke-ku-anao'a's physique and now disciplined temperament showed promise of his becoming a war chief. He was sent for several months to Napuauki's lua school.*[58:68-69] This was followed by vigorous training in javelin-throwing (lono maka-ihe), spear-thrusting,

---

* Pukui/Elbert dictionary (p. 196) defines lua as hand-to-hand fighting that included bone-breaking, quick turns and twists of the spear, noosing and leaping.

pole-vaulting (ku-pololu), single-stick (kaka-laau), rough-and-tumble wrestling (kaala) and boxing (kui-alua).[83:65]

Ka-mehameha endeavored to conciliate the angry god who had caused the failure of his invasion of Kaua'i. Upon the advice of priests, he rebuilt the Papa'ena'ena heiau on the slopes of Leahi (Diamond Head). There was a 10-day kapu when the work was completed, and a ceremonial sacrifice of 400 hogs, coconuts, and bananas, and three men.[131:23]

Half of Ka-mehameha's counselors had perished in the mai okuu epidemic and they were replaced by their sons. His astute and favorite queen, Ka-'ahu-manu, began attending council meetings and her power increased. Some of her lands were proclaimed pu'uhonua, places of refuge (from any death penalty).[70:313] Ka-lani-moku became chief counselor. Westerners began calling him the "Iron Cable of Hawaii" and "William Pitt," the name of the long-serving British Prime Minister.

Ka-mehameha still had his eye on the island of Kaua'i. Conquest by diplomacy was attempted, based primarily on the advice of three trusted westerners: John Young, Isaac Davis and William Shaler. A number of chiefs went back and forth negotiating.

The ruler of Kaua'i, Ka-umu-ali'i, came to Honolulu in 1810 aboard and under the protection of a western vessel. No doubt realizing that he couldn't win a war against such enormous odds, he offered his island and people. Ka-mehameha told him to return to Kaua'i and retain his power, subject to acknowledgment of fealty to Ka-mehameha. It was agreed.[77:50 70:196 80:29]

Ke-ku-anao'a reached age 16 in 1810, a full-grown, husky and mature young warrior chief versed in weapons, warfare and leadership. He'd even had some training on cannons and muskets, which Ka-mehameha had utilized so effectively. He continued as a companion to Liholiho, and began to periodically train the militia – where every able-bodied man was required to serve.

As in his later life, he probably had the same boundless energy. He also must have started to perform junior management and administrative tasks. (A decade later he was selected to accompany Liholiho to Great Britain as treasurer, so had to have gained experience earlier on.) These tasks were under the authority and direction of Ka-lani-moku, now functioning as prime minister. Here is the connection to him being Ke-ku-anao'a's mentor. Here is where the youth began to absorb the older man's integrity.

3

WHITE MEN

WHITE MEN. THEY WERE NO LONGER RAR-ities but still objects of curiosity and interest. How different than the Hawaiians. So different that Ka-mehameha had exempted them from the kapu, other than those concerning religious structures. By 1810, there must have been close to a hundred white men living in the islands off and on.

Chiefs prided themselves on having one or more people skilled in working iron, boatbuilding, and the use and repair of muskets and cannons. Ka-mehameha had two white men, John Young and Isaac Davis, both forcibly detained from their vessels. During the ruler's warfare, they had been in charge of the very effective cannons. Ka-mehameha thought so highly of John Young that he was given the ruler's niece as a wife and made governor of the home island of Hawai'i.*

Ke-ku-anao'a took a great interest in western vessels. A vast number of trees had been laboriously shaped into planks, and some were somehow curved. It took a lot of doing! They were fastened together and caulked watertight with a strange black substance. The tall masts, yards, the superior material of the sails and bewildering number of ropes! The ships appeared seaworthy and obviously required great skill to operate. These vessels were greatly respected and admired. He no doubt understood that they had sailed many days from some far off unknown place to get here.

Almost a dozen ships were now coming each year. Some were large vessels on what were called exploring expeditions. Most were smaller, and most were American. The reason they came was to stop briefly for water, firewood, salt, hogs, foodstuffs – especially fruit – and women. The men who came ashore after many days at sea were wild for female company, and the Hawaiian women were receptive

* He became one of Queen Emma's grandfathers.

9

to these strange light-skinned men. Ke-ku-anao'a certainly noticed that some children being born today had lighter skins. Some were darker, as some of the seamen were popolo (blacks).

Almost all ships visited briefly before heading north and northeast to secure furs to take to a place called China, where they were much in demand for garments during cold weather. Ke-ku-anao'a was allowed to stroke a pelt. So much hair so close together and smooth to the touch. The pelts were certainly warm when wrapped around his arm. Some said that the fur trade had been good for 20 years but animals were now getting hard to find.[22:72]

Hawaiian sandalwood was probably discovered by westerners when their ships' cooks burned the fragrant wood. There were two varieties in the islands: ili-ahi (Santalum), a small shrub to a medium sized tree; and naio (Myoporum sandwicense, bastard sandalwood). Ili-ahi wood was found to be desired in China. The trade began about the time Ke-ku-anao'a was born and flourished to about 1825.[25:219]

Chiefs sent their men to the uplands and mountains to laboriously cut trees for export. The usual two to eight inch diameter trunks were cut into pieces three to four feet long. The logs were then carried to the shore and tied into bundles weighing a picul (133½ pounds). Agriculture suffered due to the absence of farmers, and there was often hunger and even famine. Of course those who labored securing the ili-ahi were not compensated.

In early days sandalwood could be secured from individual chiefs, but soon Ka-mehameha made it a royal monopoly (except for Kaua'i). Early barter was for pieces of iron, clothing, muskets, cannons, gunpowder, beads, rum, and so forth. Later trading was for more armament, ships and Chinese silks, furniture, beads and ceramics. Exchange was sometimes unscrupulous and often to the advantage of traders when they supplied liberal amounts of lama (rum) during the negotiations. Great quantities of high-priced Chinese goods (i.e., silks, etc.) were stored away and allowed to decay.[5:156]

The Hawaiians quickly acquired a taste for rum and its effects. They knew awa (Jambosa), an intoxicating drink whose roots were chewed and mixed with saliva, then put in a bowl with some water for a short time. With no more preparation, the fluid was ready for drinking. The effect was more of a narcotic, and stupefying if taken in any great quantity.[25:216] [17:530]

When white men began to stay in the islands, they started distilling lama (rum) from sugar cane, 'okolehao (hard liquor) from the cooked roots of the ti (Cordyline terminalis), and ʻuwiʻuwi (swipes) from sweet potatoes. A mash would be prepared in an iron pot from a ship, and a musket barrel was used as a tube to conduct the vapor.[5:157]

These ardent spirits became very popular with the Hawaiians as a means of excitement and wildness. Excessive use was stupefying, just as with awa. Ka-mehameha, like other aliʻi, indulged to an excess until John Young dissuaded him.[5:157]

Among the white man's marvelous possessions was what they called "paper." It was in sheets, finer than kapa (bark cloth), and mostly "bound" into what they called "books." Small marks filled each paper and they could tell you what the marks meant. Ke-ku-anaoʻa tested this by having them "read" a sheet several times. It was the same each time!

He discerned the social order of aliʻi and makaʻainana aboard the ships with their officers and crew. But there was very little respect shown and the penalty for infractions of their kapu was not death. Maybe he figured that's why white men didn't follow the Hawaiian kapu – they were not used to living that way. Ka-mehameha accepted this…they were different…and this was probably why he exempted them from Hawaiian kapu.

Ke-ku-anaoʻa talked to those Hawaiians who had gone with the ships as seamen and traveled many days to strange places beyond the horizon. They told amazing stories about the "Northwest" – green and chilly, and filled with sea otters and land animals that were not difficult to catch; or about getting pelts from the local people, the "Indians." Those who had gone to China told tales of the teeming numbers of slant-eyed people who had such great things and lived in large groups. Those who had visited where the ships came from told of a cool green country with lots of people who lived in wooden and stone houses. Such marvelous things that the Hawaiians did not have! These others did not know taro or poi, but grew what they called "wheat" and "corn" in large fields. There were lots and lots of horses. Hawaiians knew about these strong animals – Captain William Shaler of the *Lelia Bird* and Richard J. Cleveland, supercargo, had brought a few horses to Hawaiʻi back in 1803.[64:10] The returned local seamen kept repeating, how many more people than Hawaiians…

Ke-ku-anaoʻa probably grew uneasy about Hawaiian women who went off with white men to isolated areas. He began to suspect the unbelievable – some of them, he was almost sure, were violating the kapu against men and women eating together. Worse, no doubt he had heard that some women were eating bananas and coconuts which were forbidden to them! There had been no apparent psychic harm... But this was a difficult situation for responsible ali'i. Ke-ku-anao'a was an orderly man, and it might have caused him to *almost* question the merits of such kapu! If so, he would have squirmed internally, because thoughts of that kind were close to heresy.

He would *never* question Ka-mehameha's judgment in allowing white men to disregard the kapu, but, the question kept arising: were not *all* men supposed to follow the kapu? That had been true for generations.

Ke-ku-anao'a was a disciplined young warrior chief. These matters must have been disquieting to him because he liked peace of mind and normalcy. The tide of incoming white men kept increasing with no sign that it might decline. So, if this was going to influence Hawaiian life, it behooved him to prepare for closer and more important contacts. He might have said to himself, let's face it, these changes are essential for the future. So he must listen more, and learn how to communicate fluently. After all, it was *his* country! There *may* be more unimaginable changes, and he wanted to be ahead of them instead of being dragged along behind them.

Ka-mehameha got restless and tired of Honolulu. He had enjoyed trading with the white men, especially acquiring western vessels, but the pleasure of that no longer attracted his interest. Some chiefs had begun to build bases of power in the newly acquired lands – he had heard about and sniffed at potential conspiracies, which were normal among Hawaiian ali'i. He moved his court to Kai-lua, Hawai'i in 1812. Potential traitors were required to come too, and remain under the ruler's eye. All cannons and muskets were brought to Kai-lua. In all ways, it was a strategic and powerful withdrawal.[70:197-98]

Boki, younger brother of Ka-lani-moku, was appointed Governor of O'ahu.[36:67] It is not known when Ke-ku-anao'a began working and supervising for him, although probably at this time.

Dr. Igor Sheffer of the Russian-American Company in Alaska was sent to the Hawaiian Islands to establish a foothold during the years 1815-17. He was also to seek restitution for a company vessel which had been recently wrecked and looted on Kaua'i. Sheffer arrived on November 7, 1815 and, as a medical doctor, had the good fortune to succor Ka-mehameha and his favorite queen, Ka-'ahu-manu. The ruler granted Sheffer the right to use a structure in Honolulu for a trading post.[94:5-8] There he was reinforced the following year by two vessels and 30 or more Aleut hunters, and went to Kaua'i.

Dr. Sheffer successfully negotiated with that island's ruler. Ka-umu-aliʻi, who pledged allegiance to the Emperor Alexander I, granted the Russian-American Company a monopoly on Kauaʻi sandalwood, allowed the Russians to establish trading posts, and guaranteed to restore what remained of their ship's cargo.[94:11] In return, Dr. Sheffer promised the protection of Russia against Ka-mehameha. This tantalizing shift of power included talk about a combined force to conquer the islands.[94:12] The Russian flag was flown over Kauaʻi. Several hundred Hawaiians began to build an octagonal fort at Wai-mea Bay, which was named Fort Elizabeth.[94:13]

In Honolulu the Russians expanded their trading post into a blockhouse with a mounted cannon and boldly flew their flag from the top. This caused an uproar among the westerners. John Young became alarmed, and, with a little urging, so did Ka-mehameha. He sent Ka-lani-moku and his first-born son, Pauli Kaʻo-lei-o-ku, with the Okaka "regiment" of Hawaiian warriors to Honolulu.[70:206 41:15] When the small number of Russians woke one morning, they found themselves surrounded by a large number of menacing armed soldiers. They capitulated peacefully and were permitted to go to Kauaʻi.[94:14] There they constructed two redoubts at Hanalei, which had been given to Dr. Sheffer.

John Young and Ka-lani-moku built a more substantial fort to guard Honolulu.[41:11-25] When quickly completed by the labor of thousands, it was a rectangular structure about 340 by 300 feet. The walls were 12 feet high and 20 feet thick at the base. They were faced with coral blocks cut from the nearby reef and filled with dirt and rubble. It was named Ke-kua-noku (thorny back) because of the 40 or more cannon mounted on the walls.

On November 24, 1816, Captain Otto von Kotzebue arrived at Kai-lua, Hawaiʻi, in the Russian Navy brig *Rurick*. The appearance of yet another subject of the Czar caused considerable excitement and apprehension. It took some talking to convince Ka-mehameha and his council that this was a friendly visit.★ Von Kotzebue repudiated any and all of Dr. Sheffer's actions.[75:19]

Ka-mehameha sent a number of messages and threats to Ka-umu-aliʻi, who finally expelled the Russians from Kauaʻi the following year.

★ We are indebted to this 1816 visit especially for the magnificent sketches and illustrations of the ship's draftsman, Louis Choris, and notably for the watercolor of Ka-mehameha in his red vest. (Located at the Honolulu Academy of Arts.)

CULTURAL
REVOLUTION

4

KE-KU-ANAOʻA WAS 25 AT the start of the year 1819, which proved to be a dramatic turning point.

Ka-mehameha had been failing for some time. He was about 61, an old man, compared with men all over the world. Just short of mid-year, he became seriously ill. Aliʻi began coming quietly to Kai-lua to maintain the customary vigil at the demise of an eminent per-sonage – out of respect, to appease the offended god, and so that the afflicted one would not be alone at the second great occurrence of his life. Ke-ku-anaoʻa was certainly among them, after having not only attended Ka-mehameha, but acting as a punahele (companion) of Liholiho.

In his final days, Ka-mehameha proclaimed his highest-born son, Liholiho, as his successor and deemed that the kahu (guardian) of his war god, Ku-kaʻili-moku, was to be his nephew Ke-kua-o-ka-lani. Such separation of inherited powers was typical of rulers and had caused generations of friction and strife.[20:209 77:62]

He announced to his assembled high chiefs that his favorite queen, Ka-ʻahu-manu, was to share power with Liholiho and have the title kuhina nui (regent/premier).[77:63-64] They accepted this departure from customary aliʻi succession as sensible. With her status and great capabilities, she had practically ruled during the past weeks and months. At the age of 23, Liholiho had no experience in government. One can surmise that Ka-mehameha knew his high-born son too well and appreciated Ka-ʻahu-manuʻs strength, and he could foresee difficult times ahead for the Hawaiian rule and way of life. Ka-mehameha was very shrewd and was farseeing – he knew his people.

A kai mimiki (tsunami) occurred in mid-April 1819. The kahuna kilokilo (seers) predicted that another disaster would follow the first. The time came. Ka-mehameha, conqueror of all the islands, joined his forebears at 2 am May 8, 1819. His final words were "Move on in my good way…" [56:228]

The assembled ali'i were the first to announce their ruler's death by wailing "Au-we! Au-we! Au-we!" (Alas! Alas! Alas!) This keening was heard and repeated by others until it spread from village to village and across the mountains to every part of the island. As early historian James J. Jarves stated (1843): "Night and day was the dismal sound prolonged; its first notes were low, gradually swelling until one full passionate burst of grief filled the air, and resounded among the neighboring rocks and hills, whose echoes threw back the cry. During the night its effect, as thus borne from party to party, from one valley to another, now rising into almost a shriek of bitterness, then subsiding into a low, murmuring sound, was startling and impressive. Watch-fires, surrounded by groups of both sexes, wailing and weeping violently, tearing their hair, and giving way to other more barbarous demonstrations of their sorrow, completed the scene." [40:68]

Final ceremonies for such a distinguished person were discussed. The subject of human sacrifices came up: [56:229]

> "If you obtain one man before the corpse is removed, one will be sufficient; but after it leaves this house, four will be required. If delayed until we carry the corpse to the grave,* there must be ten; but after it is deposited in the grave, there must be fifteen. Tomorrow morning there will be a Kapu, and if the sacrifice be delayed until that time, forty men must die."

Liholiho said "No" to these sacrifices, citing an earlier statement by his father, "The men are sacred to the ruler." [56:227]

The body was taken to a new small, thatched hale lua (house of the dead); wrapped in banana, wauke and taro leaves; placed in a shallow trench and covered with dirt. A fire was started over the trench to assist decomposition.

The remains were exhumed on the 10th day of the kumakena (mourning period). The bones were carefully arranged, wrapped in kapa, and then a sennit casket (ka-ai) was woven around the bundle. It was covered with red feathers and two round shells affixed to indicate eyes. The remaining residue was carefully collected and laid to rest far out at sea.

The evening of that last night the island was placed under a strict kapu for all to remain in their houses under penalty of death. Around

---

* The grave referred not to the final resting place of the ruler, but to what was done in the hale lua.

midnight High Chief Hoapili and a retainer took the ka-ai to a secret hiding place. Only the stars of the heavens know the location of Ka-mehameha's final resting place.[7:165]

As was traditional, the heir moved to another district during the kumakena. This was for his safety and so he would not participate in the frenzy of mourning. Liholiho went to adjoining Kohala, which was controlled by his cousin Ke-kua-o-ka-lani.

The kumakena was a time of uncontrollable grief and madness. The kapu were not observed. Many lost control and became pure savages. Liquor and awa flowed freely. Some took advantage of this lawless period to resolve old feuds. Every vice and crime occurred.[60:73]

A difficult situation arose when some sorcerers performed the kuni (burn) ceremony to discover who had caused the late ruler to die. There was a spellbound audience when the intoxicated High Chief Ke'e-au-moku, Ka-'ahu-manu's brother, broke several staffs around the fire. The sorcerers immediately concluded that Ka-'ahu-manu herself had been instrumental in the death. This startling conclusion indicated that there must have been strong ali'i political maneuvering and backing to permit the sorcerers to be so bold.[70:214]

As the mourning continued toward its peak, there was self-mutilation. Ears were mangled and tongues tattooed. Ka-'ahu-manu inflicted burns and incisions on her body.[12:92] Her younger brother, High Chief Kua-kini, knocked out two of his teeth,[86:368] and High Chief Boki lost four.[50:136]

There was a grand accession ceremony and feast at Kai-lua following the kumakena. Liholiho wore a red military uniform and a cocked hat trimmed with gold lace and feathers. He also wore an 'ahu'ula (feather cloak). He was escorted by two tall high chiefs carrying spears, his spittoon bearer, another carried his kahili (tall staff topped with a feather cylinder indicating his rank), and his chanting genealogist. Ka-'ahu-manu wore Ka-mehameha's feather cloak and helmet and leaned on a tall spear. She was flanked by the council of high chiefs and Ka-mehameha's other queens.

Ka-'ahu-manu made it clear to all that Ka-mehameha had established she would share the position of ruler. The council nodded concurrence. Liholiho agreed and also stated that his father's awards of lands to the chiefs should continue. The council appeared to be very pleased. Each chief could sell sandalwood from the land he controlled. This made them even more pleased. Ka-lani-moku would continue as "Prime Minister." High chiefs were confirmed to govern each island.

Ka-'ahu-manu casually asked if the kapu could continue to be ignored beyond the kumakena – especially the one prohibiting men and women eating together. To this Liholiho said, "No," and abruptly left. He returned to his cousin Ke-kua-o-ka-lani at Kohala – who favored total adherence to the ways of old. All kapu were to be enforced.

The French navy corvette *Uranie*, on an exploring and scientific expedition, arrived in August 1819 and visited for three weeks.[64:77] Captain Louis de Freycinet was accompanied by his wife, who had been smuggled aboard. She was a great curiosity, the first white woman the Hawaiians had seen. One may imagine their initial reaction to be – how many clothes! Among other events that took place, Abbe de Quelen baptized Ka-lani-moku as a Catholic in an impressive ceremony.[46:29] Later his younger brother Boki was also baptized.[46:41] Captain Freycinet concluded that political affairs were in a state of very uncertain equilibrium.[77:65] They depended on who now assumed power following the demise of a very strong ruler.

A great philosophical confusion was probably going on in the uneasy minds of all Hawaiians. On one hand, white men who had such marvelous things and did not observe the kapu or religion seemed to suffer no psychic harm. On the other hand, wasn't the age-old Hawaiian way of life inviolable? And...the always nagging question, were not the Hawaiian gods and kapu for *all* men? An intrusion had upset this ancient system and strangers came from places way beyond the horizon where there were many, many more people than in the islands. These white men were human beings *like us*, why should they have freer and less restrictive lives? It must have seemed that there was something basically *not* right.

Determined and powerful chiefesses such as Kuhina nui Ka-'ahu-manu and the highest-born Ke-opu-o-lani (Liholiho's mother) deplored kapu that placed them in secondary roles to men, both Hawaiian and white. The chiefesses were especially vehement about the prohibition of men and women eating together *and* the ban on any female consuming consecrated pork or the plentiful bananas and coconuts. They questioned the logical reason for these kapu. And, why couldn't women go into the heiau venerating the Hawaiian gods which were restricted to men? Chiefs and kahuna found these questions disquieting, and quite impossible to answer. This included the senior kahuna-pule (religious priests).

 Hawaiian leaders were logical and pragmatic, and not afraid to address these immense, all-important questions. After many small, informal discussions, a consensus gradually came about that few would object to change – if it should occur. This included the most powerful high priest, Hewahewa of the order of Holoa-e.[71:7]

 Because Ka-mehameha had designated Liholiho as head of the worship of the gods at age five, back in 1801,[70:187-88] he had been thoroughly indoctrinated in all aspects of the Hawaiian religion. Many kapu were intertwined with spiritual beliefs, so any change had to take religion into consideration. Liholiho had to be the instrument of change and convincing him must have been a tremendous task, yet he too was pragmatic and liked to discuss logic. He did recognize that traditional moral forces had been weakened.[9:38] Liholiho did a lot of soul-searching and, at the same time, a lot of drinking. Many different pressures were brought to bear, some very well coordinated. Liholiho was slow to yield. As the saying goes, it took lots of doing, and the progressive forces were finally successful.

There was a great 'aha'aina (feast) at Kai-lua about the first of November 1819.[77:65] Liholiho came in his double canoe and was greeted by Ka-'ahu-manu, Ke-opu-o-lani, Hewahewa, Ka-lani-moku, counselors and other high chiefs. He was escorted to a large halau (open-sided thatched structure). Two long tables laden with food had been prepared, one for the chiefs and one for the chiefesses. The halau was surrounded by a large crowd of commoners,[9:41-42] drawn by rumors that something significant was about to happen. Liholiho walked around, suddenly sat between Ka-'ahu-manu and Ke-opu-o-lani and began to eat rapidly. Those assembled were stilled. There were shouts. "Ai noa – the eating kapu is broken!"[27:68] "The kapus are at an end, and the gods are a lie!"[9:42] Hewahewa went to the nearby heiau and lit a torch to the structures and idols. He and Ka-lani-moku then sent messengers to all parts of the island and the other islands announcing that the gods and kapu had been overthrown, and to burn the religious places.[9:42] The fact that a torch and messengers were on hand suggests careful preparation and giving in to an inevitable decision. The feast continued long into the festive night. All women, whether chiefesses or commoners, ate pork, bananas, coconuts and other foods that in the past could have resulted in a death sentence.

But…not all agreed with losing their gods. Some idols were rescued, stolen and hidden away. Not all were so sure about losing the kapu. Most religious priests were placated by the continuing use of heiau lands for their benefit.

Ke-kua-o-ka-lani, guardian of the war god, was violently against the drastic actions that had overthrown both spiritual beliefs and laws. His solution to all questions was to absolutely go back to the ways of old, and kill all the white men in the islands and permit no more to land.[46:20] He went to Ka-'awa-loa and was gradually joined by a sizable number of dissenting chiefs, kahuna and commoners.[27:69] Others gathered at Hamakua. A pervasive opinion of the time was, "No sin of ungodly rulers, by which they lost their kingdoms, is equal to this sin of Liholiho."[9:42]

A delegation led by Ke-opu-o-lani went to Ka-'awa-loa to reason with Ke-kua-o-ka-lani, but to no avail.[38:154-55]

On both sides men were armed and formed into combat units. There had been no fighting for 23 years, and most of these men were barely trained militia who had not been blooded. Ka-lani-moku was Liholiho's war leader and Ka-'ahu-manu commanded a flanking force of swivel cannon armed double canoes. One may be sure that Ke-ku-anao'a, a tough, trained warrior chief, led a fighting group.

The battle over kapu occurred at Kuamo'o on or about November 21, 1819. Kekua-o-ka-lani and his wife were killed. Amnesty was granted to his fleeing warriors; some 60 men died and more of the wounded succumbed later. The Hamakua insurrection was suppressed with ease.

After this news spread, people were convinced that the religion and kapu had really been struck down. The discontinuance of priest-led religious services contributed to the general demise, and yet it can be said that the old beliefs died slowly.

Ka-mehameha, 1816.
Watercolor by Louis
Choris. (von Kotzebue,
Otto. Voyage of
Discovery in the South
Sea... London: Sir
Richard Phillips & Co.,
1821)

RIGHT. Ka-'ahu-manu, 1816. Sketch by Louis Choris. (von Kotzebue, Otto. Voyage of Discovery in the South Sea... London: Sir Richard Phillips & Co., 1821)

BELOW. Liholiho, 1816. Sketch by Louis Choris. (von Kotzebue, Otto. Voyage of Discovery in the South Sea... London: Sir Richard Phillips & Co., 1821)

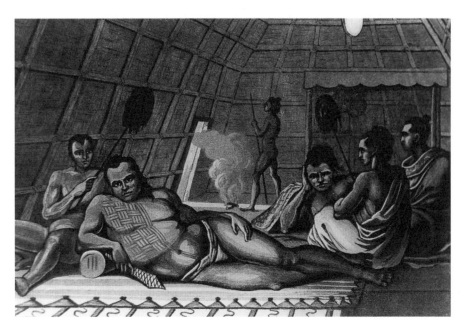

On the afternoon of March 30, 1820, the American brig *Thaddeus* rounded ʻUpolu Point on the island of Hawaiʻi. When she came into the lee of the high mountains, she ran out of wind. The captain ordered a ship's boat ashore to discover the current state of affairs and the whereabouts of the ruler. Sailors shortly returned with astonishing news:[133:26]

> *Ka-mehameha is dead; — his son*
> *Liholiho is king; — the kapus*
> *are abolished: — the images*
> *are burned; — the temples are*
> *destroyed. There has been war.*
> *Now there is peace.*

The American Protestant missionaries fell to their knees — two clergymen, two teachers, a medical doctor, printer and farmer — along with their wives, five children and three Hawaiian helpers who had somehow wended their way to New England.

DIVINE PROVIDENCE! All prayed in gratitude for the unexpected Hawaiian spiritual void, and the unforeseen open path ahead.

But it wasn't to be all that easy...

Light breezes brought the brig to anchor off Kai-lua on April 4, 1820, after 164 days from Boston. The missionaries went ashore and met the ruler and Hewahewa, the former high priest. Hewahewa, a learned man in his own culture, stated that he had always believed in one supreme god, such as the white men did, and cordially welcomed his brother priests.[133:28] Rev. Hiram Bingham regarded him as "an object of pity."[17:88]

The main observation of all the missionaries concerned the *very* scanty dress of the Hawaiians. The men wore a malo (narrow girdle around the waist and loins that exposed their backsides); the women were clad in a pa'u (bark cloth wrapped around the hips to the knees but leaving breasts bare). When the weather was cool, both sexes added a kihei (mantle similar to a Roman toga), which provided not only warmth but also some modesty. Many chiefs and chiefesses had secured some coveted western garb. Commoners had partial clothing gotten from seamen by trading.

The missionaries did not realize that the chiefesses considered large size a standard of beauty and stature. As an example, Lucy Thurston recorded that Kalakua, one of Ka-mehameha's dowager queens, had "limbs of giant mold" and estimated her weight "at three hundred lbs., and even more." She wore a pa'u "consisting of ten thicknesses of the bark cloth three or four yards long, and one yard wide wrapped several times round her middle, and confined by tucking it in on one side" [133:31] and wore a loose dress over the pa'u.

Talks began. The next eight days were frustrating. Rev. Bingham addressed Liholiho and the assembled high chiefs and chiefesses: [17:86]

> "As ambassadors of the King of Heaven, having the most important message to communicate, which could be received, we make... the offer of the Gospel of eternal life, and propose to teach Liholiho and his people the written life-giving Word of the God of heaven...we ask permission to settle in his country, for the purpose of teaching the nation Christianity, literature and the arts."

The impressive and ambitious charge of this small band of missionaries was to convert some 140,000 Hawaiians for the purpose of "raising up the whole people to an elevated state of Christian civilization." [59:27]

Liholiho was slow to consent. He had just abolished their age-old religion and was not so sure another should be accepted. But, he agreed to consider it.

Meetings over the next few days brought forth some unexpected questions. Liholiho had five queens. He is reported to have said, "If I receive and patronize these missionaries I shall not be allowed but one wife." [17:88] It is easy to imagine he had other considerations; maybe our great friends, the English, would be averse to American missionaries in Hawai'i; we understand that the white man's religion of France is the only true religion.

There were comparisons of great Hawaiian gods with Christian gods (i.e., the Holy Spirit). Difficult questions to discuss at any time, but especially so when the missionaries knew only elementary Hawaiian and the Hawaiians only elementary English, and both discovered that interpreters left much to be desired.

Eventually, on April 11, 1820, the king and kuhina nui granted the missionaries permission to land and stay for one year on probation. Liholiho wanted one clergyman, the doctor and two of the Hawaiian helpers to stay with him, the rest could go to Honolulu, where most white men wanted to be. By ballot Rev. Asa Thurston stayed with the ruler's court and Rev. Hiram Bingham went to Honolulu. This must have been a difficult choice. On one hand, the importance of being with the ruler was that conversions must start with the ali'i leaders; on the other hand, Honolulu was becoming the commercial center of the islands and planned headquarters of the mission. (Unbeknownst to Liholiho was a plan to send the two teachers to the island of Kaua'i.)

The missionaries established three priorities. First, become fluent in the Hawaiian language so they could completely communicate Christianity. Second, reduce the spoken language to written words, and third, teach the Hawaiians to read and write. They had learned the bare rudiments of Hawaiian by rote from the few Hawaiians in New England and those who were on their vessel en route to Hawai'i. The only written Hawaiian words available were the various phonetic spellings of locations and important personages which had been recorded by earlier visitors.

The year of probation passed rapidly. There was some initial schooling in English for the chiefs and chiefesses. They were used to memory knowledge, and readily absorbed more than the few action words they already knew. Missionary wives were much in demand to make garments for the chiefesses. Each covered most of the body and have come down to us today called mu'umu'u (similar to a Mother Hubbard).

The missionaries proved to be acceptable good people and were permitted to stay. Hawaiian humor nicknamed them ai oeoe (long necks) as the women's bonnets gave their heads a long appearance.

It took over two years before Rev. Bingham concluded that they had progressed to the point where 24 chiefs and chiefesses "in some sense acknowledged Christianity." [17:174]

Sufficient Hawaiian words had been established by January 7, 1822 for a language primer to be printed. Liholiho was intrigued with the printing press. The missionaries were still having problems with reducing Hawaiian sounds to writing. He was asked if "L" or "R" ought to be used in spelling his name. He gave it thought, and stated that he preferred "R." However, the missionaries had settled on a 12-letter alphabet consisting of five vowels and seven consonants. "R" as not among them, so the ruler's name was spelled "L"iholiho.[17:158] The press never seemed to stop, and printed thousands of pages in Hawaiian, culminating 17 years later with the tremendous achievement of missionary translation and printing of the Bible in Hawaiian.

Kuhina nui Ka-'ahu-manu became interested in Hawaiian reading and writing. She ordered the entire adult population to become students. Missionaries, teach them all! Bright young men were made available to become teachers. They were schooled up to a certain level, went out and taught small groups of people, returned for more instruction and went forth again. This was a challenge to organize. It has been estimated that 500 Hawaiians were being schooled by September 1822[60:230] and that several thousand could read and write their own language by 1824.[7:188] Reading and writing was accepted with much interest and enthusiasm. Many soon began to exchange short letters.

The missionaries were greatly pleased, as it was a maxim with them that in order to preserve and raise the Hawaiian people and nation they must first save its language.[69:79] Literacy had come to the islands – the numbers of those who learned the skills increased by leaps and bounds.

The frugal missionaries were aghast at the huge prices chiefs paid for vessels, silks, furniture, and a variety of needless things. Payment was made in sandalwood. All men in a chief's district would be ordered to the mountains to secure the diminishing wood. This sometimes took days, and often caused hunger and even famine in their lowland home areas. Missionaries counseled the chiefs to use moderation and caution.

A growing antagonism grew between missionaries and traders who had such different goals in the islands. And the missionaries advocated moral values that curtailed white men's intercourse with Hawaiian women! Relations became bitter at times, and occasionally even violent.

In 1820 Liholiho bought *Cleopatra's Barge*, an elegant 83-foot yacht, for $90,000 worth of sandalwood. The ship had been built in

1816 for $50,000 and auctioned for $15,400 in 1818.[22:62] Her name was changed to *Haaheo o Hawai'i* (Pride of Hawai'i).[73:23-24] He also purchased the brig *Thaddeus*, which had brought the first missionaries to Hawai'i, for $40,000.[7:177 22:62] Both were in poor condition.[77:91n]

The missionaries at Honolulu had been allowed use of land at Ka-wai-a-ha'o, on the plain about half a mile from the harbor. In July of 1820 seven small thatched structures were put up for them.[48:82, 242] They received a prefabricated two-story wood house from Boston in February of 1821 and asked Liholiho for permission to erect it. His reply was: "No, my father never allowed a foreigner to build a house in his country except for the king." [17:126, 132 126:113] Some anti-mission-ary white traders spread rumors that the cellar of the house was for storing firearms and ammunition to be used against the ruler.[126:114] Several more requests to the ruler received negative responses. Missionary wives urged the ruler's queens to assist in getting approval. Eventually Liholiho said yes and the house was built. After that came the first Honolulu church, a 54 by 21 foot thatched struc-ture, erected between August 9 and September 15, 1821.[17:133 22:130]

Liholiho and Ka-'ahu-manu had moved their Court to Honolulu on February 4, 1821.[48:246] Apparently there were two major reasons. First, Honolulu was rapidly becoming the commercial center and contact point with important westerners. Second, it conformed to the significant adage that rulers kept unruly chiefs and chiefesses in their Court for better control. Boki was governor of O'ahu, and one can image that relations with his elder brother, the "prime minister" Ka-lani-moku, precluded his replacement. But there appears to have been a conflict of power between Ka-'ahu-manu and Boki.

At this time, Ka-'ahu-manu was described as being "tyrannical, haughty, disdainful and unfriendly." [10:128] After all, was she not kuhina nui? She would not tolerate any insubordination or partial compliance with her orders. This attitude must have put the missionaries on guard.

Boki was attracted to and yet repelled by the white man's world. Unsuccessfully, he sought a middle ground, and ended up with a lax administration that accepted westerners' excesses.[103:74 36:66] He enjoyed boisterous living and "became attached to those foreigners who were hostile to the mission." [70:276]

Ke-ku-anao'a was a senior administrative officer under Governor Boki in 1821.[58:146] He had the important task of levying and collecting foodstuffs from all over the island to support the Court. No small undertaking, as the Court sometimes exceeded a thousand persons.[7:180]

Ke-ku-anao'a was also in overall charge of weighing and delivering sandalwood. By this time he could speak passable English, and his burly, tough appearance no doubt precluded some cheating by traders and ship captains.

Like all ali'i, he married a number of times (five wives are recorded by history). His first was Ka-lehua of unknown parentage, "who had been his from the time of Ka-mehameha" and by whom he had a son, Pa'a-lua.[70:347] His second wife was Kauhi, daughter of Chief Mailou, "she was his wife when he went to Great Britain in 1823."[14:349-52] This chief could have been from Waialua and had his name variously spelled Maio[103:92-93] or Maiao.[70:248]

Liholiho came readily under Boki's influence. He too liked to party most of the time. It is easy to imagine that the ruler tried to escape the realities of the Hawaiian evolution which meant joining the world. His upbringing as titular head of the Hawaiian religion had not prepared him for such active considerations. Various contemporary writers described Liholiho as frank and humane, agreeable, inquisitive, idle, restless, dissipated and dissolute. Comments in Don Marin's 1821 journal included such as:[48:248-49] "10 March, king drunk; 12 March, the king not very drunk; 1 May, the king began to drink; and 3 May, the king sober." Ka-'ahu-manu's veto power over any of his independent actions vexed him. He respected her, but was he not ruler in his own right?

Liholiho did manage to personally change the course of events on July 21, 1821.[48:253] He was aboard a small sloop sailing to Ewa, and off Ka-lae-loa (Barbers Point), he instructed the helmsman to continue on to the island of Kaua'i. The sloop was very overloaded with some 30 passengers, and the rum bottle had passed freely. The wide channel was noted for being rough and had strong winds; the small craft had no compass, water or provisions. The passengers were aghast, except for the half-intoxicated ruler:[7:177]

"...spreading out the fingers of one hand, (he) said, 'Here is your compass; steer by this.' Twice the boat was nearly capsized, the seas broke over them, and his companions begged him to put back. 'No,' said the king, 'Bail out the water and go on. If you return with the boat, I will swim to Kauai.'"

The small craft, crammed with exhausted and thankful people, finally landed at Wai-mea early the following morning. The island's ruler, Ka-umu-ali'i, greeted Liholiho cordially, provided great hospitality, and confirmed his allegiance.

Shortly after, the *Haaheo o Hawai'i* came to Kaua'i with kuhina nui Ka-'ahu-manu and high chiefs and chiefesses for a lengthy visit and tour of the island.[73:31] When Liholiho and Ka-'ahu-manu returned to Honolulu, they were accompanied by Ka-umu-ali'i and his son and heir, Ke-ali'i-a-honui. (Some sources suggest that guile was used.)

Lucy Thurston recorded on O'ahu October 9, 1821:[133:64]

> "That night Kaahumanu associated with the king in the government of Hawaii, Maui, Oahu & c., and Kaumualii, tributary king of Kauai, reclined side by side on a low platform, eight feet square, consisting of between twenty and thirty beautiful mats of the finest texture. Then a black kapa (native cloth) was spread over them. The significance of it was, it now pronounced the royal pair to be husband and wife. An important political union was likewise peacefully effected, between the windward and leeward islands under one crown."

Kuhina nui Ka-'ahu-manu later also married Ke-ali'i-a-honui.[73:32] With a large entourage, they toured the windward islands May–June 1822, and went on to Kaua'i that August. The two brigs and two schooners were so loaded with people that there was barely standing room on the decks.[7:180] One may be sure that Boki went on these grand tours, while Ke-ku-anao'a probably remained in Honolulu to keep that island administration operating.

The fourth anniversary of Ka-mehameha's death was celebrated during the fortnight April 24–May 8, 1823.[7:181-82] Levies and gifts of foodstuffs such as fish, poi, bananas, chickens, dogs, and pigs were received by the Court. One can imagine that Ke-ku-anao'a achieved an almost impossible distribution for the many feasts. There was a grand procession of great splendor on the last day.[117:92-93]

Ka-mamalu, Liholiho's favorite queen and half-sister, rode in a highly decorated model whaleboat on a 30 by 12 foot platform of light spars on the shoulders of 70 men. She wore a red silk pa'u, was shaded by an immense Chinese umbrella, and attended by Ka-lani-moku (prime minister) and Na-ihe (national orator).

The Queens Kina'u and Ke-kau-'onohi were similarly borne in a double canoe. Queen Pauahi was carried on a couch. Queen Ke-kai-ha'a-kulou might have also participated. The ruler's younger brother, Kau-i-ke-aouli, and younger sister, Nahi-'ena'ena, were conveyed on four small bedsteads and escorted by High Chiefs Hoapili and Ka-iki-o-'ewa.

Ka-'ahu-manu wore 72 yards of scarlet and orange double kerseymere wrapped around her body so many times that her arms were supported horizontally.[26:11-12] Her husbands must have been in attendance, but history doesn't mention them on this occasion. Liholiho and companions, under the influence, rode horses bareback up and down the parade route. A bodyguard of 50 to 60 soldiers endeavored to keep pace with them in a shambling run.[7:182] Groups of singing and dancing men and women serenaded their leaders along the uncertain path of the procession. And then there were final feasts.

High Chief Hoapili was appointed Governor of Maui in March 1823.[73:41] His wife, Ke-opu-o-lani (Liholiho's mother) accompanied him to La-haina. She had been ailing, and Liholiho was very solicitous when she left Honolulu on the *Haaheo o Hawai'i.* The 83-foot long vessel was loaded with 200 passengers and took three days beating to windward to arrive.

Among those on board were the Revs. William Richards and Charles S. Stewart,* who were to establish a mission station at La-haina. Ke-opu-o-lani was the highest caste ali'i and was most important to the missionaries. She had become receptive to Christianity – and now had a personal chaplain, Tau-'a, a Tahitian "Native Teacher" who had come to Hawai'i with the Rev. William Ellis.[22:18] The London Missionary Society had stationed Ellis in Tahiti, where he acquired fluency in a language similar to Hawaiian. Now he was in the islands to assist the American missionaries.

Ke-opu-o-lani made earnest inquiries concerning the way to heaven. She gave up a second husband.[73:41] [100:20] As a sign of commitment, she had two thatched houses erected for the missionaries, and a small church, which was dedicated August 24, 1823.[17:191-93] [117:143-44] [159] Both she and Hoapili took a firm stand against vice. She reproved Liholiho for his habits of dissipation and their relations became strained.

On Maui she became very ill and messengers were sent to the ruler and ali'i. Liholiho hurried to La-haina and was with his mother day and night. Chiefs and chiefesses began to assemble in the traditional way.

* Newly arrived second company April 27, 1823.

Toward the end she expressed a desire to be baptized a Christian. The Reverends Richards and Stewart were not fluent in Hawaiian, but fortunately Rev. William Ellis was present and able to assist. He baptized Ke-opu-o-lani on her death bed.[17:195] [117:167] She died September 16, 1823, surrounded by her family, the missionaries, and no less than 50 chiefs and chiefesses.[117:160] [100:36]

Ke-opu-o-lani had left instructions that she wanted a Christian service and burial. Little remained of the old ways, and only three days of wailing were permitted.[17:196] [60:239]

6

ENGLAND

LIHOLIHO WAS DEPRESSED, RESTLESS, IRRI-
table and pensive all at the same time. The course of events disturbed
him, and he really couldn't envision where they were taking him and
his people. He should have control over the forces that were changing and evolving the Hawaiian way of life. After all, he was ruler
along with Ka-'ahu-manu, and the responsibility weighed heavily
upon him.

He received lots of advice and was realistic enough to evaluate
the source and motivation of who was giving it. The great friendship
his father, Ka-mehameha, had shared with British Naval Captain
George Vancouver must have been an inspiration. In 1794, on advice
from the captain, Ka-mehameha had allowed the island of Hawai'i to
be placed under British protection.[77:41-42] It would be reasonable to
follow his father – but get advice from his brother ruler, the King of
England.

Had not the British king last year sent the schooner *Prince Regent*
to Ka-mehameha as an expression of friendship?[22:97] Liholiho had
signed a letter of thanks to King George IV, advising him that Ka-
mehameha had died and he was now ruler, "the former idolatrous
system had been abolished," and "(I) beg leave to place them all
(islands) under the protection of your most excellent Majesty."[60:233-34]

With this in mind, Liholiho called a council meeting at La-haina
in October 1823.[95:1-2] He announced his intention to go to England
and see his brother sovereign, King George IV. He stated that he had
two goals: solicit counsel on the best way to operate the government,
and on how to conduct commercial activities.[95:98]

There was considerable discussion about Liholiho's plan. Kuhina
nui Ka-'ahu-manu was initially against the idea and had no previous

knowledge of it. She wanted nothing that smacked of foreign entanglement, or agreements that didn't require her approval. Ka-lani-moku, the prime minister, favored the plan, which seems to indicate his involvement in prior discussions.[95:1]

The high chiefs were suspicious that the result of any such meeting might usurp some of their power. Ka-lani-moku was able to keep the customary dissension among the ali‘i under control. High Chief Kahala-i‘a (son of Ka-mehameha's half-brother, Kalai-mamahu, and Ka-lani-moku's sister, Wahine-pio) was apparently a leader of opposition to the present rule. He was quoted as telling Ka-lani-moku, "I have refrained from taking the kingdom while you are alive, but after you are gone I shall take it."[70:275] He and kuhina nui Ka-‘ahu-manu did not get along with each other at all.

Finally, Liholiho announced that Captain Valentine Starbuck, American master of the English whaleship *L'Aigle*, had offered to take him to England *free* and that Liholiho had accepted. This seemed to tip the scales. The council at last agreed to the trip, then had to decide who would go with the ruler. After further discussion, a list was agreed on:[70:256 346 75:2]

Liholiho would take only one of his queens, his favorite and half-sister, Ka-mamalu. It was the white man's style to have just a single wife! Kahala-i‘a "took under his protection" the Queens Pauahi and Kina‘u, which may well have been an astute political maneuver. Queen Ke-kau-‘onohi was left "without a husband to care for her," and nothing has been recorded about Queen Ke-kai-ha‘a-kulou, who may have returned to Kaua‘i.

High Chief Boki, governor of O‘ahu, would head the ruler's entourage as Chief Counselor. His wife Liliha would accompany him and act as Lady-in-Waiting for Queen Ka-mamalu.

Ke-ku-anao‘a was to be the ruler's Treasurer.

"Admiral" Kapihe, punahele (companion) of Liholiho, who had been on a vessel to China and commanded the *Haaheo o Hawai‘i*, was assigned the position of Aide-de-Camp.

Manuia, son of Ka-ulu-nae, was to be Steward.

James Kanehoa Young, son of John Young, was Interpreter.

Three young ali‘i were to be kahili bearers and attendants: Ka-uluhai-malama, younger brother of High Chief Hoapili; No-ukana, son of High Chief Ka-manawa; and Na-‘ai-weuweu, son of Ke-kumu‘ino.

It was understood at the council meeting on November 15

that: [47:284] Ka-'ahu-manu and Ka-lani-moku would continue to operate the government in Liholiho's absence; his younger brother, Kau-i-ke-aouli, was designated heir to the rule, with Ka-'ahu-manu as kuhina nui.

Ka-lani-moku had raised $25,000 in specie for expenses, and the sum was hoped adequate for the return trip, as well. [95:8] [73:45] Captain Starbuck safeguarded the money chests on his ship.

Rev. William Ellis' wife was ailing and he indicated a desire to join the trip as interpreter and guide in England. Hawaiian leaders greatly trusted him, thought the idea excellent, and asked Captain Starbuck if the Ellises could go along – they would even pay for their passages. The captain refused on the grounds that there was no room for more people. [95:45] One wonders how even the approved passengers were quartered on the whaleship. Rev. Ellis had a low opinion of Captain Starbuck's character and his activities in the islands – a man distinguished "by his disorderly conduct" – and this may have been a deciding factor.

Once the final arrangements had been made, there was a flurry of activity: Captain Starbuck wanted to set sail as soon as possible, Liholiho was even more eager to start such an important voyage. They left La-haina for Honolulu on November 17 as all ships anchored in the harbor fired cannon salutes. [95:5] There had been no room for Rev. Ellis and his wife, but Captain Starbuck found room for Jean Rives, occasional secretary and interpreter for the ruler. He had arrived in 1801 and become fluent in Hawaiian. Rives was a diminutive Frenchman known to the Hawaiians as Luahine (old woman). He acted as the king's interpreter when the French Captain Freycinet visited in 1819. Mme. Freycinet recorded that Rives was "an impudent fripon (rascal), small in stature, but large in ideas." [95:4]

The ship stayed at Honolulu a short time to assemble supplies and gifts for the trip. Missionary wives were busy making dresses in the latest fashion for Ka-mamalu and Liliha. Black suits were a norm for the chiefs – alterations must have been made day and night by the probably very few tailors who were available in Honolulu.

At 10 am November 27, 1823, the royal party embarked in shore boats to go aboard the L'Aigle, which was plying on and off the harbor. Cannon salutes thundered from the fort and other vessels lying at anchor. A huge crowd commenced wailing their farewell to their ruler as he began this momentous trip. Queen Ka-mamalu made a moving farewell address: [95:7] [17:203-04]

> *"O skies, O plains, O mountains and oceans,*
> *O guardians and people, kind affection for you all!*
> *Farewell to thee, the soil,*
> *O country for which my father suffered;*
> *Alas for thee. Farewell!*

(Then almost a prayer to her late father, Ka-mehameha)

> *"We both forsake the object of thy toil (kingdom).*
> *I go according to thy command:*
> *Never will I disregard your voice.*
> *I travel with thy dying charge,*
> *Which thou didst address to me."*

Ke-ku-anao'a was not a good sailor,[95:5] and it took several days before he got his sea legs and the sight and smell of food did not revolt him. With the captain's permission, he carefully examined all parts of the ship (except for the captain's cabin and private lazaret which, among other things, contained the specie chests). He talked to everyone constantly and absorbed a lot of new information.

The heavily laden whaleship sailed southeast at about seven knots. Liholiho was kept well entertained with rum bottles. The airs were light in the Doldrums, and heavy seas began about 45° south latitude. The temperature dropped to the forties in the Cape Horn "summer," when the weather was comparatively mild. It took the *L'Aigle* about a week to make her way through the gales of the Drake Passage to the Atlantic Ocean. After 81 days, they sailed into Rio de Janeiro harbor on February 15, 1824. The *L'Aigle* remained at anchor in the comfortable 75-80° temperature for three weeks, as provisioning and refitting were completed, and the passengers were entertained.

Emperor Don Pedro I invited Liholiho and his entourage to a levee at the palace. The king wore his red uniform tunic, Ka-mamalu and Liliha were in their best dresses. High Chief Boki had on his new black suit. The remainder of the men were in black suits, as well. It appears that on this and all other formal occasions, Ke-ku-anao'a was also clad in a black suit, with certain dramatic additions: an 'ahu'ula (feather cape), a mahiole (feather helmet), and carrying a javelin. His imposing physique made him an impressive bodyguard for his Hawaiian Majesty.[95:11] [44:10] The entire royal party was at their most dignified, and did not miss a single thing they saw or heard. The emperor and the king had an enjoyable conversation and exchanged gifts – a sword and a feather cape.

The Hawaiians must have buzzed with comments after they left the first meeting of their ruler with another monarch. Such a magnificent palace and throne room, the strange new band music, the immaculate soldiers, AND the town of sturdy stone buildings, abundant markets, the colors, religious processions of children, so many peculiar people and languages… How different – and more spectacular – than Hawai'i!

The British consul general gave a large ball in honor of the visitors, and Liholiho presented him with a feather cape and kahili.[50:55-56] As Jean Rives interpreted for the event, the consul general didn't care for him and requested James Kanehoa Young perform that duty. Revenge occurred later when the *L'Aigle* sailed for England and Young was left stranded in Rio – at the connivance of Jean Rives aided by Captain Starbuck.[95:8] But Young was able to get on another ship and follow his king. Yet he was in Liholiho's bad graces because, presumably, he had defected from his ruler. Such intrigue…

The *L'Aigle* departed from Rio de Janeiro March 7, 1824.[95:7] The thrills and success of the visit were marred just weeks later, when Kauluhai-malama died en route on May 13, 1824, and the Hawaiian royal party witnessed their first burial at sea.[95:14] To everyone's relief, the ship anchored safely at Spithead, just offshore of Portsmouth, May 17, 1824. The entire trip from Honolulu had lasted almost six months.

On the following day, Captain Starbuck took the Hawaiians by carriages to London. The bulk of the baggage and the specie, under the care of Manuia, remained on the *L'Aigle* which proceeded on to London. Without great fanfare, King Liholiho and his entourage were installed at Osborne's Hotel (later named the Caledonian) on Robert Street, Adelphi Terrace.

Captain Starbuck reported to the owners of the ship, Messrs. Boulcott of Wapping-wall, that he had arrived in England with a shipload of whale oil *and* the Hawaiian royal party. Needless to say, they were most surprised, and immediately notified the British Foreign Office. This was the first notice the British had of the royal visitors. The Hon. Frederick Gerald Byng, known as "Poodle Byng," was assigned as official host.[95:9 50:58] He called on King Liholiho to inform him that he and his retinue were honored guests of the British government and as such would incur no expenses during their visit.[95:10]

As most of their clothes were still on the *L'Aigle*, the first order of business was to provide the visitors with the latest of London fashions. Their first outing on May 23 was to attend Whitsunday services at Westminster Abbey. Liholiho's attention was focused mostly on the roof; Ka-mamalu had to be restrained from making a hasty exit when the organ blasted full volume. Liholiho refused to enter the Chapel of Henry VII, as kings were buried there and he considered it sacred ground.[95:10] [73:48] [50:62]

Foreign Secretary the Hon. George Canning gave a reception for the Hawaiian royal party on May 28 at Northumberland House. Some 200 influential people were invited. There was a strong English curiosity, mostly snobbish and cruel, to see these savages from almost half way around the world. They found them decorous, self-possessed and well-dressed. Lord Byron concluded that:[50:61] "...the laughter and exclamation which seem to have been ready prepared for the royal strangers soon died away when it was perceived that not the slightest embarrassment or awkwardness was displayed by them, and that the king knew how to hold his state, and the erees (ali'i) to do their service, as well as if they had practiced all their lives in European courts."

When the specie chests were opened at the Bank of England, only $10,000 of the original $25,000 was found.[73:48] Ke-ku-anao'a must have been overwhelmed – was he not treasurer and thus responsible for the money? Yet...he had not had custody of the specie. Captain Starbuck had safeguarded the chests, what did he have to say about this? He stated that he had expended $3,000 in Rio de Janeiro for needed supplies and things.[95:8] That left $12,000 unaccounted for...oh yes, there were also travel expenses from Portsmouth to London.[50:56-57] He denied any knowledge of the remainder of the missing money.

This wasn't the only trouble the captain was in. Messrs. Boulcott fired him for misusing their whaleship, not taking the cargo where it was supposed to be sold, and brought suit against him.[50:57] [44:29]

Somehow Captain Starbuck remained in King Liholiho's favor and was given a feather cape and one of Queen Ka-mamalu's dresses made of kapa (bark cloth).[95:15]

According to London social custom, the Hawaiian monarchs received visitors and in turn called on dignitaries. On the 31st they enjoyed Pizarro from the Royal Box at the Covent Garden Theatre, went to the races at Epsom, where the "horses flew," attended

Drury Lane in the Royal Box June 4 to see Rob Roy McGregor, went to the British Museum, watched a balloon ascension at White Conduit Gardens, attended the Opera, etc. A full and enjoyable schedule.[95:12] [73:48] [50:63-64]

History has recorded an instance of purely Hawaiian delight. One member of the entourage came back to the hotel in great excitement with a fresh grey mullet. The others could scarcely believe that "it had not swam hither on purpose for them, or be persuaded to wait until it was cooked before they ate it."[50:60] Their diet in London was mostly fish, clams, poultry and fruit.

Then...amidst all this fun and great activity, Manuia came down with measles on June 12. Liholiho fell ill the following day at a Royal Academy Exhibition. By the 17th, all the Hawaiians were sick with measles. An audience with King George IV was canceled.[95:13] [73:51]

Queen Ka-mamalu died July 8, 1824, and her devoted, despondent husband, King Liholiho, followed his love barely a week later on July 14.[95:15-17] [73:52] [44:11-14]

The British government graciously offered to return the royal bodies and the remainder of the Hawaiians to their home. This was gratefully and tearfully accepted.

High Chief Boki fired Jean Rives as Interpreter. That night the Hawaiians, who had been drinking mostly cider in England, celebrated by consuming 20 bottles of wine.[50:60] The vengeful Rives stole the king's gold watch before departing, but it was recovered.[73:53]

A final meeting was held with King George IV on September 11, 1824[50:60] and Ke-ku-anao'a reported the following:

"These are the words which we heard in Great Britain at a conversation when we met King George IV after the death of Liholiho and Ka-mamalu his wife.

"At that time Boki informed King George IV of what was said by Ka-mehameha I to Vancouver.

"We first entered the Palace of the King, and afterwards the King entered with his friends, and then came also two chiefs, one of whom was called Kalaimoku (Mr. Canning) and another besides him. We then were introduced. King George IV stood before Boki and said to him and we heard it.

"I exceedingly regret the recent death of your king and his wife. The chiefs of people will think perhaps that I have been inattentive to our King, but it is not so, for the same medicine and the same Physicians have been employed as are employed by the chiefs of this nation. On account of the severity of the disease he died.

"Then James Young, the Interpreter, told all these words to Boki and we all heard them.

"Then King George asked Boki the chief thus. As you have come to this country, and the King has died here, who will be the King of the land?

"Boki answered thus to him – His Majesty's younger brother will be King, but it is for Kaahumanu and Kalaimoku to take care of the country.

"The King then asked Boki what was the business on which you and your King came to this country?

"Then James Young interpreted the words to Boki and we all heard the question of the King to Boki.

"Then Boki declared to him the reason of our sailing to Great Britain – We have come to confirm the words which Kamehameha I gave in charge to Vancouver thus – go back and tell King George to watch over me and my whole Kingdom. I acknowledge him as my landlord and myself as tenant (or him as superior and I inferior) should the foreigners of any other nation come to take possession of my lands, then let him help me.

"Then James Young told all these words to King George, the ancient words which King Kamehameha I gave in charge to Vancouver. These he told to King George.

"And when King George had heard he thus said to Boki – I have heard these words, I will attend to the evils from without. The evils within your Kingdom it is not for me to regard: They are with yourselves. Return and say to the King, to Kaahumanu and to Kalaimoku, I will watch over your country, I will not take possession of it for mine, but I will watch over it, lest evils should come from others to the Kingdom. I therefore will watch over him agreeably to those ancient words.

"Then James Young told Boki the words of the King – then we heard all these words, Boki, Liliha, Kapihe, Naukana, and James Young heard these words. I also, Kekuanaoa – we all heard the words of the King to Boki."*

Thus the first brave attempt by a Hawaiian ruler to make contact with an imperial monarch in his own country ended in tragedy. The repercussions of this sadly failed mission would be felt for years.

---

* Rev. William Richards Record of Kekuanaoa's Testimony of What Was Said at the Court of St. James (Archives of Hawaii FO; & Ex 1824)

7

BOKI

THE BRITISH GOVERNMENT RESPECTFULLY had the frigate H.M.S. *Blonde*, commanded by Captain the Right Hon. Lord Byron, take the king's and queen's coffins to Hawai'i along with the remainder of the royal party.[73:52] [19:3] There was one additional passenger, John Wilkinson, whom Boki had engaged to help improve Hawaiian agriculture.[82:34]

The *Blonde* made a leisurely trip. After leaving Portsmouth on September 28, 1824, the frigate visited Madeira, Rio de Janeiro, and rounded Cape Horn to Valparaiso.[50:79] Kapihe died there of apoplexy on February 8, 1825.[50:86] The grieving passengers continued on to Callao and the Galapagos Islands. Boki partook of the Sacrament on Easter Day,★ and Liliha, Ke-ku-anao'a, and the other Hawaiians were baptized by Rev. R. Bloxam and received into the Church of England on May 1, 1825.[19:19] Lord Byron surmised that this was "probably induced by example of Boki and anxious to carry home with them every possible mark of civilization..."[50:95]

When the ship stopped briefly at La-haina on May 4, the returning travelers found that three preceding vessels had already brought the news of the deaths of the king and queen. Since their departure, Ke'e-au-moku, kuhina nui Ka-'ahu-manu's brother, had died; and Ka-umu-ali'i, Ka-'ahu-manu's husband, had also passed away. A rebellion on Kaua'i, led by one of Ka-umu-ali'i's sons, had been suppressed. Ka-'ahu-manu and the chiefs were presently in Honolulu because Prime Minister Ka-lani-moku was seriously ill.

The *Blonde* anchored in the Honolulu Roads (sea lanes) on May 6, 1825, and fired a salute of 15 guns which was returned by the

★ Boki had been baptized as a Roman Catholic aboard the French navy corvette *Uranie* in 1819.

fort.[50:109] The following day Lord Byron and the ship's officers formally called on the kuhina nui and prime minister. Each was escorted arm-in-arm by a chief. The Englishman noted that the Hawaiian Royal Guard was uniformed in "the native maro (malo), and a dark European frockcoat, without shirt, waistcoat or trowsers."[50:112-13] Boki and Ke-ku-anao'a were resplendent in "uniforms of Blue, turned up with red and gold lace, with long slashing basket hilted swords: lofty plumed cocked hats upon their heads..."[61:36] There was a formal reception at which Lord Byron presented impressive gifts from England.

The funeral was held on May 11 with great ceremony. Crowds of Hawaiian mourners admired the coffins covered with crimson velvet and ornamented with silver gilt plates and handles. The procession to the church was stately.[19:36-37] [50:128] A detailed list gave the exact order of participation:

1　Twelve native warriors clad in their beautiful feather war-cloaks and helmets, and each trailing as in mourning a kahili or ensign.*
2　The marines of the *Blonde*, their arms reversed.
3　The band playing a dirge.
4　Chaplain and surgeon of the *Blonde*, and two missionaries.
5　The funeral cars, each drawn by forty chiefs.
6　Kiaukiauli (Kau-i-ke-aouli), brother and successor of 'Iolani, in Windsor uniform, crape on his arm & c. with the British consul (Richard Charlton).
7　The princess Naheinaheina (Nahi-'ena'ena), supported by Lord Byron.
8　The (high) chiefs, male and female, in deep mourning, according to rank, each supporting a British officer.
9　Foreigners, resident agents, masters of vessels, & c.

And lastly, 100 seamen from the *Blonde*, dressed in white, with black handkerchiefs, two and two.

The procession was accompanied by minute guns and watched by thousands of impressed Hawaiians. At the door of the thatched church, there was a brief burial service, in English, by Rev. Bloxam of the *Blonde*, and in Hawaiian by the missionary pastor, Rev. Hiram Bingham.[17:266] [117:285] The coffins were then moved to Ka-lani-moku's house, a temporary resting place while the Royal Tomb was constructed on the present 'Iolani Palace grounds.†

---

* There is also another version of this.
† Hawaiian customary mourning had been forbidden.

Don Marin recorded in his journal on May 23 that "The English surgeon (Dr. Davis) tapped the minister (Ka-lani-moku) and drew off a galon & a half of water."[50:13] [47:295] He had dropsy. This small detail seems to demonstrate a kindly interest in the health of individuals, and not merely a concern over the fates of nations.

There was a great council meeting on June 6, 1825.[50:152-57] [17:268-70] The 12-year-old Kau-i-ke-aouli was confirmed the next ruler with Ka-'ahu-manu continuing as kuhina nui. Boki spoke eloquently for an hour and a half about their visit to England, the audience with King George IV, and expressed great appreciation for the English hospitality.[82:43] [50:153] There were a few favorable responses by Hawaiian leaders.

Lord Byron was called upon. He had done a lot of research into Hawaiian practices, and made the following suggestions for the islands' government:[50:56-57]

1 That the king be the head of the people.
2 That all the chiefs swear allegiance to the king.
3 That the lands which are now held by the chiefs shall not be taken from them, but shall descend to their legitimate children, except in cases of rebellion, and then all their property shall be forfeited to the king.
4 That a tax be regularly paid to the king to keep up his dignity and establishment.
5 That no man's life be taken away except by consent of the king, or the regent, for the time being, and of twelve chiefs.
6 That the king, or regent, can grant pardons at all times.
7 That all people shall be free, and not bound to any one chief.
8 That a port duty be laid on all foreign vessels.

The subject of American missionaries came up.[50:155] Lord Byron was asked if the King of England had any objection to American missionaries in Hawai'i. No, he responded, as long as they did not interfere with the laws or commerce. He did mention that the missionaries were reported to have drawn up a proposed code of laws. Rev. Hiram Bingham replied that they had neither the design nor wish to do so and were precluded from such by their directives.

One of the first actions Boki took was to confiscate the lands used by Jean Rives.[73:53] John Wilkinson, brought from London, fared better. Because of his experience as a planter in the West Indies, he had been solicited as advisor to Hawaiian agriculture, and Boki set him up to farm in Manoa Valley. He was granted the use of 200 acres in the vicinity of Pu'u-pueo above the taro patch areas.[92:220-21]

Wilkinson sought Lord Byron's assistance at the council meeting to have land tenure defined and hopefully made permanent. Prime Minister Ka-lani-moku stated that it was Hawaiian practice to allow the use of such land to foreigners, and "he could have it until the ground may be wanted by themselves."[82:43]

In July, Wilkinson began clearing land and planting coffee beans and seedlings brought from Brazil and sugar cane from local sources.[82:43] He also planted corn, potatoes, bananas, and other staples which were in demand to supply visiting ships.

Ke-ku-anao'a was in charge of securing and supervising Hawaiians for this work.[58:145-47] Western farming tools were rare and the Hawaiians mostly used their familiar o'o' (digging sticks).

Boki's voyage to England as Chief Counselor had given him immense prestige.[36:74] He continued as Governor of O'ahu, and was appointed kahu (guardian) of the young King Kau-i-ke-aouli.[58:147 72:87] Having been exposed to the most respected white man's civilization and way of life, England, his observations and experiences were sought by both the ali'i and commons. He grew in stature, recommended the Bible and said he would observe its teachings himself.

Ka-'ahu-manu was so impressed with the monumentous happenings that she declared her desire to be baptized a Christian and become a member of the church. Ka-lani-moku and eight other chiefs and chiefesses joined her in this request. They were provisionally accepted by the missionaries but placed on six months' probation. The Mission had established this rule to be sure of a Christian's commitment, otherwise the number of converts might not be validly reported. The group from the Court was baptized and became church members on December 4, 1825.

As proof of piety, in June the leaders of the council were determined to outlaw vice, drunkenness, theft and non-observance of the Sabbath, and in August added the requirement that all must attend worship, go to the schools to learn to read and write, and observe the Sabbath.

Boki split from Ka-'ahu-manu and his brother Ka-lani-moku, and did not support the effort to have the moral code of the Ten

Commandments become the law of the land. He felt that his experience with white civilization did not include such regulations. He was joined by most of the traders, and the measures were defeated.[36:69-70]

Ke-ku-anaoʻa also had increased prestige. He related his experiences of places, buildings, horses and carriages, people and events. In fact, he became quite a storyteller. The chiefesses were fascinated by the visit to England, and interested in this manly, 31-year-old enterprising figure. There were affairs, one of which became serious. He married Pauahi, a former queen of Liholiho, on November 28, 1825.[58:147]

Pauahi was the daughter of Pauli Ka-ʻo-lei-o-ku, Ka-mehameha's first-born son. It took some influence for this marriage to occur between such different levels of aliʻi caste – the fact that Ka-lani-moku was Pauahi's foster father obviously had considerable bearing.[58:147] As may be recalled, when Liholiho left for England in 1823, High Chief Kahala-i-ʻa "took under his protection" Queens Pauahi and Kinaʻu.[70:346]

Unfortunately, after less than a year of marriage, Pauahi died in childbirth on June 17, 1826.[47:307] [58:147] [70:347] [14:316] Her daughter, Princess Ruth Ke-ʻeli-kolani, was said to be poʻolua (a child of two fathers), considered to be an honor.[70:347] Ruth was hanai (adopted at birth) by Ka-ʻahu-manu.

John Wilkinson had 50 acres under cultivation by May 1826. He had made a dam on a small stream to be used for a future mill.[92:220] When he died on September 17, 1826,* he had more than 100 acres in coffee and sugar. Boki took over the budding plantation, placed Chief Kinopu in charge of day-to-day work, increased the number of laborers and paid them $2 a week.[70:278] [77:172]

Ke-ku-anaoʻa continued to supervise the plantation and frequently rode out from town on horseback. Prime Minister Ka-lani-moku built a house at Makiki near the road which he named Kilauea. He used to intercept Ke-ku-anaoʻa and have lengthy conversations. Ke-ku-anaoʻa often stayed the night there.[58:146-47] His continued close relationships with the highest officials indicated that he was valued for a variety of reasons.

---

* Elisha Loomis and Stephen Reynolds journals. Several 19th century writers state that he died in March 1827.

About a year later, Boki got into financial difficulties, and leased the plantation to traders in 1828 who intended to distill rum from the sugar cane. The following year the moral and temperance guardian Kuhina nui Ka-'ahu-manu placed a kapu on this venture. The cane was destroyed and replaced with potatoes.[17:339-40] The traders lost a sizable investment, which led to resentment and growing opposition.

The moral laws created friction with the some 150 whalers coming to Hawai'i in the spring and fall en route to and from the whaling grounds. When the rough, tough whalemen came ashore after being months at sea, they wanted immediate relaxation, mainly in the form of women and liquor. They felt free to do anything in the heathen, uncivilized Pacific Ocean, and had "hung their consciences on Cape Horn when they entered the Pacific."[18:29] They rightfully saw the missionaries as the instigators of prohibitions that began appearing in the 1820s.

The English whaleship *Daniel*, under the command of Captain Buckle, anchored in La-haina Roads on October 3, 1825. About 20 angry whalemen had a difficult confrontation with the resident missionary, Rev. William Richards. The sailors threatened to burn him out, and kill him and his wife if he did not procure the repeal of the obnoxious laws. Captain Buckle was requested to restrain his men. He refused. On October 7, the entire crew marched, following a black flag, to the mission's thatched structures. They were faced with a large number of Hawaiian warriors under the command of island Governor Hoapili. There were no overt acts, and the whalemen returned to their ship and soon sailed away.*[17:274-75 70:281 7:194]

There was another so-called "outrage" the following year. The first American Navy warship to come to Hawai'i, the U.S. schooner *Dolphin*, under Lt. John "Mad Jack" Percival, arrived in Honolulu on January 16, 1826, and stayed four months for refitting.[92:xii 196] Lt. Percival assisted American traders in collecting sandalwood debts from the chiefs, and obtained an acknowledgment that the creditors should be paid by the government.[92:xiv] He was not sympathetic to the edicts restricting intercourse with Hawaiian women.

---

* Captain Buckle later sued Rev. Richards for slander.[70:281] The chiefs determined that Rev. Richards had been telling the truth.[22:189 7:199]

A riotous conflict occurred on Sunday, February 26, 1826. A group of sailors broke into Prime Minister Ka-lani-moku's house and demanded, "Where are the women?"[92:xv] More than a hundred sailors and whalemen went after Rev. Hiram Bingham. One of Kamehameha's dowager queens, Na-mahana, fended off a blow with a club aimed at the minister. Many Hawaiians had gathered and they surged forward to defend their ali'i and overwhelmed the seamen and whalemen. "Kapu, Thou shalt not kill!" was shouted by the chiefs and missionaries, and this undoubtedly saved lives.[92:xvi] [225-26] Lt. Percival came ashore, freely used his whalebone cane, and got his men back on board the schooner.*

But...the end result was that Governor Boki relaxed the law. Women were again permitted, and some swam to the ships at anchor.[22:179] [7:195] The decree was again enforced on April 1 by order of the council.[22:180]

There was another lesser "outrage" at La-haina in October 1826.[7:196] The U.S. schooner *Dolphin* was the first of a number of western warships visiting Hawai'i to apply "Gunboat Diplomacy."

H.B.M. sloop *Blossom*, commanded by Captain Frederick W. Beechey, arrived in Honolulu on May 20, 1826 and stayed for 10 days. Later he returned on January 26, 1827, and visited for two months. He commented that Honolulu was advancing rapidly toward civilization – "The number of wooden houses, the regularity of the town laid out in squares..."[22:88] The captain apparently basked in the good relations that existed between the Hawaiians and the English. There were only minor complaints about British subjects in the islands, brought to his attention by Consul Richard Charlton.

Foreign seamen began to appear with greater frequency. The U.S. sloop-of-war *Peacock*, under Captain Thomas ap Catesby Jones, arrived in October 1826 and stayed three months. One purpose of his visit was to investigate and rectify, if necessary, an earlier whaleship owner's complaint that some 150 American seamen were "prowling about the country, naked and destitute, associating themselves with the natives, assuming their habits and acquiring their vices."[22:105] The Hawaiians wanted to get rid of these unemployed vagrants who were leading their people into evil ways.

Captain Jones apprehended and removed 30 runaway sailors. He

* At the instigation of the missionaries, Lt. John Percival faced a Court of Inquiry when he returned to the east coast of the United States. He was acquitted.[92:xvii]

influenced the resolution of petty differences between Americans and the kingdom which were the responsibility of John Coffin Jones, who since September 1820 had the title of "Agent of the United States for Commerce and Seamen."[116:2] On his own initiative, Captain Jones prepared a treaty of friendship and favorable commerce between the United States and the kingdom of Hawai'i. The Hawaiians signed it and strictly followed the provisions. It was never ratified by the United States government.[77:99]

8

POWER RIVALRY

A LETTER FROM GOVERNOR BOKI TO British Admiral Otway January 24, 1826 was published in the London Quarterly Review (March 1827 issue). Among other things, it expressed the differences between the Christian Kuhina nui Ka-'ahu-manu and the council, which was under the influence of the literal American missionaries, and Boki's more worldly, indifferent Christian viewpoint.

Rev. Charles S. Stewart took umbrage at "the most injurious misrepresentation" of the missionaries by this "fabricated" message. Lord Byron was quoted that he did "not believe Boki ever wrote or dictated that letter. It is not his manner of expressing himself, and you are aware that he can scarcely form his letters." Rev. Stewart concluded that it had been written by a semi-literate Englishman or American and Boki *may* have signed it. [117:xxiii-iv 342-46]

> "Mr. Bingham the head of misheneres is trieng evere thing in his pour,to have the law of this cuntry in his own hands; all of us ar verrey happy to have sum peopel to instruct us in what is right and good, but he wants us to be intirely under his laws, which will not do with the natives. I have done all in my power to pre-vent it, and I have don it; as yet ther is Cahomano (Ka-'ahu-manu) wishes the misheneres to have the whole athority, but I shall prevent it as long as I can, for if they have, ther will be noth-ing don on thes islands, not even cultivation for their own use. I wish the people to ried and write, and likewise to worke, but the misheneres have got them night and day, old and young, so that ther is verrey little don her at present; the people in gineral are very discetisfied at the misheneres, thinking they will have the laws in ther own hands."

This curious document was to have far-reaching consequences. In certain ways, it set the stage for a conflict that lasted for decades.

Prime Minister Ka-lani-moku had not been blessed with robust health for some time and became quite ill in early 1825. As mentioned before, he had been diagnosed with dropsy and was "tapped" to remove fluid by the surgeon of H.M.S. *Blonde*. He was "tapped" four more times by various doctors every two–three months at Honolulu.[47:299 300 302 305] Ever the realist, he left Honolulu on January 11, 1827 via La-haina for Ka-maka-honu, Kai-lua, Hawai'i, where his lord and great benefactor, Ka-mehameha, had died in 1819.[58:146] Dr. Pelham, his personal physician, accompanied him. Ka-lani-moku was "tapped" twice more before the "Iron Cable of Hawaii" died on February 8, 1827.[70:277 17:307] The ali'i had assembled as was customary and Kuhina nui Ka-'ahu-manu had a difficult time restraining their mourning.[70:277-78]

Ka-lani-moku had been the powerful and respected leader who had "held fast the nation," and tempered and resolved ambitions and rivalries among the high chiefs. There was apprehension about future power and leadership. Levi Chamberlain expressed the missionary evaluation in a letter to the American Board in Boston:[17:308]

> "The right of controlling the king and directing the affairs of the nation, belongs to Kaahumanu; and even Boki has acknowledged his power is vested in her. I had feared that the death of Kalanimoku would be the signal to resist Kaahumanu, but the present appearance of things is that peace and order are likely to prevail. Boki has discovered a disposition to act contrary to the wishes of the higher chiefs, particularly of Kaahumanu, and his conduct has actually excited the apprehension that he is aiming to usurp the regency. But this strange course is to be attributed more to foreign influence than to the independent actings of his own mind. Indecision is a natural trait of his character, and he is just such a tool as would suit the purposes of an artful and designing person who had an interest to promote by creating civil dissensions."

Ka-lani-moku's death had been long anticipated, all Hawaiians were prepared for it, and there appears to have been contentment with the present leadership and system. British Consul Richard Charlton reported to the British Foreign Office on February 27, 1827 that "the islands are perfectly tranquil, and I am happy to inform you that there does not appear to be any inclination among the other chiefs to disturb the peace." He also stated that Boki had succeeded to Ka-lani-moku's position as prime minister – although in fact the position remained vacant, and Boki continued to be the influential Governor of O'ahu.[34:18]

Early historian James J. Jarves adds an interesting note (1843):[60:271]

"At his death his stone house (at Kai-lua), the best built and most
costly in the island, was dismantled in accordance with a supersti-
tion that still lingers among them. Upon the death of a high chief,
it was not uncommon even at so late a period, to destroy much of
his property, that none other might possess it; and valuable loads
of satins, velvets, broadcloths, and other rich goods were taken to
the seaside, cut into small pieces and cast into the surf."

Boki's good behavior, induced by his elder brother's death, did
not last long. Revelry began again with the enthusiastic support
of such traders as British Consul Richard Charlton, American representative John C. Jones, Stephen Reynolds, and others.[70:275] The more
respectable traders did not participate. Fourteen-year-old King Kau-i-
ke-aouli followed his guardian Boki.

The O'ahu governor owned several stores, saloons, and a hotel in
Honolulu. The drinking places did a vigorous and noisy business.
Kuhina nui Ka-'ahu-manu soon took action to stop excesses. Boki,
Liliha and others were charged and fined in May 1827 for miscon-
duct, intemperance, fornication and adultery.[36:75] This slowed the
pace of life in Honolulu – for a while.

And Ke-ku-anao'a? He continued as a steadfast and senior
administrator of the island of O'ahu, and was loyal to his superior,
Governor Boki. It is hard to determine how much he participated in
various revelries, the only clue being that in later years he was a
leader in temperance activities. One may safely assume moderate
involvement at the most.

When Ke-ku-anao'a returned from England, he had been
appointed commander of the Hawaiian military, some 200-300
poorly trained, uniformed and equipped men.[58:148-49] [17:320] He made
great improvements. When the American Navy Captain William
Finch officially called on the king on October 15, 1829, there were
200 troops completely uniformed in white with scarlet cuffs and col-
lars and black caps. They presented arms perfectly en militaire.[118:121]

Commerce was a continuing concern in Honolulu. For some
businessmen, there were fortunes to be made. British Consul Richard
Charlton reported to the Foreign Office October 15, 1827:[34:19]

"Riho-Riho (Liholiho), the late King, had contracted debts to the
amount of 14,000 peculs (133-½ lbs. each) of sandal wood, for the
payment of which a tax of half a pecul of sandal wood, or four

dollars each man, and one dollar each woman, has been laid on the people. After payment of this tax every man is at liberty to cut and sell sandal wood on his own account (this is the first time the common people have been allowed to sell it); by these means upwards of 20,000 peculs of sandal wood have already been collected, 12,000 of which have been shipped for China: the price of sandal wood may be estimated at seven dollars per pecul.

"British calicoes, printed cottons, coarse blue broad cloths, hardware, good silks, and large English blankets, will at all times command high prices.

"There are now in this harbour eight American and two Mexican merchant-ships, also nine British and twenty American whale-ships; three of the American merchant-ships are loading for China, two for the coasts of Mexico and Columbia, and one for Manilla; the Mexican vessels are loading for the coasts of California and Mexico."

The startling evolution of the Hawaiian way of life was the introduction of free enterprise for the commoners – for the first time they could keep some of the results of their labor and not just provide it for the benefit of their chiefs. The earliest tax law of Hawai'i was written December 27, 1826. There was a limitation on sandalwood: a man could cut only one picul, half would go for the tax and half to himself to sell for his own benefit. Women age 13 and up were to pay a mat 12 feet by 6 feet or a kapa of equal value for $1 Spanish.[48:82-83]

The chiefs kept making new purchases, payable in sandalwood, and still had some old debts outstanding. The traders had quite a time balancing the "old" and "new" obligations. The government had promised to pay major debts at the end of 1826 totaling 15,000 piculs of sandalwood.

This tax law had a strong social impact as most of the able-bodied men were constantly in the mountains collecting wood. This led to an adverse effect on agriculture, fishing, and taxes owed to the ali'i. It also resulted in less attendance at church services and literary classes.

The French merchantman *La Comete*, commanded by Captain La Plassard, anchored off Honolulu harbor on July 7, 1827. This arrival was due to the exertions of Jean Rives after he returned to France following the ill-fated voyage of Liholiho.

Aboard were the first Catholic missionaries – Fr. John Alexis Bachelot, appointed Apostolic Prefect of the Sandwich Islands; Frs. Abraham Armand and Patrick Short; Brs. Theodore Boissier, Melchior Bonom and Leonore Portal; and several mechanics under the leadership of M. Morineau, a French lawyer.[142:31] The ship carried cargo to be delivered to Jean Rives and paid for in sandalwood. But he was no longer in Hawai'i, so they faced a dilemma.

Governor Boki advised them that permission to land and live in the islands must be obtained from the kuhina nui. In the meantime, he would ask if these new missionaries could come ashore. They did, rented three thatched houses, and local Catholics who were westerners gathered around to support them. The first Holy Mass was conducted on July 14, 1827.[60:228]

Kuhina nui Ka-'ahu-manu refused to receive or admit "the Papal Teachers" into the islands and ordered Governor Boki to eject them. By coincidence, *La Comete* weighed anchor on July 27, 1827, two hours before the order could be carried out.[17:31] [142:36-37] So the French sailed away and the priests were left in Hawai'i.

The American missionaries did not appreciate Catholics in their chosen area and made their opinions known. Ka-'ahu-manu and most of the influential chiefs accepted the American Protestant teachings and moral code, and that form of Christianity was now practically a state religion. In the rites of the Catholic church, the chiefs perceived a revival of idolatry which had been abolished in 1819.[77:141] The Catholic response was that they never prayed to but often prayed *before* images.[142:45] The Protestant missionaries took a broader view of objection – they considered Catholic doctrines to contain fundamental errors and evils.[77:140] An understandable viewpoint, because Protestants came into being as a sect after secession from the Church of Rome at the time of the Reformation.

Some chiefs also feared that two separate religious teachings could be divisive in terms of government.[77:141] This *may* have been the result of adverse experiences with the differing orders of Hawaiian priests under the old Polynesian religion.

Ka-'ahu-manu was quoted as saying:[69:81]

> "We do not want you. We have put away our idols, and abandoned our old system of religious forms and penances. We have received the Word of God by the hand of teachers whom we love, and with whom we are satisfied. Our kingdom is a little one. We do not wish the minds of our subjects distracted by any other sect. Go away and teach destitute countries, which have not received the bible."

There were mild overtures of acquaintanceship between American and French missionaries. The result was just barely cordial. Boki gave the Catholics some protection and assistance.[38:361] The priests carried on their work quietly and without interference. They diligently began to learn the Hawaiian language, aided by school materials published by the American Protestant Mission Press. The seemingly peaceful situation did not last long. A new quarrel erupted over the conflict between ancient customs and new moral values.

"Heard She (Ka-'ahu-manu) had given orders for Tuanou (Ke-ku-anao'a) to be banished for being busy with Tenow (Kina'u)" was an entry in Stephen Reynolds' journal August 19, 1826.[74:148] The rumor of banishment was unfounded, but Ka-'ahu-manu was furious.

In her zeal to adhere to Protestant Christian moral values,[72:160] she had been trying to curtail the ancient practice of chiefs and chiefesses "sleeping here and there." And this was personal – Kina'u was her niece. a high chiefess of great lineage, being a daughter of Ka-mehameha, half-sister and a queen of the late Liholiho.* Moreover, no matter how stalwart and attractive Ke-ku-anao'a was, by comparison he came from an insignificant ali'i caste. Kina'u could do much better in selecting a mate.

Following Liholiho's death, Kina'u had made a proper marriage with Kahala-i-'a, nephew of Ka-mehameha. As mentioned before, when the king left for England in 1823, Kahala-i-'a "took under his protection" Queens Pauahi and Kina'u. In 1826, Stephen Reynolds recorded in his journal: "March 23. Kalaiia (Kahala-i-'a) was Married yesterday to Tenow (Kina'u)."[74:128] "April 26. Kenow (Kina'u) was bro't to bed of a son," and "April 28. Last night Kalia (Kahala-i-'a) died with Cramp in Stomach."[74:133] (At the time there was a whooping cough epidemic in the islands.[70:347])

In status Kina'u was second only to her half-sister, Nahi'ena'ena. A union of the young king to either of these chiefesses would result in the highest caste of offspring, ali'i ni'aupio'o. There were reports that Kau-i-ke-aouli (age 14) had been sleeping with both Kina'u (age 22) and Nahi'ena'ena (age 11).[36:78][74:174] The one great barrier to this Hawaiian traditional practice was that the Protestant moral code had no tolerance for incest – and Ka-'ahu-manu was becoming a strong Christian.

Ke-ku-anao'a and Kina'u had been living together for some months[†] when Ka-'ahu-manu, aided by Ka-heihei-malie (Kina'u's

---

* And would become kuhina nui when Ka-'ahu-manu died, and the mother of Kings Ka-mehameha IV and V.
† Hawaiian marriage (ho'ao)?[70:374]

mother), Ke-ka-ulu-ohi and other high chiefesses applied pressure for her to either leave Ke-ku-anao'a or have a Christian wedding. She refused to separate from him, and consented to marry.[29:] The ceremony was held at Ka-wai-a-ha'o Church on September 19, 1827, with a large number of people in attendance.[29:]

Their first son, David Ka-mehameha, born on May 23, 1828, was immediately adopted by Ka-'ahu-manu.[58:347] A little over a year later, a second son arrived, Moses Ke-ku-aiwa, born July 20, 1829. He was adopted at birth by High Chief Ka-ike-o-'ewa.[70:348] [14:343] Rev. Charles S. Stewart recorded on October 31, 1829 that next to Kina'u at a formal occasion were "seated the son and daughter of Kekuanao (Ke-ku-anao'a), in expensive European dresses." [118:179] Both were infants[118:182] and to have them treated like the offspring of European royalty must have been confusing to anyone with a western background.

Governor Boki became more and more depressed with the policies and dictates of the kuhina nui and council. His excesses now took a political form. Soon there were rumors of intrigue and possible revolt. He assembled armed men at Wai-kiki in early April 1829.[70:290] [22:191]

Ke-ku-anao'a did not participate in Boki's intrigues. In fact, he probably was not aware of, to use poetic Hawaiian, "those drops of rain that denote war." [58:145] He went courageously to Wai-kiki to attempt to dissuade Boki:[70:291]

> "Here am I, your younger brother, whom you commanded to remain at Ka-'ahu-manu's house and to be obedient to the voices of those whose house it was. I would not have gone there except for your command because I do not wish your words to be in vain. I have found no fault in the house of the aunt-in-law (Ka-'ahu-manu). I have heard that you were coming to kill Ka-'ahu-manu and I have left her weeping over this plot of yours." Boki answered, "I will not put those of her household to death, but I am jealous of her because of our Lord (the king)."

This potentially explosive issue was resolved without violence. In 1829 Governor Boki led the bustling construction work in Honolulu town. He built a fine new thatched palace for the young king at Pelekane, the Hawaiian version of "Britannia," in the vicinity of the present St. Andrews Episcopal Cathedral. It was "100 or more feet in length, 50-60 feet broad and 40 or more high." [70:277] [118:121] The palace was named Hale-uluhe, as it was beautifully lined and trimmed with uluhe ferns. [70:280] A new thatched Ka-wai-a-ha'o Church was constructed that year, 196 feet by 63 feet, able to accommodate 4,000 people, and opened for worship on July 3, 1829. [17:344] [7:210-2] Prefabricated wooden two-story structures imported from New England were much in demand. Some Hawaiians were learning to become carpenters.

And yet Boki was beset with all sorts of difficulties. His commercial activities were not doing at all well. He coveted western things and made frequent purchases of new goods on credit. The O'ahu government share of the sandalwood tax did not entirely go for payment of past debts but also for new things. Boki was generous, and considerable goods were given to those ali'i who supported him in opposition to kuhina nui Ka-'ahu-manu and the council.

He was required by them to proclaim in the streets on August 8, 1829 that Hawaiians were prohibited from attending Catholic services and harsh penalties were announced. [142:50] Armed guards were posted at Catholic structures and Don Francisco de Paula Marin's complex to prevent contacts. [74:274] But when the guards were soon removed, Governor Boki did not enforce the order.

Troubles continued with foreigners who felt they were above any Hawaiian law. The so-called "cow case" brought this to a head. Cattle that grazed in the common pasture on the plains sometimes broke down fences surrounding cultivated areas, entered and ate what was available. The farmers had little success in securing redress. One trespassing cow was fired upon, escaped back to its own pasture and there slain. Its owner, British Consul Charlton, took action – caught the Hawaiian farmer, tied his hands and dragged him with a rope around his neck behind his horse to Governor Boki in town. [77:129] This humiliating spectacle was not only a demonstration of anger and power, but also a public event.

On October 5, 1829, Charlton got up a petition signed by British residents demanding protection for their lives and property, and presented it to the governor. [34:20] The king and council declared protection under the general laws on October 7, and found that the cow had damaged a fenced cultivated area. The council also stated that *all* were subject to the law "…the same for every foreigner and for the people of these islands; whoever shall violate these laws shall be punished." [34:21]

U.S. Navy Captain William B. Finch of the *Vincennes* came to Honolulu on October 2, 1829 and stayed for a month and a half. Like others before him, he got involved in helping American traders with sandalwood debt collections. Boki agreed to pay a considerable portion. Sandalwood was getting scarce and of poor quality. His commercial efforts became almost frantic. Partly due to this, he was more and more alienated from the kuhina nui and American missionaries.

A ship arrived in Honolulu from New South Wales in November of 1829, bringing news of a New Hebrides island rich in sandalwood. Boki, now desperate, grasped at a way to extricate himself from overwhelming debts. He decided to go there, take over the island, and secure the fragrant wood.[36:80-1] He assembled his supporters, armed them, and engaged western captains to sail and navigate two kingdom ships – the brig *Kamehameha* loaded with 300 men and the smaller *Becket* with 179 men.[7:203]

Ke-ku-anao'a delivered the king's order for Boki to return to shore, then returned alone after a long discussion.[58:157] Boki's wife, Liliha, and others tried to dissuade him not to go, without success.

The ships sailed on December 2, 1829. Eight months later, the *Becket* limped into Honolulu harbor on August 3, 1830, with only 12 Hawaiians and eight foreigners aboard. The rest of the people on the ship had been stricken with an unnamed disease and died.[36:81] The *Kamehameha*, with Boki and most of his followers, had disappeared. It was conjectured that the ship was either lost in a severe gale, or exploded when there was careless smoking amidst the large amount of gunpowder.[60:289 36:82] Boki's final resting place remained a mystery. This was a sad end of an ambitious, talented but deeply conflicted man who once wielded great power as governor of O'ahu.

LEFT. Rev. Hiram and
Mrs. Sybil Bingham,
1819. Arrived Hawai'i in
First Missionary
Company April 4, 1820.
Pastor Ka-wai-a-ha'o
Church 1821-1840.
Leader of the Hawaiian
Mission. (Archives of
Hawaii)

BELOW. Honolulu Harbor, 1821. Copy of
watercolor by C.E. Bensell. Honolulu
Fort, *center*, Punchbowl Battery, *right
center*. Large thatched structure, *right*, is
Ka-wai-a-ha'o Church and adjacent
frame missionary house. Ship, foreground,
is the Nantucket whaler *Russell*. (Howay,
F.W. ed) Reynolds, Stephen. The Voyage
of the New Hazard... Salem: Peabody
Museum, 1938.

Fourth Anniversary of
Ka-mehameha's death,
Honolulu, May 1823.
Cartoon by unknown
artist. (Eveleth, Rev.
Ephraim. History of
the Sandwich Islands…
Philadelphia: American
Sunday School
Union, 1831.)

Wailing at Ke-opu-o-lani's death, La-haina, September 16, 1823. Cartoon engraving by unknown artist. 1) Kua-kini, governor of Hawai'i. 2) Hoapili, husband of Ke-opu-o-lani. 3) Kau-i-ke-aouli, youngest son of Ke-opu-o-lani (Ka-mehameha III). 4) Nahi-'ena'ena, daughter of Ke-opu-o-lani. 5) Ka-mamalu, Liholiho's favorite queen and half-sister. 6) Wahine-pio, sister of Ka-lani-moku. 7) Kalakua, mother of Ka-mamalu. 8) Kaiko, relative of Ke-opu-o-lani. 9) Keoua, wife of Governor Kua-kini. The flag at left was adopted by Ka-mehameha in 1812 as Hawaiian colors – it endeavored friendship with the British combatants (the union), and American combatants (the field). ((Richards, William.) Memoir of Keopuolani, Late Queen of the Sandwich Islands. Boston: Crocker and Brewster, 1825.)

Ka-lani-moku, 1819 and 1825. He functioned as Prime Minister, was nicknamed "William Pitt" after the famed British Prime Minister, and known as "The Iron Cable of Hawai'i."

TOP. 1825: Pencil portrait by Robert Dampier, artist and draftsman with Captain The Right Hon. Lord Byron in Hawai'i May–July 1825. (Archives of Hawaii)

BOTTOM 1819: By J. Alphonse Pellion, draftsman with Captain Freycinet in Hawai'i August 1819. (Bassett, Marnie. Realms and Islands. London: Oxford University Press, 1962.)

ABOVE. Queen
Ka-mamalu, London,
1824. Portrait by John
Hayter. (Archives of
Hawaii)

BELOW. King Liholiho,
London, 1824. Portrait
by John Hayter.
(Archives of Hawaii)

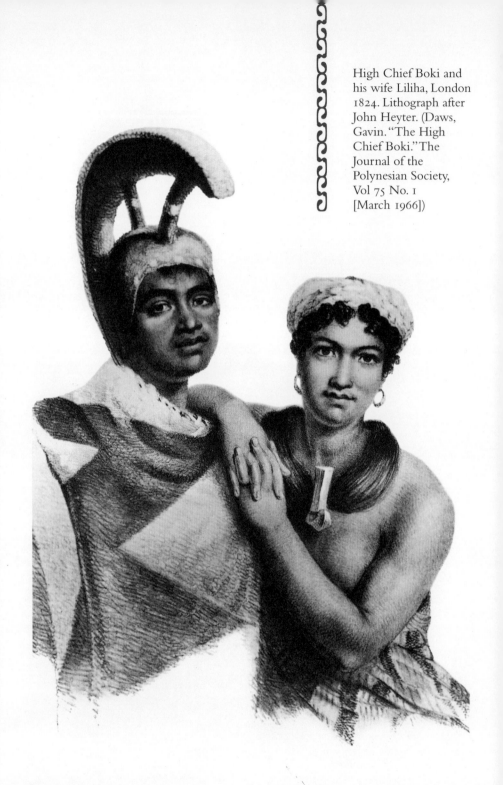

High Chief Boki and his wife Liliha, London 1824. Lithograph after John Heyter. (Daws, Gavin. "The High Chief Boki." The Journal of the Polynesian Society, Vol 75 No. 1 [March 1966])

9

KA-'AHU-MANU

Ke-ku-anao'a and Kina'u joined Ka-wai-a-ha'o Church on March 7, 1830.[17:371] Their third son, Lot Kapu-aiwa (later Ka-mehameha v), was born on December 11, 1830, and adopted by High Chief Hoapili, Governor of Maui.[70:348]

When Boki left on his ill-fated sandalwood venture, he designated his wife, Liliha, to act as Governor of O'ahu.[70:297] [22:196] She appointed Chief Ku-ho'oheihei Paki to be her "Chief Captain" and placed him in charge of Honolulu Fort and other fortifications. He also shared her bed.[70:298] [37:87-8] Liliha continued Boki's antagonism against the kuhina nui and council, and did not enforce moral laws on O'ahu.

Ka-'ahu-manu seized on a weakened power situation when Boki and many of his supporters were absent. At a public meeting in Honolulu on June 16, 1830, she declared that O'ahu would be temporarily governed by Liliha and Kina'u.[17:372] She then took the young king on a three-month visit to his windward islands, thereby removing him from Liliha's and Honolulu influence.[7:204] Liliha and Kina'u must have been uncomfortable with each other – they were of opposing philosophies and Kina'u had no experience in governing. Fr. Bachelot called Kina'u "our greatest enemy" in the O'ahu government.[142:56] Ke-ku-anao'a was now working partly for his wife.

The news that Boki had apparently perished along with his ship triggered discussions among the chiefs about future governing of O'ahu. The October 1830 council quietly concluded that Liliha should be replaced.[70:303] A decision such as this was impossible to keep secret. One may be sure that Liliha very soon became aware of it because she stated that she would not surrender her position unless ordered to do so by the king.[22:197]

He, kuhina nui and high chiefs were at Kai-lua, Hawai'i, in mid-January 1831, when they heard alarming rumors: Liliha was making warlike preparations to take over the kingdom, had secured and was purchasing more arms and ammunition, and assembling men in training at Honolulu Fort and other fortifications.[17:405 37:88]

At La-haina in February, Ka-'ahu-manu received a letter from Kina'u:[17:406]

> "This is my word to you, which I declare that you must know. The language or threatening of war is here. The fortress is occupied by the men of Waianae. When you approach and anchor outside, a boat is to go out for the king, and force him away from you. That is it. Attend to this small matter. But this is what we ought chiefly to do, to rely on God. Therein let us make fully manifest our regard to him with whom is the power and the wisdom. And pray ye to God for those who do us evil. Thus also do we at this place."

Diplomacy was tried and proved successful. Maui Governor Hoapili, Liliha's father, came to Honolulu and "dissolved the rebellion with words." He invited his daughter to come home with him – it must have been a powerful conversation to make Liliha acquiesce – and she and Paki sailed for La-haina on March 7, 1831.

At a public meeting in Honolulu on April 1, 1831, the king and kuhina nui announced that Kua-kini, the Governor of Hawai'i and Ka-'ahu-manu's younger brother, was appointed Governor of O'ahu.[17:407 37:87]

Kua-kini was an autocratic high chief of imposing presence and stature, weighing some 350 pounds. As a strong member of the church, he was known for enforcing the kingdom's moral codes recently adopted from the teachings of the American Protestant missionaries. Kua-kini was used to being obeyed immediately and without question by Hawaiians. Newly arrived (1828) American missionary Dr. Gerrit P. Judd recorded in his journal that at a public meeting Kua-kini arose and addressed primarily the foreigners, saying in part:[67:20]

> "My thought for you white men, especially those who sell rum is this – today you expect to pay money for your licenses – I will not receive it – keep your money, but I affirm that if you sell any more rum I will strip you of your property and tear down your houses. Break off altogether selling spirits – you have heard the complaint that the former governor would not execute the laws. I am resolved to enforce them."

Liquor and gambling were forbidden, no amusements on the Sabbath, and prostitution and unmarried people living together were prohibited. Enforcement was harsh. At least 30 grog shops were closed and several hundred white men lost their jobs. A number of foreigners were angered by these restrictions of their "rights" and became difficult.[37:88] Kua-kini put them down with an iron fist. There was no question that Honolulu's pace of life had changed, and it took months before the laws were relaxed.

The new governor met the Catholic question head on. The day after his appointment, he sent for the Catholic priests and read them an earlier order to leave Hawai'i in three months: [142:60 67:21]

> "This is our decree for your banishment. Begone from this land. Dwell not upon these Hawaiian Islands for your doctrine is at variance with the religion which we profess. And because of your teaching your religion to the people of this land, some of us have turned to your sentiments. We are endeavoring to spread among the people the religion which we profess – this religion we plainly know to be the true. This is what we earnestly desire.
>
> "When you arrived here, we did not invite you. But you came of your own accord. Therefore we send you away. Begone.
>
> "We allow three months to prepare for your departure, and if within that time you shall not have gone, your effects will be confiscated, and you will go destitute; and if you wait until the fourth month, and we see you delaying, then, you will be imprisoned, and we shall do unto you, as do the Governments of all nations to those who disregard their commands. So will we constantly do to you."

To make a long difficult story short, the Catholic Mission was forcefully expelled on December 24, 1831. Ke-ku-anao'a led a drummer and armed men who escorted the Catholic missionaries to the kingdom schooner *Waverly*, commanded by Captain William Sumner, and they were taken to California.[37:89 142:74]

British Consul Richard Charlton heatedly queried Ka-'ahu-manu on this action and received the following letter in succinct Hawaiian writing:[34:27]

> "I answer to your asking me the cause of this condemnation – it is for the division and the opposition. I do not consent to their residing in the beginning, I ordered them off again; they remained firm – they said there was no ship.

"There is a ship now ready for them. I send them to another country. Be quiet you. This is our business, of me and the king."

Hawaiians who would not recant Catholicism were put into prison at hard labor or otherwise persecuted. To the credit of the American Protestant missionaries, they objected to these actions – without avail.

Among other actions, Kua-kini rebuilt Honolulu Fort.[70:304] He constructed a two-story building against one of the interior walls that served as his office and residence. This was later used for the same purpose by Ke-ku-anao'a when he became governor. An article in the *Pacific Commercial Advertiser*, October 1, 1857, relates:

> "All who intended to commit matrimony must present themselves before the stern old governor for his consent to the bans – Here taxes were paid, in poi, fish, tapas, sandalwood and Dollars – Here captains came for permission to ship sailors and for help to catch runaways – Here criminals and offenders of all sorts were summarily disposed of – In short here was transacted all and every kind of Government business, for then the 'Governor' was the factotum of the powers that be."

High Chief Haiha Na-ihe, who had been appointed acting governor of the island of Hawai'i while Kua-kini was on O'ahu, died on December 29, 1831.[17:427] [7:297] Kua-kini returned to the island of Hawai'i to resume his governorship. It was considered more important than O'ahu, being the home of the Ka-mehameha line and having the largest population of all the islands.

Kua-kini and the younger Ke-ku-anao'a apparently got along well. They had similar convictions, viewpoints and were both authoritative Christian chiefs. Ke-ku-anao'a was loyal to Ka-'ahu-manu and had married her niece. It was difficult for many chiefs to govern and have relations with white men, who quite often ignored Hawaiian laws and argued back. The chiefs were wary of confronting them. Ke-ku-anao'a was fluent in English, understood foreigners better, and was used to dealing with them firmly. He had no inhibitions about upholding the laws.

Ke-ku-anao'a now became Governor of O'ahu undoubtedly based on Kua-kini's high recommendation.[58:177]

In mid-may of 1832, Ka-'ahu-manu came to Honolulu in a depleted and ailing physical condition. She was then about age 55,[119:43] and the only earlier mention of her medical history was an "apoplectic shock" suffered on March 15, 1831.[67:18] Dr. Gerrit P. Judd consulted with newly arrived missionary Dr. Alonzo Chapin and they diagnosed chronic dysentery – an illness for which the Hawaiians had little or no resistance – and concluded that there was little they could do.[53:139]

Ka-'ahu-manu was carefully borne on a manele (palanquin) by her solicitous attendants to her favorite retreat in upper Manoa Valley, three miles above Punahou. Her choice thatched house with green shutters, Puka-'oma'o, was on the edge of 'ohia, kukui and koa groves.[70:308 42:42]

"Here a bed of sweet scented maile and leaves of ginger was prepared, over which was spread a covering of velvet, and on this she lay down to die."[69:47]

The ali'i began to gather, as was traditional, out of respect and so that the afflicted would not be alone at the second great occurrence of that person's life. It wasn't long before a large village of 100-200 thatched houses had sprung up in the vicinity.[42:42]

The king and more senior ali'i were constantly at her side, as well as her doctors and favorite missionaries.

Rev. Hiram Bingham gave her a special red morocco bound copy of the New Testament in Hawaiian that had just been printed. She inspected it carefully and clasped it to her bosom. Toward the end Rev. Bingham prayed on his knees at her bedside, "In my Father's house are many mansions…" and was weakly responded to with, "I will go to Him and be comforted…aloha."[17:432]

Kuhina nui Ka-'ahu-manu passed away at 3 am on June 5, 1832 – and joined her beloved husband, Ka-mehameha, who had died 13 years before.

> "The tidings of her death passed from lip to lip in a few moments, and the voices of the multitude were lifted up in one doleful wail, that echoed from the hills and mountains' sides with appalling reverberations. After a brief indulgence in this expression of grief, Governor Adams (Kua-kini), brother of the deceased, issued an order for silence, and requested Mr. Bingham to offer prayer. As the people were spread over the space of a square mile, the almost immediate stillness that prevailed seemed magical and mysterious."[69:48]

Ka-'ahu-manu's body was carried to her Honolulu house and placed in an ornate coffin covered with crimson velvet fastened with many large brass-headed nails spelling out her name. There was a short but impressive procession from her house to Ka-wai-a-ha'o Church, attended by multitudes. There Rev. Hiram Bingham preached the funeral sermon from the text, "I have fought the good fight, I have finished my course, I have kept the faith." [42:50-51] The casket was then interred in the almost adjacent Royal Tomb.

Ka-'ahu-manu, King Kau-i-ke-ouli and the council had earlier determined that Kina'u would succeed her as kuhina nui with the title Ka-'ahu-manu II. This was announced on July 5, 1832. [7:210] Ka-'ahu-manu had been childless and gave Kina'u her extensive land holdings. [72:120]

Ke-ku-anao'a must have asked himself, So WHERE ARE WE NOW? The strong, dominating Hawaiian rule he had known for the past 38 years was gone. Not many of the high chiefs of the Ka-mehameha generation were left: Kua-kini, who had returned to his governorship of Hawai'i; Hoapili, governor of Maui; and Ka-iki-o-'ewa, governor of Kaua'i. The young King Kau-i-ke-aouli had some experience in ruling but had loose standards. Kina'u, Ke-ku-anao'a's wife, had higher standards, but was absolutely inexperienced to share the rule as kuhina nui. The future of rule seemed uncertain, at best.

The few American missionaries had made a count of the people in the islands as well as they could. They estimated about 46,000 on the island of Hawai'i, 43,000 on Maui and adjacent islands, 30,000 on O'ahu, and 12,000 on Kaua'i and Ni'ihau – a total of a little over 130,000. These large numbers were almost incomprehensible figures to Ke-ku-anao'a, but he knew that there were far less people than when he had been a boy. The strange new diseases that Hawaiians seemed unable to combat had taken their toll – especially the mai oku'u (cholera or bubonic plague of 1804), which by some estimates killed half the population, and the recent influenza (1826). [72:24 36-37] Families had fewer children – a concern for the future. About 400 foreigners were counted as residents in the islands. [72:42]

Ke-ku-anao'a might well have thought the following at this time: The American Protestant missionaries have certainly made an impact on our lives during the dozen years they have been here. Some have come and gone, but 31 remain scattered in 10 locations on all the islands.[85:16] Despite all of our learning about Christianity, a waiting period is required to join the church. They say it is to make sure. Today there are almost 600 church members in good standing.[106:42]

What a change from our old religion, which was intertwined with the kapu system. Infraction used to mean death, but now most penalties are chastisement or silent scorn. Because many of the missionaries are fluent in Hawaiian, we can understand the teachings of the One Christian God. We overthrew our old beliefs for the solace of Christianity. Ka-'ahu-manu was a great driving force to have all learn the new religion. The Ten Commandments as a way of life is a good one, the moral codes much stricter than our old ways, but we have accepted them. That is, most of us. The new way is different, there isn't as much laughter, amusements, sports and so on as before. But Christianity intends good, is good and Kina'u and I embrace it.

Our customs of life and death are changing. When an ali'i dies now there is not the gross grief as before, and no human sacrifices at the passing of a high chief or high chiefess. We no longer fear sorcerers or somebody displaying the bones of the deceased. Instead of hiding body remains, the entire body is now placed in the ground with the respect of all who witness the event. Under the Christian system marriages are more permanent, and singular. "Sleeping here and there" is discouraged – but continues.

The missionaries brought another kind of communications, reading and writing. How valuable! They reduced our speaking to written words – and printed thousands and thousands of pages in pamphlets and books in Hawaiian. How right it was for Ka-'ahu-manu to require all adults to learn to read and write. It took lots of missionary planning and effort to make this come about, but they did it. About 53,000 people, 40% of our population, are being taught today.[17:70] About a third of our people can now read and write to some degree, and are considered literate.[79:128] This in a dozen years!

When I was a boy we were only concerned with growing enough food and harvesting the shore and sea for our own needs. With the coming of the white men, we are now also concerned with provisioning their ships. They need food that they can eat today, as well as for their long voyages.

Most of the white men living here are traders who supply the wants of visiting ships. These are satisfied partly with what we produce and partly from what is brought to Hawai'i. Aside from foodstuffs, they provide ships' stores such as canvas, ropes, spars, barrels, tools and ironwork.

Only a few fur traders visit Hawai'i now, and I understand that our remaining sticks of sandalwood do not sell for enough to pay the freight. Who knows how the kingdom will ever be rid of its sandalwood debts? Some 200 whalers are coming in the spring and fall, principally to Honolulu and La-haina. To fill a whaleship's hold with 2,000 barrels of whale oil now takes almost two years. About 40 merchant ships will also arrive, bringing cargo, and a few will return to New England with whale oil.[87:67 77 225]

Some of the konohiki (land division) chiefs complain that they are losing control over their people. The kapu system used to keep commoners in line, now each chief enforces kingdom dictates as he sees fit. With sandalwood almost gone, the law requiring male taxes in sandalwood must be relaxed. Many people spend time in classes to learn reading and writing – this cuts down on manual labor, and the chiefs' share of their efforts has been greatly reduced. Some men have left the islands to be seamen. Some have left the land and moved to port centers to become independent craftsmen like carpenters and blacksmiths. A few have even managed to leave a konohiki and work on their own for ships needing repair.

Of most importance, we must recognize that the world no longer belongs to just us. Our horizon has been lifted. We know that far beyond where we can see are different people, many more than in our islands. They have great things superior to our possessions and they live differently. Those of our people who have sailed away on ships tell us these things. I know it to be true, for I have been to Rio de Janeiro, London and Valparaiso. We are also aware of other people and how they live from our new ability to read and see illustrations.

That's the way things are – we can't change them, and must make them work for us. To just look backwards is not helpful. We must continue to evolve and join the world.

Now I am Governor of O'ahu, a position of great stature and honor. I am proud to have attained it, and credit the appointment to my experience, record of integrity, loyalty and accomplishments. I will strive to perform well without the direct supervision I have been used to. I will diligently work to attain kingdom goals with high standards.

I married far above my wildest ali'i dreams…and now my wife has the highest power…I will apply all my will and knowledge to help her.

IMUA! (FORWARD!)

10

KING
KAU-I-KE-AOULI

ONE COULD EASILY IMAGINE KE-KU-anao'a thinking that King Kau-i-ke-aouli felt as if a heavy 'ahu'ula (feather cloak) had been lifted from his shoulders when Ka-'ahu-manu died. Yes, she had been his foster mother guardian for years. Yes, she had ruled the islands as kuhina nui since he was a young prince. But, now he was almost 18, a king in his own right, and his conquering father's son. No, he was not an absolute monarch, Kina'u enjoyed the same positional succession kuhina nui power of co-rule as Ka-'ahu-manu had, and the powerful council possessed the right to issue authorizations and exercised checks and balances. Currently the main difference between them was that the kuhina nui and council accepted and directed the missionary Christian religion and moral codes – while the king was indifferent to the first and disliked the second, as if still in parental revolt. The young monarch reverted to the revelry he had shared with Boki, Liliha, British Consul Richard Charlton and others. He liked the old singing and dancing and plea-sures, especially *every* day of the week. Life had been more enjoyable in yesteryear, why not now?

The high chiefs returned to their islands, the council was held at La-haina, Maui, and the king remained at Honolulu town. They could do as they pleased on their islands, he was where he wanted to be.

His example and pronouncement of the noncompliance with many of the moral laws resulted in their nonenforcement. Everything was relaxed, particularly in Honolulu, except for the laws against murder, theft and rioting. Grog shops and liquor distilleries multiplied, gambling flourished, prostitution resumed openly, and drunken revels became commonplace.[7:212] For a half dozen years the king had owned a tavern and billiard room and they now did a brisk business.[37:92]

Evolution from the old Hawaiian values to the new western and Christian valued had its ups and downs, and the path was not always smooth or straight. Hawaiian leaders were groping for their identities in the rapid changes of cultural ways and external pressures. Several noted historians have called this period the "troubled thirties" or the "turbulent thirties" – apt expressions for Honolulu and environs, less so for the other islands where most Hawaiians lived. The king was the king, and some Hawaiians followed him. The chiefs were the chiefs and closer to the people – most were Christians, and their views and dictates prevailed over the majority. Nevertheless, school and church attendance decreased throughout the islands.[60:300] The king declared that all could go or not go to churches, as they pleased.[72:158]

King Kau-i-ke-aouli liked to "sleep here and there" and considered it a royal prerogative. He was young and personable. Early journals are replete with reports of liaisons.[37:92, 430] He was deeply attached to his younger sister, Nahi-'ena'ena, and had been sleeping with her for years in the old Hawaiian style. The Christian high chiefs and missionaries tried to keep them separated according to the new prohibition on incest, and she lived at La-haina, Maui. The king also had a liaison with his older half-sister, Kina'u. Ke-ku-anao'a beat his kuhina nui wife for this intimacy.[37:92]

Kau-i-ke-aouli had some 18 punahele (companions) who were known as Hulumanu (bird feathers). They all liked to party – during one early celebration with the king, 32 barrels of spirits were consumed in a week.[37:92] For his companions he purchased Boston Cadets uniforms, which had been brought to the islands by Captain John Dominis.[120:44] A special favorite was Hawaiian-Tahitian Kaomi, a smart young former teacher, healer and rejected convert. He acquired such influence over the young ruler that he became known as Ke-li'i-kui (Engrafted King).[17:447] Kaomi was given power over loans extended by the government.[70:335] The Hulumanu mocked Christianity when the king's pet baboon died by staging a funeral for the animal, complete with coffin and prayers.[37:92]

Governor Ke-ku-anao'a was placed in an impossible position. His office required him to uphold and enforce the laws. His king told him to disregard them. The kuhina nui and council took no action. He must have sought advice from the senior high chiefs, and their counsel was undoubtedly ho'omalie (keep calm), conditions will improve – in time. It was still difficult. He had his integrity, and was very distressed.

Kuhina nui Kina'u also had her own difficulties. The young king made it very clear that he did *not* allow his will to be questioned or negated. When he wanted to buy a ship for $12,000, the kuhina nui and council refused to add to the kingdom debt by authorizing the money.[7:211] [103:122] The king was so irritated that he refused to see Kina'u for any purpose.

She called upon her friend Laura Judd, wife of missionary Dr. Gerrit P. Judd, for solace and advice, saying:[69:52]

> "I am in straits and heavy-hearted, and I have come to tell you my thought. I am quite discouraged, and cannot bear this burden any longer. I wish to throw away my rank, and title, and responsibility together, bring my family here and live with you, or we will take our families and go to America; I have money."

In this particular instance the Judds could but counsel patience and cited examples from the Bible. This was abstract and not very helpful.

Kina'u and Laura had become good friends, although of very different social backgrounds. Laura had been a teacher before marriage and was a quiet, observant and determined woman. Kina'u especially appreciated Laura instructing one of her attendants on how to make bread, cake, custards and puddings.[69:57]

The friendship had almost been jeopardized when Laura gave birth to a daughter on July 5, 1831. Kina'u wanted to hanai (adopt) the baby right then and there. The Judds said, "No, we don't give away our children." Kina'u replied, "But you are poor, I am rich, I give you much money." The answer was still "no" and she left in high dudgeon.[138:7] When the baby was baptized by Rev. Hiram Bingham on August 7, Kina'u came and elbowed Dr. Judd aside, and told Rev. Bingham to name the little baby Kina'u "sending at the same time a haughty glance" toward the parents.[138:7-8] The baby was baptized Elizabeth Kina'u Judd – a diplomatic solution, as Kina'u's Christian given name was also Elizabeth.*

There are numerous entries in Laura's journal about having tea and socializing with Ke-ku-anao'a and Kina'u. The two husbands were compatible, both were authoritative (one a chief, the other a medical doctor), shared mutual values and respected each other. This relationship was to continue for the betterment of the kingdom.

---

* Kina'u and Ke-ku-anao'a wanted a girl child and later adopted the newborn daughter of Konia and Paki, to be named Bernice Pauahi.[69:57]

High Chiefs Hoapili*, governor of Maui, and Kua-kini, governor of Hawai'i, came to Honolulu to confer and reason with King Kau-i-ke-aouli. He was adamant about having attained his majority and not needing a regent or co-ruler. Kuhina nui authority in the form of a premier would be acceptable. The council would be consulted on laws. Hoapili insisted that he himself would have to be killed before he allowed Liliha or Kaomi to be named kuhina nui. A compromise was reached, for neither the king nor high chiefs could do without each other.[72:160 17:447]

Kaomi, in military uniform, delivered a king's note to Kina'u on March 15, 1833, advising her that he was taking over all authority relating to "...life and death, right and wrong, the amusements, the laws and all doings..."[103:123]

Later that day the king addressed a large mass meeting in Honolulu town, saying:[72:159 77:135]

> "These are my thoughts to all ye chiefs, classes of subjects and foreigners respecting this country which by the victory of Mokuohai was conquered by my Father and his chiefs – it has descended to us as his and their posterity. This is more – all that is within it, the living and the dead, the good and the bad, the agreeable and the pleasant – all are mine. I shall rule with justice over all the land, make and promulgate all laws: neither the chiefs nor the foreigners have any voice in making laws for this country. I alone am the one."

After a moment's hesitation, he announced that Kina'u would remain as kuhina nui but charged with only enforcing the laws.[22:273] Kina'u responded with, "We cannot war with the Word of God between us."[7:212]

It was one thing to claim absolute power, quite another to attend to all matters, large and small, that were presented or came to mind. King Kau-i-ke-aouli soon found that his followers could handle little

---

* Maui Governor Hoapili was the most influential high chief. He was the son of Kame'eiamoku, one of the four stalwart Kona chiefs who supported Ka-mehameha's rise to power. When Ka-mehameha died, Hoapili married Ke-opu-o-lani, the sacred queen mother of Kings Liholiho and Kau-i-ke-aouli. Hoapili was thus the young king's stepfather. He was also Liliha's father. Hoapili had been supportive of Ka-'ahu-manu and was a strong Christian.

of the details of governing, so these were passed on to Premier Kina'u. By virtue of taking charge, she accrued authority of decisions and accomplishments.

In about May of 1833 the king wanted to remove Ke-kua-anao'a as military commander of troops and the fort. After all, control over armed men was power and King Kau-i-ke-aouli wanted that essential for himself.[103:123] Compliance was questionable.

The king proposed a redistribution of lands in June of 1833. Kina'u objected firmly, saying that their father's awards were just and proper. (And she didn't want the king dabbling with the many lands Ka-'ahu-manu had bequeathed to her.) The high chiefs were satisfied with their present holdings and didn't support any change. The idea was dropped.[72:159]

Power seesawed amidst continuing ambiguity and ill will. Rumors were rampant.[22:274] Two almost equal factions arose – the anti-Christian moral code led by the king, and the Christian chiefs led by Kina'u.[72:159] Ke-ku-anao'a staunchly backed his wife, the kuhina nui.

As a demonstration of their position, King Kau-i-ke-aouli and his followers made a riotous circuit of O'ahu in August–September 1833.[103:124] In retaliation, Hoapili and other chiefs made the same circuit six months later and destroyed distilleries in March 1834.[7:213]

Kina'u gave birth to Alexander Liholiho on February 9, 1834. The king left a note in the thatch of her house stating that the child was his (hanai, adopted). This was interpreted as a sign of reconciliation between the king and his half-sister.[69:59]

Without Ka-'ahu-manu's strong backing and leaders being divided, the school system throughout the islands practically came to a halt due to nonattendance of both teachers and students.[103:124] On Maui, however, Hoapili insisted that all people above age four attend school, and that no one could marry if unable to read.[17:474]

In another show of independence, the king ordered the jail to be opened and freed all the imprisoned seamen. The high chiefs responded to this disorderly act by having Kaomi arrested in his sleep and locked in the fort on March 15, 1834. The king had to come personally and free him.★[37:93]

A few months later two Hawaiians were found guilty of piracy and murder on the high seas. They were hung from the yard arm of

★ There is also another version of this event.[72:160]

the kingdom brig *Niu* in Honolulu harbor on July 29, 1834. This was watched by awed multitudes, and proved to be a sobering realization of law and order enforced by Kina'u.[7:213 34:36]

Things had really come to a head earlier in June of 1834. King Kau-i-ke-aouli was at Pearl River and reported to be needing medical attention. Dr. Thomas C.B. Rooke, Dr. Gerrit P. Judd, Rev. Hiram Bingham and the chiefs in Honolulu rushed to the king. He had apparently made an unsuccessful attempt at suicide by cutting his throat and trying to drown himself. The reason given was that he was depressed about his sister Nahi-'ena'ena,[37:93-94] and his condition had been aggravated by the excessive consumption of liquor.[103:125]

King Kau-i-ke-aouli and his sister, who was two years younger, had been close since childhood. He still wanted to marry her. Both had very high ali'i status, and any offspring would be ni'aupi'o, the purest concentration of Hawaiian bloodline. He loved his sister and had been sleeping with her periodically.[103:124]

Nahi-'ena'ena was being brought up as a Christian by her stepfather, Hoapili. The incestuous relationship with her brother was a clear violation of the Christian code. She didn't know which conduct to pursue – love for her brother or religious conviction.

They were formally joined in the ancient Hawaiian style of matrimony at a large party in Paki's house on July 21, 1834.[103:125 112:142] Both reclined on a low platform, a black kapa (bark cloth) was spread over them, and the marriage consummated.[133:64]

The missionaries and Christian chiefs were aghast. Negative opinions resulted in tugs and pulls on the couple. Nahi-'ena'ena was uneasy and Hoapili prevailed upon her to return to La-haina in mid-January of 1835.[112:146] There her unhappiness continued, she led a dissolute life, and defied the missionaries. Nahi-'ena'ena was eventually excommunicated from the church on May 24, 1835.[112:151]

This conflict and discord overwhelmed the now 22-year-old King Kau-i-ke-aouli. He practically abandoned the direction of affairs of state, and even moderated his revelry.[37:94] After making concessions to the kuhina nui and council, the laws and punishments were republished:[130:49]

MURDER OR HOMICIDE – death, imprisonment of four years or a fine of $50-100.

THEFT – double the amount stolen or imprisonment.

ADULTERY OR FORNICATION – $15-50 or imprisonment for a few months.

FALSEHOOD OR PERJURY – to fit the crime.
DRINKING SPIRITS – $6-50.

A partial solution of face-saving in the eyes of others came about when Nahi-ʻenaʻena was married as a Christian to Lele-io-hoku, son of the late Prime Minister Ka-lani-moku, in November 1835.[72:165] A son born on September 17, 1836 was considered po-olua, the result of two fathers. Unfortunately, the infant died a few hours after birth.[112:157]

The tragic and unhappy mother died three months later, on December 30, 1836.[112:158] The king was disconsolate with grief and guilt. He built a mausoleum at Mokuʻula, La-haina, for her and their mother, and lived beside it for seven years after abandoning pleasures of Honolulu.[72:165] [70:342] During this time he was dispirited and changed to quieter ways.

The chiefs urged King Kau-i-ke-aouli to marry…and produce rulers to follow him. They recommended Ka-manele, daughter of Hawaiʻi Governor Kua-kini, and the offspring of other high chiefs. This amounted to a short list, as the senior aliʻi had few children.[17:428]

As if bowing to the wishes of others, the king was married to Kalama on February 14, 1837 by Rev. Hiram Bingham. She was the daughter of I-ʻahu-ʻula and Na-ihe-kukui,[70:341] also known as "Admiral" Kapihe. He had been a punahele (companion) of King Liholiho and accompanied him to England, and died on the return trip at Valparaiso. The chiefs grumbled that Kalama was of low lineage. But she had been adopted at birth by Ke-ka-ulu-ohi, a queen of Ka-mehameha and Liholiho, and was to become a future premier. The royal couple, Kau-i-ke-aouli and Kalama, had two sons, both of whom died in infancy. This familiar pattern of early deaths was common all over the world at this time, yet the Hawaiians were particularly in need of children who survived because their people had been so terribly decimated by imported diseases.

THE BRIG *Garafilia*, UNDER
Captain Seymour, arrived in Honolulu from Valparaiso on September
30, 1836. Aboard was Father Arsenius Robert Walsh, an Irish Catholic
educated in Paris. Catholic Mission historians described him as
a "most zealous priest" who became known as the "Apostle of
Hawaii."[142:93]

Although a member of a French mission, Walsh was a British
subject, and British Consul Richard Charlton took him to see
Kuhina nui Kina'u.[77:94] She granted him initial permission to land
and reside in the islands, subject to approval by the king and council.
When Walsh appeared before the council on October 3, 1836, they
deferred consideration of his case until the imminent arrival of a
British warship. However, a decision was made October 7 and Kina'u
directed the Catholic priest to leave the islands.[142:94 60:303]

A day later, the French naval corvette *Bonite*, commanded by
Captain Auguste Nicolas Vaillant, arrived in Honolulu and stayed two
and a half weeks.[77:45] The warship came the day before the U.S.N. ship
Peacock under Commodore Edmund P. Kennedy departed. Captain
Vaillant got involved in the Catholic question and secured the king's
agreement to protect French subjects in the islands, and permit them
to exercise their religion. Father Walsh came under this latter consideration – his expulsion order was withdrawn and he was permitted to
stay, *provided* he not give religious instruction to Hawaiians.[142:96 77:147]
This created an impossible situation for the priest, who might be *asked*
for instruction rather than volunteering information.

The same day the French warship left, the British sloop-of-war
Acteon under Captain Lord Edward Russell came into Honolulu harbor on October 24, 1836. He also got involved in the Catholic question by urging that any British priest should and could give religious

solace to any British Catholics residing in the islands. Lord Russell concluded a treaty with the king on November 16, 1836, mostly about the "rights" and protection of British subjects, and left three days later. Kau-i-ke-aouli had assumed a new name, and this treaty was signed by him as Ka-mehameha III.[60:389-90 77:148]

A now established trend of sympathy for Catholics continued to grow. The British brig *Clementine*, commanded by Captain Wm. J. Handley, arrived from California on April 17, 1837. On board were 16 horses and two passengers. A crowd came down to the wharf to see the horses, and the passengers were recognized as Catholic priests, Frs. Bachelot and Short,[142:99] banished from the islands six years ago on Christmas Eve.[142:74]

Father Bachelot had received a Papal brief in 1835 advising him not to give up hope of establishing a Hawaiian mission. Father Walsh had written him in February 1837 of the support of French and British warship captains on his behalf, and stating that he was in Honolulu with impossibly limited powers. At any rate, he felt it was now more favorable to try and re-introduce the Church in the islands.[142:98]

Reaction to the arrival of more Catholic priests was fast and furious. Governor Ke-ku-anao'a summoned Captain Handley and *directed* him to get his passengers back on board and out of the islands. They were prohibited from being in Hawai'i. The captain refused on the grounds that control of the *Clementine* was about to change. Captain Jules Dudoit, owner of the vessel, had chartered it to Captain William B. Hinckley for this trip, and was re-chartering to William French for another voyage.[142:101]

Kuhina nui Kina'u came to Honolulu and confirmed Governor Ke-ku-anao'a's actions, as did the king, who issued a public proclamation April 29, 1837:[142:100]

"Ye strangers all from foreign lands, who are in my dominions, both residents and those recently arived, I make known my word to you all, so that you may understand my orders.

"The men of France whom Kaahumanu banished, are under the same unaltered order up to this period. The rejection of these men is perpetual, confirmed by me at the present time. I will not assent to their remaining in my dominions.

"These are my orders to them, that they go back immediately on board the vessel on which they have come, that they stay on board her till that vessel on board which they came, sails; that is to me clearly right, but their abiding here, I do not wish.

" I have no desire that the service of the missionaries who follow the Pope should be performed in my kingdom, not at all.

"Wherefore, all who shall be encouraging the Papal missionaries,
I shall regard as enemies to me, to my counsellors, to my chiefs, to
my people, and to my kingdom."

Copies were printed 10 days later, issued widely, and sent to the
"French priests" on May 10, 1837. Father Short sent his back – he was
British and law-abiding in accordance with the recent Lord Russell
treaty. Father Bachelot appeared before the kuhina nui the next day to
say he would willingly leave if the *Clementine* sailed for Valparaiso.[142:101]
There was no money for such a charter.

Two Hawaiian officers escorted Frs. Bachelot and Short to the
Clementine on May 20, 1837. The priests insisted that they were
touched when entering a small boat – "force" was used and witnessed. They were refused permission to board the brig, and the boat
returned to shore. Governor Ke-ku-anao'a angrily sent his men back
to carry out their orders, and had two cannons on the fort parapet
uncovered in preparation to fire at the ship. This time the priests were
"forced" on board. Captain Dudoit stated that his vessel had been
"forcibly seized," hauled down his British colors, and went ashore
with his crew.[142:103] [48:148] He delivered the insulted flag to the British
consul, who burned it in front of a large crowd,[34:2] then demanded
reparations of $50,000 on behalf of Captain Dudoit.[34:10] This sum
was later reduced to $20,000.[34:17]

One American Honolulu merchant concluded:[34:2]

> "The chiefs think that they have not taken possession of the vessel
> in such a sense as to involve their national honor, but have placed
> these passengers on board by force, because they refused to go
> voluntarily, and in pursuance of a right which they claim of pro-
> hibiting any vessel from leaving on shore obnoxious residents."

Gunboat diplomacy exerted full pressure a few days later. H.B.M.
ship *Sulphur* under Captain Sir Edward Belcher arrived on July 8,
1837, and the French naval frigate *Venus*, commanded by Captain
Abel Du Petit-Thouars, came two days later. When the captains called
upon Kuhina nui Kina'u, they were received with military honors by
Governor Ke-ku-anao'a, dressed in his British General uniform.[142:107]
Both foreigners actively addressed the Catholic question.

Captain Belcher had a difficult and heated discussion with Kina'u
about releasing the priests on the *Clementine*. Rev. Hiram Bingham

was interpreter, and the captain realized that he was speaking for himself, as well as the kuhina nui,[16:54] by referring to American rather than Hawaiian resolve. When Captain Belcher threatened to forcibly remove him, Rev. Bingham remonstrated, and intimated "that blood will flow from this act." Captain Belcher shook his fist and shouted at the clergyman "that his life should answer for the first drop of British blood which his agency would cause to flow."[16:54] British Consul Richard Charlton added fuel to the discussion by stating that "Mr. Bingham is the cause of this trouble." Rev. Bingham dissented, "That is not so." Charlton responded with, "Mr. Bingham, if you insult me again, I will horsewhip you." Captain Belcher reportedly increased his threat, this time to have Rev. Bingham hanged at the yard arm.[17:508]

Captain Belcher ordered a marine detachment to "recapture" the *Clementine* and have the British colors re-hoisted.[16:54] The two priests were escorted back to land, where they were taken to their dwelling by Captains Belcher and Du Petit-Thouars.[77:149] So much for "gunboat respect" of Hawaiian sovereignty. A seemingly insignificant series of events had gotten out of control.

The king arrived from La-haina, Maui and there was a meeting on July 21, 1837 at Hale-kauwila House between the Hawaiian leaders and the two captains and their staffs. There were difficulties with interpreters (Hawaiian-English-French). The captains didn't want Rev. Bingham to have any influence, the king did. The captains fully supported Father Bachelot, but the king said he could not understand him. Several other interpreters were used, even American missionaries Rev. Lorrin Andrews, Rev. William Richards, and Dr. Gerrit P. Judd.[17:508-09]

Discussions were long and involved, and eventually an acceptable consensus was reached. The king remained within his rights to exclude the priests if he so insisted, and he did. They could remain at Honolulu, with no preaching, until passage elsewhere became available.[77:149] Damages due to Captain Dudoit would be determined later.

Captain Du Petit-Thouars appointed him French Consular Agent on July 24, 1837, subject to confirmation, which followed. Interestingly enough, Dudoit had been born a French citizen on Ile de France (Mauritius) in 1803, and, as the British took over that island in 1810, he was technically also a British subject.

Both warships left Honolulu several weeks later. Father Short departed on October 30, 1837 for Valparaiso, via Tahiti, on the American brig *Peru* under Captain Henry A. Peirce.[142:112 65:28]

The entire complicated issue was still not resolved. The American ship *Europa*, commanded by Captain Shaw, arrived in Honolulu on November 2, 1837.[17:512] Among the passengers were Frs. Louis Desire Maigret and Columba Murphy. Their arrival had been anticipated, and Governor Ke-ku-anao'a came aboard in the roads and secured a promise that they would "not interfere with the laws and regulations" and would "leave the islands the first favorable opportunity."[142:115] Father Bachelot purchased the schooner *Honolulu* (formerly *Missionary Packet*) from Captain Jules Dudoit and renamed it *Notre Dame de Paix*.[142:117] She sailed on November 23, 1837, taking Frs. Maigret and Bachelot.[77:150][65:29] Father Murphy left Honolulu in October 1839[142:46] and Father Walsh remained at the Honolulu Mission.

King Ka-mehameha III promulgated a lengthy Ordinance Rejecting the Catholic Religion on December 18, 1837. The first and last paragraphs follow:[60:390-92]

> "As we have seen the peculiarities of the Catholic religion and the proceedings of the Romish faith, to be calculated to set man against man in our kingdom, and as we formerly saw that disturbance was made in the time of Kaahumanu I, and as it was on this account that the priests of the Romish faith were at that time banished and sent away from this kingdom, and as from that time they have been under sentence of banishment until within this past year when we have been brought into new and increased trouble on account of those who follow the Pope, and as our determination to keep away such persons is by no means recent, and also on account of the request of foreigners that we make it known in writing, Therefore, I, with my chiefs, forbid, by this document, that any one should teach the peculiarities of the Pope's religion, nor shall it be allowed to any who teaches these doctrines or those peculiarities to reside in this kingdom; nor shall the ceremonies be exhibited in our kingdom, nor shall any one teaching its peculiarities or this faith be permitted to land on these shore; for it is not proper that two religions be found in this small kingdom. Therefore we utterly refuse to allow any one to teach those peculiarities in any manner whatsoever. We moreover prohibit all vessels whatsoever from bringing any teacher of that religion into this kingdom.
>
> "If any one, either foreigner or native, shall be found assisting another in teaching the doctrine of the Pope's religion, he shall pay to the government a fine of one hundred dollars for every such offence."

The language of this Ordinance is not similar to the writings of other Hawaiian leaders. It must have been prepared or heavily edited by someone more erudite. The hand of American Protestant missionaries appears most probable.

Although not clear, it appears that Father Walsh was excepted from this Ordinance because of Captain Vaillant's agreement with the king in October 1836, which allowed religious freedom for the French, on condition that the priest not give instruction to Hawaiians.[142:96 77:147]

Events negated this Ordinance, as will be seen later in the Edict of Toleration issued June 17, 1839, which resulted from the French Captain Cyrille La Place's hostile visit during July 9–20, 1839.

Meanwhile…by 1837 there were almost 50 American Protestant missionaries scattered in 17 Mission Stations throughout the islands. About half were clergymen, most of the rest were teachers.

Missionary study of spoken Hawaiian had reached a point where Rev. Lorrin Andrews was able to publish a Hawaiian-English dictionary in 1836. Rev. Sheldon Dibble, relying on La-haina Seminary scholars securing widespread memory knowledge, wrote the first Hawaiian history (1839). The Mission Press was printing thousands of pages in Hawaiian. A formidable 15-year challenge was completed on May 10, 1839 – 10,000 copies of the Bible translated into Hawaiian were printed.[17:531] The question sometimes arises, why the effort to teach Hawaiians to read and write their own language? Laura Judd put it succinctly: "It was a maxim with the Mission that in order to preserve the nation, they must preserve their speech."[69:79]

At the time of Kuhina nui Ka-'ahu-manu's death (1832), there were some 50,000 mostly adult students being taught to read and write Hawaiian by 900 teachers.[11:254] As may be recalled, without her emphasis schooling practically ceased. It was slowly implemented again with mostly children as students. There were probably 12–15,000 being instructed in the latter 1830s.[77:110]

The task of missionaries having to educate vast numbers of teachers lessened, and efforts were made to improve the quality of instructors. Classes were started on September 5, 1831 at the La-haina Seminary (later La-haina-luna School) to prepare students to become teachers and assistant teachers of religion. The O'ahu Charity School, in English and for westerners' children, began in 1833. Boarding academies for boys and girls were opened during 1836–38. A separate institution for chiefs' children was established at Honolulu in 1839 (later Royal School).[137:21-26]

There was steady progress on the part of the Protestants. The life led by Rev. William P. Alexander at the Wai-'oli Mission Station, Hanalei, Kaua'i, offered a good example of their activity in a country setting. Like his parishioners, he and his wife lived in a thatched hut, which was infested with cockroaches, rats, mice, fleas and mosquitoes. Fortunately, the Alexanders had mosquito netting for their bed.[3:88 4:190-91 230]

He preached at least three times a week in his not-yet fluent Hawaiian, held daily classes for teachers in the forenoon and children in the afternoon. Mrs. Alexander conducted a daily school for women. The clergyman periodically made a visitation of his assigned area. He would walk on the narrow paths to six or seven small villages a day, preaching, performing marriages, inspecting schools, and so forth.

His congregation numbered between 800-1,000 out of a population of 3,107. Rev. Alexander reported that there had been 80 births and 164 deaths from September 1834 to September 1835, and sadly noted: "What we do for this nation we must do quickly – they are rapidly melting away."[4:195-96] And because there was no doctor available, Rev. Alexander delivered a boy born to his wife on January 29, 1835.[4:188]

The population decline was true all over the islands. As well as they could, the missionaries conducted another census during 1835-36. They tallied 108,579 Hawaiians versus 130,313 in 1831-32 – a decrease of 21,734 (17%).[105:42] There were an estimated 600 foreigners in the islands,[105:43] still a relatively small number.

▨

Rev. Titus Coan, Hilo Mission Station, was indefatigable and an impassioned preacher. During the hour of evening prayers (7 pm) on Tuesday, November 7, 1837, he recorded that:[37:99]

> "We were startled by a heavy thud, and a sudden jar of the earth. The sound was like the fall of some vast body on the beach, and in a few seconds a noise of mingled voices rising for a mile along the shore thrilled us like the wail of doom…The sea, moved by an unseen hand, had all of a sudden risen in a gigantic wave, and this wave, rushing in with the speed of a racehorse, had fallen upon the shore, sweeping everything not more than 15 or 20 feet above the high-water mark into indiscriminate ruin…Through the great mercy of God only 13 were drowned."

Fortunately an English whaler in Hilo harbor was not damaged and lowered its boats and helped rescue many who were being swept rapidly out to sea.[35:89-90]

The strong earthquake and consequent tsunami (tidal wave) were felt throughout the islands of Hawai'i and Maui. There was considerable damage. Honolulu harbor, 217 statute miles from Hilo, had an eight-foot rise and fall of water level.[35:88]

Rev. Coan preached to his impressed listeners that this natural phenomenon was a Sign from God. He baptized 639 Hawaiians by June 30, 1838. Religious fervor spread to Rev. Lorenzo Lyons' Waimea Station and he baptized 2,600 within the same eight-month period.[17:528] The feeling of inspiration, perhaps mixed with fear, spread rapidly to other islands and became known as the Great Revival. Hawaiian church members in regular standing jumped from 1,049 at the end of 1837 to 3,341 in 1838; 15,915 in 1839; and 18,451 (18% of the population) in 1840.[106:42]

The missionaries had been conservative and now required probation of up to several years before admittance to a church to assure that the supplicant was worthy. They were very honest about the size of their congregations – to exaggerate church numbers seems to have been practically a sin. The Great Revival modified this philosophy and time proved there were not many backsliders.

Some missionaries influenced the course of events in the islands, as well as living the evangelism they preached and advocating moral values. Several became trusted advisors to the chiefs and chiefesses. Although precluded from decision making, they were forceful at times when recommending a position or action. The missionaries had earned this trust because they were obviously trying to help, were of the highest order of western civilization, and wanted not material gains for themselves. Rev. William Richards at La-haina Mission Station, where many of the chiefs lived, was particularly of assistance to the important governor, High Chief Hoapili. Rev. Hiram Bingham, leader of the Hawaiian Mission, served the king and kuhina nui well, and was often interpreter in meetings with important westerners. There were numbers of others who should be mentioned in this context for providing good sense, especially about dealing with westerners – let just one suffice, Levi Chamberlain, Secular Agent at Honolulu.*

★ Levi Chamberlain was the greatest chronicler of his time. His journal is remarkably complete, reasonably unbiased and objective. A typewritten copy can be found at the Hawaiian Mission Children's Society library.

Missionary leaders decided that the time had come to rebuild the fourth thatched church at Ka-wai-a-ha'o, Honolulu. Pastor Hiram Bingham designed the present "stone" (coral block) edifice in the mid-1830s. The king became enthusiastic and headed a subscription list. On November 28, 1868, the P.C. Advertiser recorded the following anecdotes:

> "The Governor (Ke-ku-anao'a) insisted that it should be 160 feet long – the pastor of the church, also a determined man, said 120, and set the stakes of one end further in. The Governor set those of the other end ahead; the missionary followed up from behind, and the site would have walked rapidly down town, had not a happy compromise arisen as to the required dimensions. (*ed*: 144 feet!)
>
> "In those days the labor of the people was in great measure at the command of the chiefs, and it was but for the chiefs to say, Come and let us do this, and the thing was done. The planning and execution and procural of material however, for that massive edifice required an amount of energy and thought, and the credit is due to the (Governor), to the late Hon. A. Paki, and the Rev. Mr. Bingham."

The cellar of the 144 feet by 72 feet structure was dug by July 31, 1837.[52:7] Chief Paki provided the half-ton cornerstone from Wai-'anae which was laid June 8, 1839.[129:44] Thousands were organized into gangs for cutting the two to three feet long coral blocks from Honolulu harbor's reef, and carrying them to the building site. The church took three years to construct.

Rev. Hiram Bingham did not see it completed. His wife's health was failing, and one suspects that she had been worn out by 21 years of demanding missionary life and bearing seven children. After *great* soul searching, they returned to New England August 3, 1840.

He had led and dominated the Hawaiian Mission by his dynamic personality and stubbornness for over 20 years. He was greatly trusted by the ruler, kuhina nui and principal chiefs. His advice was freely and forcefully expressed. Although he was strongly disliked by some westerners for his intolerance and insistence on morality, these were normal traits for a committed missionary.

A respectful tablet on the outside front wall of Ka-wai-a-ha'o Church states in part:

"This slab is placed here in grateful remembrance of a pioneer missionary by descendants of Hawaiians…among whom he preached Christ for more than twenty years. He preached the first sermon ever delivered in this city April 25, 1820 from 'Fear not for I bring you glad tidings of great joy.' Here he taught confiding kings, queens and chiefs, faced danger, bore calumny from abroad, aided in reducing the language to writing, translated much of the Bible, composed hymns and tunes, here he baptized a thousand converts, planted this edifice and with his loving people on June 8, 1839 laid this adjoining cornerstone…"

Almost two years after the Binghams departed, Ka-wai-a-haʻo Church was completed on July 21, 1842. It still stands in the center of Honolulu, and services and community work continue to this day.

H AWAIIAN LEADERS WERE especially disturbed and uncomfortable by the confrontation with the British Captain Belcher and French Captain Du Petit-Thouars in July 1837. The islanders had maintained their position but were embarrassed as to how it came about. They hadn't expected to be challenged on matters within their own authority. At the same time, they hadn't wanted to tempt the powerful cannons of the warships. That would have been awful. In an attempt to organize and govern more in the western way, Hawaiian leaders turned to their trusted missionaries for guidance and assistance.

The missionaries were precluded from government decision making and actions. Yet the basic objective of the Mission was to raise up the whole people to an elevated state of Christian civilization.[59:27] This recognized the need to teach two secular concerns beyond missionary injunctions: 1) a better means of government on the principles of civil liberty, rights of the people, and law, and 2) better control of commercial and gainful activities.[17:492]

Both Hawaiian leaders and missionaries had earlier (August 23, 1836) written to the American Board in Boston requesting teachers and assistance in these areas. The Board did not consider these requests favorably – their charter was for evangelism.[17:496-97]

Rev. Lorrin Andrews of the Mission Seminary at La-haina was asked to leave the Mission and join the kingdom in 1837. This did not come about. Rev. William Richards did accept the following year, with the backing of his missionary brethren. He resigned from the Mission and became Chaplain, Interpreter, Teacher of Political Economy, Law and the Science of Government on July 3, 1838.[17:529 64:66]

Rev. Richards started giving the chiefs daily lessons in Political Economy. He also translated writings of western leaders on the subject, then compared the governments of the western powers and how they operated. Soon the chiefs began to say: "So this is it! Here is the way to gain wealth and honor." [70:343-44] The king, now living at La-haina, was becoming more conservative and receptive. The seeds of improving Hawaiian government were planted and flourished.

A description of Honolulu as being "narrow, crooked and filthy lanes" summed up the port in 1838. The village of some 6,000 people stretched from Ka-pa-lama to Ke-walo, and from the sea to the beginning of Nu'u-anu valley. There were some 11 mercantile firms, numbers of shops and places of leisure. One hundred whalers could crowd into the harbor deck to deck[52:4] if they were tightly berthed.

Kuhina nui Kina'u issued a proclamation at the beginning of 1838: [33:5]

"I, Kaahumanu II,
do hereby explain to you, O people of the foreign land and also to those of these islands the work to be done on this year of ours. Here is the work. I shall widen the streets in our city and break up some new places to make five streets on the length of the land, and six streets on the breadth of the land...

"That is why some of our streets are closed. Because of the lack of streets some people were almost killed by horseback riders and the ruler of the kingdom barely escaped in 1834...Because the streets lack yards, therefore that may be the reason for the filth and stench and the too close living that cause people of the city to be sick. Because of the lack of streets, there is much foul odor to offend the nose, therefore, perhaps causing dull headaches... Therefore do not hinder with evil hearts..."

Governor Ke-ku-anao'a was given the task of laying out the town.[33:5] That he did with great vigor. Work began in February 1838 with surveys, then gangs of men began pulling down houses and fences. There *were* lots of arguments and compromises. It took almost the whole year to provide wide and dusty streets. One report claimed it was done with great carnage among houses and fences.[52:6]

The council became actively temperate and passed two liquor laws with strong penalties in 1838.[52:12] A notice to foreigners was published on March 13 stating that beginning on April 1 the 12-14 O'ahu liquor licenses would be reduced: "But two houses only will be left where liquors may be sold, the two houses where billiard-tables are now kept, but the most of the grog-shops are taboo, and must sell no more." A week later another law: "Permitted sales of spirits by the barrel or large cask." [77:162]

Further: "Any house having been licensed for retailing spirits, may sell by the glass, but not by any larger measure; and its doors must be closed by ten o'clock at night, and all visitors must go away until morning. And on Sunday such house shall not be opened from ten o'clock on Saturday night until Monday morning. We prohibit drunkenness in the licenses houses." [77:162]

Distillation of spirits within the kingdom was not allowed, and a law enacted on August 21 prohibited the import and purchase of spirits, and a duty of 50¢ per gallon on wines imported after January 1, 1839. [52:13]

Governor Ke-ku-anao'a had the task of enforcing these laws in Honolulu, which were most unpopular with those who did not receive licenses. He had lots of troubles with his judgments on visiting seamen who were drunk or unruly, and their obstreperous consuls. (American Agent for Commerce and Seamen John C. Jones was replaced by more respectful Peter A. Brinsmade on April 9, 1839.) The governor was the last word on what to do about prostitutes (usually fined $10), cattle stealers (flogged and fined), civil disputes, wife beating, theft, pranksters – all of it was the governor's responsibility and maintaining order kept him a busy man. [52:20-21]

Kina'u gave birth to a daughter, Victoria Ka-mamalu, on November 1, 1838. [58:161] [69:76] She was not adopted, as apparently Kina'u considered that no family was superior in lineage and thus advantageous. John I'i, her secretary at that time, became the infant's kahu (guardian). [58:164]

Amidst all the exciting activities of rebuilding and maintaining order in the large town, there was a mumps epidemic. Kina'u became ill and succumbed to this disease on April 4, 1839. [58:164] [72:119]

As kuhina nui, she had been heir to the extensive lands of her predecessor, Ka-'ahu-manu, and now these fell to the infant Victoria Ka-mamalu – it appears the council had determined that the office of kuhina nui was hereditary, like the king. Thus her baby daughter had the title of Ka-'ahu-manu III. [22:124] The lands were administered by her father, Ke-ku-anao'a, and John I'i. [72:107]

Because Victoria Ka-mamalu was still so young, High Chiefess Miriam Ke-ka-ulu-ohi was appointed to act as kuhina nui (premier). She was the daughter of Ka-mehameha's half-brother Kalai-mamahu, had been one of Ka-mehameha's queens and a queen of Liholiho, was also the niece of Ka-'ahu-manu and Kina'u's half-sister (and mother of a son afterwards to be King Luna-lilo).[72:117] [124] These extremely complex relationships were nevertheless typical of Hawaiians, who understood all the nuances of an extended family.

Rev. William Richards' teaching the king, kuhina nui and council about political affairs resulted in the Declaration of Rights on June 7, 1839. They were drafted by Hawaiian graduates of the La-haina Mission Seminary and discussed by the king and council until finalized. The Declaration contained two important principles:[77:159-61]

> "Chiefs and people* may enjoy the same protection under one and the same law.
>   "Protection is hereby assured to the persons of all the people, together with their lands, their building lots, and all their property, while they conform to the laws of the kingdom, and nothing whatever shall be taken from any individual except by express provision of the laws."

Ten days later, on June 17, 1839, the king announced what has been termed an Edict of Toleration. It stopped the persecution and punishment of Hawaiians who professed the Catholic faith. Visiting naval captains had strongly urged religious toleration, and American Protestant missionaries advocated the same. This edict was apparently in the form of an order, and not announced by crier or printed.[77:163-64] Sixty or more Hawaiian Catholics were released from jail in Honolulu.[60:317]

However, there were unexpected repercussions. News was received in June 1839 that French Captain Du Petit-Thouars had gone to Tahiti in August–September 1838, and secured a treaty, apology, salute and indemnity of $2,000 for the expulsion of two French Catholic priests.[77:165] Now rumors circulated that one or two French warships were coming to Hawai'i.

Indeed, Captain Cyrille P. T. La Place of the French frigate *L'Artemise* arrived in Honolulu on July 9, 1839. Barely consulting with French Consular Agent Jules Dudoit, he presented a scornful Manifesto to Governor Ke-ku-anao'a. In substance:[7:225-26]

> "His Majesty, the king of the France, having commanded me to come to Honolulu in order to put an end, either by force or per-

---

★ In this context, Hawaiian commoners.

suasion, to the ill-treatment to which the French have been victims tims at the Sandwich Islands, I hasten to employ the latter means as more comfortable to the noble and liberal political system pursued by France towards the powerless. Misled by perfidious counselors, the principal chiefs of the Sandwich Islands are ignorant that there is not in the whole world a power capable of preventing France from punishing her enemies, or they would have endeavored to merit her favor instead of incurring her displeasure, as they have done in ill-treating the French...They must now comprehend that to tarnish the Catholic religion with the name of idolatry, and to expel the French under that absurd pretext from this archipelago, was to offer an insult to France and to her sovereign...Among all civilized nations there is not one that does not permit in its territory the free exercise of all religions. I consequently demand –

1 That the Catholic worship be declared free throughout the islands subject to the king.

2 That a site at Honolulu for a Catholic church be given by the government.

3 That all Catholics imprisoned on account of their religion be immediately set at liberty.

4 That the king place in the hands of the captain of the *Artemise* the sum of twenty thousand dollars as a guarantee of his future conduct towards France; to be restored when it shall be considered that the accompanying treaty will be faithfully complied with.

5 That the treaty, signed by the king, as well as the money, be brought on board of the *Artemise* by a principal chief; and that the French flag be saluted with twenty-one guns.

"These are the equitable conditions at the price of which the king of the Sandwich Islands shall preserve friendship with France...If, contrary to expectation, and misled by bad advisers, the king and chiefs refuse to sign the treaty I present, war will immediately commence, and all the devastations and calamities which may result shall be imputed to them alone, and they must also pay the damages which foreigners injured under these circumstances will have a right to reclaim."

No discussion was permitted. Captain La Place then blockaded the port and advised the British and American representatives that he would commence hostilities at noon on the 12th if his demands were not met. He also offered protection for westerners aboard his frigate with one exception: [7:227] "I do not, however, include in this class the individuals who, although born, it is said, in the United States, form a part of the Protestant clergy of the chief of this group, direct his counsels, influence his conduct, and are the true authors of the insults offered to France. For me, they compose part of the native population and must undergo the unhappy consequences of war which they will have brought on this country."

The five articles in the Manifesto, entitled Treaty, were signed by Kuhina nui Ke-ka-ulu-ohi and Governor Ke-ku-anao'a on the 12th, and later by King Ka-mehameha III.[77:166] The demanded $20,000 surety was hurriedly collected, half being borrowed from resident merchants.

A further Convention was signed on the 17th without any argument permitted. It expanded Captain Du Petit-Thouars' 1837 document and included two new significant provisions:

> "A Frenchman accused of any crime would be tried by a jury composed of foreign residents proposed by the French Consular Agent and approved by the Hawaiian Kingdom.
> "Foreign liquor could be imported into Hawaii with a duty no higher than 5% ad valorem."

This latter provision in effect repealed the previous year's Hawaiian law prohibiting the import of any "ardent spirits."[77:166]

Captain La Place led his band and several hundred armed marines and seamen to one of the king's houses for a Military Mass by Father Walsh on Sunday, July 21, 1839. The *L'Artemise* then sailed away.

This was a bitter experience for the Hawaiian leaders. The question arises, why didn't they say "no" and resist? The question of "what if" is always chancy.

"What if" the French warship had attacked the fort and town of Honolulu? From the magnificent fortification with its more than 50 cannons on the parapet, a shot had never been fired in anger. How good were the guns and artillerymen's capabilities and will to fight? Honolulu Fort served only as a military symbol and the center of Governor Ke-ku-anao'a's administration.

"What if" the Hawaiians had been able to defeat and sink the French frigate? What would they have done with any prisoners? How long would it take before a fleet of French warships came in revenge? Could the Hawaiian military cope with them?

"What if" there had been a prolonged battle? The damage would be terrific, and islanders would have to pay for it somehow in the end.

Would it have been worth it? Humiliation was galling, but, one could rationalize, better than valor, deaths and destruction. The Hawaiians had inordinate respect for the white man, his knowledge and things, and will to act. It might be difficult to admit, but the foreigners were thought to be superior. The island nation was small by comparison. And not only Hawaiians had to be considered, but also resident westerners engaged in business. They were here to stay and had to be protected as well.

All these considerations must have plagued Ke-ku-anao'a.

The islands *were* a convenient place in the middle of the Pacific to stop for water, foodstuffs, firewood and relaxation. The grand design of each major maritime power appeared to be:

FRENCH. They were primarily interested in their trade on the west coast of South America which supported their other interests in Asia, the Indian Ocean and Africa. Their goals in the Pacific lay south of the equator. Hawai'i was of minor importance compared to maintaining a strong position against the other great powers. When visiting the islands, they seemed most concerned about respect for the French, and the welfare of French residents and the Catholic religion.

BRITISH. They led in Pacific influence and commerce, and their Protestant missionaries were dominant in other island groups. They had established a penal colony on Australia in 1788 and the entire continent was a British dependency by 1829. Interest in Hawai'i, which was off the beaten track, was based only on maintaining favorable commerce and good treatment of their subjects.

AMERICAN. Both the British and French recognized that United States interests controlled the majority of commerce in the form of North Pacific whaling and, through the missionaries, greatly influenced political affairs. Their warships enforced the status quo.

Ke-ku-anao'a might have found all this an interesting summation, but not very helpful for any future potential confrontation. It would be most encouraging if the Hawaiian leadership could somehow play one great power against the other.

The onslaught of westerners continued. They came for the usual variety of reasons. Bishop Rouchouze of the Pacific area arrived in Honolulu on May 15, 1840 with three priests – Fathers Louis

Maigret, Ernest Heurtel and Dasitheus Desuault.[77:341] Over 2,000 Hawaiians were baptized Catholics by the end of 1840, and their missionaries spread to the other islands. The Catholic Cathedral was built during 1840-43.

The U.S. frigate *Columbia*, commanded by Commodore George E. Read and accompanied by the U.S. sloop-of-war *John Adams* under Captain Thomas Wyman, arrived in Honolulu on October 10, 1839 and remained for a peaceful three weeks.

A different category of official visitors came in September of 1840, the United States Exploring Expedition – Commander Charles Wilkes, in the sloop-of-war *Vincennes*, Captain William L. Hudson, in the sloop-of-war *Peacock*, and Lt. Cadwalader Ringgold, in the brig *Porpoise*. They explored and surveyed the islands until April 5, 1841. This must have been baffling to most Hawaiians, raising the question of what these men really intended.

Commander Charles Wilkes was a great observer and described his first views of Hawai'i in 1840 as:

"Honolulu exhibits, even to a distant view, many dwellings built in the European style, with look-outs, and several steeples rising above the habitations. Some edifices of large size are also seen in the progress of construction. Native houses, with thatched roofs, however, predominate, which prevent it from losing the appearance of a Polynesian town, and are associated with ideas of semi-civilization.[139:III373]

"On landing, a great uproar prevailed, and groups presented themselves to view, so motley that it would be difficult to describe their dress or appearance. There are, indeed, few places where so great a diversity in dress and language exists as at Honolulu. The majority were in well-worn European clothing, put on in the most fanciful manner; but on the whole, I should say that the crowd were scantily covered, some being half-dressed, many shirtless, none fully clothed, and numbers of them with nothing but the maro (malo, loin cloth). I had been led to expect a greater appearance of civilization. The women were all clad in long loose garments, like bathing-dresses, and many of them were sporting in the water as if it had been their native element. Some of the natives wore the simple tapa (ed: kapa, bark cloth) thrown over their shoulders, which gave them a much more respectable appearance than those who were clothed in cast-off garments.[139:III374]

"Everything is earth-colour, with the exception of a few green blinds. The streets, if they may be called, have no regularity as to width, and are ankle-deep in light dust and sand. Little pains are taken to keep them clean from offal; and, in some places, offensive sink-holes strike the senses, in which are seen wallowing some old and corpulent hogs. One of these, which was pointed out to us as belonging to the king, was tabooed, and consequently a privileged personage."[139:III375]

Governor Ke-ku-anao'a made an official call on the Commander on September 28, 1840. "He is a noble-looking man, upward of six feet in height, and proportionately large. He was in full dress uniform of blue and gold and was altogether very striking and soldier-like in his appearance and pleasing in his address…He was self-possessed, and appeared quite used to the etiquette on such occasions…is possessed of much energy of character…"[139:III388]

The king came to Honolulu on the 29th and Commander Wilkes called upon him the next day. "The king was dressed in a blue coat, white pantaloons, and vest. We afterwards understood that he had prepared himself to receive us in full costume, but on seeing us approaching in undress uniforms, he had taken off his robes of state. The appearance of the king is prepossessing: he is rather robust, above the middle height, has a good expression of countenance, and pleasing manners. The conversation was carried on with ease through the interpretation of Mr. Richards, and left upon our minds a favourable impression of the intelligence of the royal family of these islands. One thing was certain, namely, that, in regard to personal size, they are unsurpassed by any family that has ever come under my notice."[139:IV3-4]

Commander Wilkes approved of Rev. William Richards, and sagely observed that: "Like other missionaries he was but little versed and had no experience in the affairs of government. He was unused to the petty squabbling of the foreign officials, and his mind was far above the ignoble task of disputing with the revilers of all law and religion."[139:IV8]

King Ka-mehameha III had a lengthy private discussion with Commander Charles Wilkes on October 2, 1840. He frankly outlined two difficulties his kingdom faced for which he solicited advice and assistance:[139:IV9] 1) The disputes with foreign nations which were unhappily finalized by threats from visiting naval captains, and 2) constant trouble with foreign residents over the Christian moral codes adopted from the teachings of the American Protestant missionaries.

Commander Wilkes emphasized that he had no authority in matters of state. He thoroughly understood and sympathized. One suggestion he made to help avoid misunderstandings – put everything in writing. He appreciated the king's desire for a close friendship with the United States, and predicted that the United States would officially recognize the kingdom as a nation. When he returned home, he would report this issue.[139:IV19] In the end, Wilkes had not been much help, but left a comfortable feeling of warm, cordial relationships.

Meanwhile, the wheels of Hawaiian law rolled on. High Chief Ka-manawa and his wife, Ka-moku'iki, were separated and he wanted to marry another woman. Having more than one wife at a time was forbidden. So he and an accomplice poisoned her. This was discovered, creating a scandal that could not be brushed aside.

Governor Ke-ku-anao'a was judge and 12 Hawaiians formed a jury who found the couple guilty and condemned them to death. Despite the fact that Ka-manawa was a high chief and favorite of the king, there was no pardon. One law for all. The convicted were hung on the Fort wall on October 20, 1840, and it was estimated that 10,000 people witnessed this execution.* [72:270 139:IV29-30]

This dramatic incident demonstrated how much Hawaiian cultural values had changed. Ali'i who only decades before had been almost god-like were subject to the same statutes as commoners.

---

* Ka-manawa was the grandson of one of Ka-mehameha's senior counselors, and grandfather of a child who would become King Ka-la-kaua.

BELOW. Kuhina nui Kina'u (Ka-'ahu-manu II), 1837. Enlargement of portion of Masselot lithograph. She was Ke-ku-anao'a's wife and mother of Kings Ka-mehameha IV & V. Prisoners at rear of illustration are either Catholics or felons. (Archives of Hawaii)

BELOW. King, kuhina nui and high chiefs confer with British and French officers, Hale-kauwila Palace, July 21, 1837. Enlargement of a portion of cartoon by Masselot. Facing, L to R: Kua-kini, governor of Hawai'i; Hoapili, governor of Maui; Queen Kalama; (in chair) King Ka-mehameha III; Rev. Hiram Bingham (interpreter); kuhina nui Kina'u; Ke-ku-anao'a, governor of O'ahu; "Captain" Francisco de Paula Marin; and unknown sleepyhead, governor of Kaua'i? (cartoon widespread)

Governor Mataio
Ke-ku-anao'a.
Unknown date.
Unknown artist.
(Alexander, W.D. A
Brief History of the
Hawaiian People. NY:
American Book Co.,
1894)

RIGHT. King Ka-
mehameha III, 1841.
Watercolor over pencil by
Alfred T. Agate. (Wilkes,
Charles. Narrative of the
United States Exploring
Expedition...Philadelphia:
Lea and Blanchard, 1845)

LEFT. Kuhina nui Ke-ka-ulu-ohi,
1840. Engraved from sketch by
A.T. Agate. She succeeded Kina'u
in this office April 4, 1839 and
served until her death June 7,
1845. Commander Charles
Wilkes described her September
30, 1840 when sketched: "This
lady is upwards of six feet in
height; her frame is exceedingly
large and well covered with fat.
She was dressed in yellow silk,
with enormously large gigot
sleeves...Her shoulders were covered with a richly-
embroidered shawl of scarlet
cape...Her feet were encased in
white cotton stockings and men's
shoes." (Wilkes, Charles. Narrative
of the United States Exploring
Expedition...Philadelphia: Lea
and Blanchard, 1845)

LEFT. Ka-wai-a-haʻo Church. Designed by Rev. Hiram Bingham. Built of coral blocks 1839-42. (Taylor, Albert P. Under Hawaiian Skies. Honolulu: Advertiser Publishing Co., 1926)

BELOW. Whaling off Honolulu, 1833. Stylized drawing by Hulsart. In early days there were some (depicted) sperm whales in Hawaiian waters. (Matthews, Leonard H. [ed.] The Whale. NY: Crescent Books, ?)

13

KANAWAI (LAWS)

THE EFFORTS OF REV. WILLIAM RICHARDS led to a giant step forward when the king and council of the fledgling Hawaiian Kingdom promulgated a Constitution on October 8, 1840.

The Preamble and Article 1 follow the theme of the June 7, 1839 Declaration of Rights: [101:10]

"It is our design to regulate our kingdom according to the above principles and thus seek the greatest prosperity both of all the chiefs and all the people of these Hawaiian Islands. But we are aware that we cannot ourselves alone accomplish such an object – God must be our aid, for it is His province alone to give perfect protection and prosperity. Wherefore we first present our supplication to HIM, that he will guide us to right measures and sustain us in our work.

"It is therefore our fixed decree,

"1. That no law shall be enacted which is at variance with the general spirit of God's law."

The Constitution established an "executive branch" and defined the prerogatives of the king, authority of the kuhina nui (premier) and the governors. A legislature came into being composed of a House of Nobles (appointed by the king and approved by this body), and a Representative Body (chosen by the people). A judiciary system began to take form. The Constitution also had a sizable section entitled "Respecting the Tax Officers."

For the first time commoners were granted a voice in their own government – on paper, at least – for any new law required the approval of the majority of both legislative bodies, and had to be signed by the premier and king. The Supreme Court was comprised of the king, premier and four judges appointed by the House of

Representatives. Despite all these new philosophies, in reality the opinions and actions of the powerful chiefs and chiefesses usually prevailed.

The first session of the legislature, held at La-haina November
1-14, 1840, was attended by the 16 nobles named in the
Constitution:[101:13] [114:26] King Ka-mehameha III, Kuhina nui Ke-ka-
ulu-ohi, Hoapili-wahine (Ka-heihei-malie), Kua-kini, Ke-kau-
'onohi, Kahekili, Paki, Konia, Ke-o-ho-ka-lole, Lele-io-hoku,
Ke-kua-anao'a, Ke-alii-a-honui, Ka-na'ina, John I'i, Keoni Ana (John
Young II) and Ha-alilio.

This body passed a law establishing seven representatives: two
from Hawai'i, Maui and O'ahu; and one from Kaua'i. Voting for "men
of wisdom and prudence" was to be by petition, with the majority
votes prevailing.[101:17-18] Elections were to come in later years.

Three representatives were in the April 1841 session: Ka-auwai
and David Malo from Maui, and Hala'i from O'ahu. The 1842 session
listed Jacob Malo and Kapae (Hawai'i), David Malo and Ka-makau
(Maui), Hala'i (O'ahu) and David Pa-pohaku (Kaua'i)[114:27] [76:37] The
House of Nobles convened with 12 members recorded present in the
1842 session.[76:37] This consistent record of attendance at a time when
interisland travel was often difficult and dangerous indicates a great
deal of effort.

The Declaration of Rights, Constitution and current laws were
codified in the Blue Book in 1842, named for the color of the cov-
ers.[77:229] Some of the 53 chapters of laws, of interest today, follow:—

Fearsome pestilence and epidemics killed many people. In an
effort to preclude their admittance, contact with a foreign vessel was
prohibited until a Health Officer pronounced that the passengers and
crew aboard were healthy. Any vessel carrying contagious diseases
was prohibited anchorage, or quarantined for at least 42 days while
flying a yellow flag at the main top.[101:39]

Three monetary taxes were established to be collected between
October and December of each year. As to be expected, there were
exceptions and penalties.[101:19-22 36]

POLL TAX. (Children under 14 and the elderly excepted)
Man, $1. Suitable substitutes: 33# arrowroot, 16# cotton, or sugar,
nets, etc., as determined.
Woman, Half-dollar proportion.
Boy, Quarter-dollar proportion.
Girl, Eighth-dollar proportion.

LAND TAX.
Large farm, A swine one fathom long at least 333# or $10.
Smaller farm, A swine three cubits long at least 250# or $7.50.
Very small one, A swine one yard long at least 167# or $5.

LABOR TAX. (Monthly)
First week, 2 days for the king, 1 day for the landlord.
Second week, 1 day for the king, 2 days for the landlord.
Third & fourth [week], none.
If important public work, 13 days per month.

In clear Hawaiian writing, Respecting Idlers:[101:23]

"As for the idler, let the industrious put him to shame, and sound
his name from one end of the country to the other. And even if
they should withhold food on account of his idleness, there shall
be no condemnation for those who thus treat idlers.

"If landlord, or chief should give entertainment to such a sluggard, he would thereby bring shame on the industrious. For three
months the tenants of him who thus entertains the sluggard shall
be freed from labor for the landlord. Such is the punishment of
him who befriends the sluggard. Let him obtain his food by labor."

The principle of Political Economy as taught by Rev. William
Richards was prevalent throughout the revised statutes:[101:28] "The
man who does not labor enjoys little happiness. He cannot obtain any
great good unless he strives for it with earnestness. He cannot make
himself comfortable, not even preserve his life unless he labors for it."
Land, the most precious asset on an island, was held in common
and use allocated by the ruler.[101:10] Inheritance of use was recognized
for property which Ka-mehamehas I and II "gave to land agents."
When a land agent died, normally one-third of his holdings was
returned to the king by the heir.[101:32] This principle of hereditary
tenure of land by the ali'i had been in force since the Council of
Chiefs declared that Kau-i-ke-aouli was to become king, June 6,
1925.[77:270]
As far as commoners and foreigners were concerned, tenure of
land was somewhat uncertain. The Declaration of Rights stated:[101:9]
"Protection is hereby secured to the persons of all the people,
together with their lands, their building lots and all their property
and nothing whatever shall be taken from any individual, except by
express provision of the laws." British and French residents had the

additional protection of the British Treaty of 1836 (due to Lord Russell) and the French Convention of 1837 (forged by Du Petit-Thouars).The commoner had limited rights according to the law of 1840:[101:24] "No man living on a farm...shall without cause desert the land of his landlord, nor shall the landlord causelessly dispossess his tenant."

The Constitution demonstrated great concern for schooling.[101:40-43] "The basis on which the kingdom rests is wisdom and knowledge...The proper ages for children to go to school shall be considered to be four years and upwards to fourteen years of age...No man...who does not understand reading, writing, geography and arithmetic shall hold the office of Governor, Judge, Tax officer nor land agent, nor hold any office over another man, nor shall a man who is unable to read and write marry a wife, nor a woman who is unable to read and write marry a husband." The government began to totally provide for Hawaiian education, which used to be partly a missionary responsibility.

Jurors for significant trials were selected from "forty, wise, reflecting, just men, not foolish men, not men of anger, not intemperate men..."[101:104-05] Foreign jurors were to be those "as are just and quiet in their lives, not angry persons nor drunkards, but such as are thought to be wise, and lovers of peace."[101:105] "If the accuser and accused be both foreigners, then the jury shall be made up of foreigners only...If there be no foreigners on either side, there shall be no foreigner on the jury...If there be a foreigner on one side and a native on the other, then in forming the jury, half shall be foreigners and half natives...But if the foreigner accused be a Frenchman, then this law respecting the formation of the jury will not be applicable, see French Treaty."[101:106]

Even the problem of public traffic came under much-needed regulation:

> "By this law is prohibited all running or swift riding of horses in roads, streets and all avenues in villages and also in all places of public assembly or public resort and in all places where the traveling is abundent...All persons riding on horseback or in a carriage in streets where people are traveling shall ride in or near the middle of the street...It is also taboo to train or teach wild and untrained horses in the streets where men are traveling...It is also

taboo to set at liberty wild cattle or permit them to go at large, or even to lead them carelessly in the streets of a village or in any place of public resort."[101:57]

To print laws was one thing, to deal with foreigners who felt that they should be exempt was another.

✦

The authority of the ruler (or the late kuhina nui Ka-'ahu-manu) to grant *use* of common land was well understood and generally accepted. British Consul Richard Charlton had a "Grant of Land" from Prime Minister Ka-lani-moku, in writing, dated December 9, 1826. The document granted a tax-free 291-year *leasehold ownership*. When Charlton asked the king about this in 1840, he was supposed to have replied that "he could not allow any person to hold land for so long a term."[34:74] This crucial issue was to become a major contention between the Hawaiian Kingdom and the United Kingdom, and is quoted in its entirety:[34:74]

> "Know all men by these Presents that I,
> "Kalaimuku, do hereby assign unto Richard Charlton, Esquire, his heirs, executors, administrators, and assigns, the piece of land situated near the north-west angle of the fort, extending 110 yards or thereabouts, in front, and running back (from the high water mark) 127 yards, to build on, improve, or to erect such warehouses as he, the said Richard Charlton, his heirs, executors, administrators or assigns, may think is proper, and to have and to hold, free of all quit rent, fees, or taxes, for the term of 291 years,★ with liberty to sell and dispose of the same for that term and no longer.
> "In witness whereof, I have hereunto subscribed my name, and set the seal, at Woahoo, this 9th day of December, in the year of our Lord 1826.
> (signed)   KALAIMOKU
> Witness:
> (signed)   BOKI
> FRANCISCO DE PAULA MARIN"

At the time, Prime Minister Ka-lani-moku did not have authority to allocate land, only the rule could do so. Ka-lani-moku died on

---

★ Cite 77:208 states 299 years, and another, 34:C.1, states 229 years. No matter which is correct, the period was over 200 years.

February 8, 1827 after a long illness. The deed was obviously written by a learned foreigner, and a seal was newly used by the Prime Minister. At the very least, one suspects coercion. The issue would remain a bone of contention.

⬚

Several British resident businessmen objected to the Constitutional labor tax upon their Hawaiian servants. The employers did pay a small "protection tax" and regular taxes for their Hawaiian servants and employees, and considered that adequate. Now the kingdom wanted 25¢ a day in lieu of three days' labor a week for the common good. British Consul Richard Charlton wrote to London that American businessmen did not mind paying for their servants' exemption, as the work was to build a stone bridge for better access to their stores and warehouses. "It was proposed by them, and a large sum of money is to be paid to the governor when completed." [34:75]

Governor Ke-ku-anao'a responded to the British Consul, February 22, 1841: [34:77]

> "I have received your communication concerning the letter of Messrs. Pelly, Henry Skinner, and Francis Greenway, complaining to you, and I understand it.
>
> "I tell you plainly that this work is for the Government. Three days in a week, and twelve days' work for the Government in a month, that is the character of the work.
>
> "Therefore, if you foreigners think to retain some natives with you to take care of your property, and this thing and that, and your houses, perhaps, you must make known the same to me, but the native must pay twenty-five cents for each day. If any native is retained without my knowledge and that of the overseers, he must pay a fine of fifty cents, according to the letter of the law.
>
> "These are the conditions that you may hear. I lay no command upon the foreigners, but upon the natives of this kingdom."

This sounds insignificant today, but the matter was reported to London with indignation. On August 21, 1841, the Admiralty sent instructions to the Admiral commanding British Naval Forces in the Pacific to send a warship to Hawai'i and "compel the Governor to refund any sum which may have been unfairly extorted from British subjects..." [34:81]

H.M.S. *Curacoa* under Captain Jenkin Jones was the next British warship to visit Honolulu – October 6-14, 1841. As usual, British

Consul Richard Charlton involved the captain in the numerous grievances of British residents. Strangely enough, no mention was made of the recent fuss about the labor tax upon the Hawaiian servants of British residents.[34:97]

Captain Jones discussed various complaints with Governor Ke-ku-anaoʻa on October 11, 1841:[34:98-9]

1 Charles Cockett was convicted of galloping his horse through La-haina village. He was confined in irons for a few hours, being violent, and discharged without being required to pay the usual $5 fine. The captain remonstrated about the use of irons.

2 The sentence of a $7 fine and confinement of Owen Jones, who took a Hawaiian woman's comb, was questioned. As the comb was estimated to be worth only 25¢, the fine was revoked.

3 A Hawaiian stole a horse from George Cruttenden, and the kingdom promised to pay him $200. (A magnificent sum.)

4 Thomas Phillips' sons had been apprehended galloping their horses on the streets of La-haina, and were admonished. As this was the least of the law, Phillips' umbrage was found to be without merit.

5 G. Lawrence had questionable land tenure but this had been resolved in his favor before Captain Jones arrived at Honolulu. A moot subject, but it was brought up anyway.

6 A civil suit by Henry Skinner (British) against Captain John Dominis (American) created great difficulty in selecting a jury. The governor had chosen one which was objected to by Skinner. The captain arranged for the king to appoint a new jury, half British and half American. (Later the king wrote to Captain Jones that if the jury was not acceptable, or the parties involved would not plead their cause before the said jury, "I will have nothing more to do with the case."[34:120])

7 British merchants' apprehensions about a new law for the recovery of debts were determined to be unfounded.

8 George Pelly complained about inadequate tonnage dues that were also based on cargo values for ships entering the harbor. A new law was passed to resolve this which established uniform harbor duties on a purely tonnage basis.

9 There were numerous loud complaints that the authorities had inimical feelings toward the British. This was important as British trade had increased over the last three years from $20,000 to $150,000 annually. The captain concluded that any Hawaiian prejudices were strongly in favor of Great Britain.

Captain Jenkin Jones made a lengthy report to his superiors, and carefully suggested that more frequent visits of British warships to the Hawaiian Islands would be advisable and in Great Britain's best interests. A British Foreign Office letter to the Admiralty dated October 4, 1842 expressed "approbation of Captain Jones' very judicious and temperate conduct in the whole of these transactions." [34:128]

Ke-ku-anao'a might not have realized that he was slowly losing ground to the English, who were so much more experienced in the subtleties of high-powered negotiation. For all of his noble intentions, the loyal governor was hardly a match for men who ran a world empire.

14

RECOGNITION?

Several years before the Constitution came into being, the broad question of recognition was already out in the open. The belligerent visit of French Captain La Place in July of 1839 had resulted in equality of the Catholic religion, preferential treatment of the few French subjects in the islands, and admittance of their "ardent spirits." Thus a law of the kingdom was negated, and the $20,000 performance bond bewildered Hawaiian leaders. They wanted to be left alone in peace to rule their own people and determine their own destiny.

At the time, their influential teachers and advisers, the Protestant missionaries, were shocked. In addition, when the captain had threatened the town, he offered protection for all foreigners *except* the American missionaries! They were apprehensive about French designs on the islands – should France take possession of them, this would be the deathblow to fulfillment of their awesome charge to raise up the whole people to an elevated state of Christian (Protestant) civilization.

One can well imagine that the United States and British businessmen were uneasy that the kingdom did not have the will or apparent capability to protect their property and commercial pursuits. The only real security was the presence of one of their nations' warships, and these visits were considered all too infrequent.

Some Britishers, particularly Consul Richard Charlton, wanted Great Britain to add the Hawaiian Islands to the empire. That would guarantee their protection of English subjects and presented exciting thoughts of tremendously increased business.

American residents felt sure that the United States would not want to acquire the islands, no matter how many American investments were involved. A consensus among them concluded that if diverse missionary and commercial interests were to be protected and to flourish, the major maritime powers must formally recognize the Hawaiian kingdom as a sovereign nation.

Hawaiian leaders became receptive to seeking recognition of their sovereignty in the hope of precluding future troubles on this issue. An initial attempt was made early in 1840. A visiting American lawyer from Illinois, Thomas J. Farnham, was commissioned Envoy Extraordinary and Minister Plenipotentiary to the United States, Great Britain and France on March 17, 1840. There was apparently not full confidence and trust in Farnham, safeguards were taken, and nothing came of this scheme.[77:187-88]

Hawaiian apprehensions increased throughout 1840. Great Britain became very suspicious of French designs on British interests in the South Pacific. The British took possession of New Zealand. This had ominous overtones because the Maoris were brother Polynesians of the Hawaiians.

The second attempt to secure recognition utilized the services of Peter A. Brinsmade, the American Agent for Commerce and Seamen. Aside from his official capacity as United States representative in Hawai'i, he was a partner in the mercantile and commission firm of Ladd and Company. Three New Englanders from Boston had formed the company in December of 1832 and arrived in Honolulu seven months later, in July. The firm prospered through diligent efforts and good fortune in speculative ventures. Cordial relations with the American missionaries were also helpful.

When these three young men cast their eyes around the islands for potential commercial endeavors, they saw a future in large scale agriculture, particularly sugar, which could be exported. A few small mills scattered around the islands ground and processed cane from small Hawaiian farms. The partners thought the island of Kaua'i would be a good location to start a sugar farm *if* they could secure the land on a long use lease, and *if* they could secure labor and financing.

At this time, the missionaries were searching for a way to have Hawaiian commoners evolve from serf-like labor to free labor. The Ladd and Company partners were moral and pious, and the missionaries favored their idea.[22:250]

Due undoubtedly to missionary influences, a 50-year land-use lease was signed by the king and governor of the island of Kaua'i on July 29, 1835, for 1,000 acres of land at Koloa. The annual rental was $300 a year, and Ladd and Company was permitted to hire Hawaiians to work on the farm with the king and governor receiving 25¢ per man per month. This employment proved to be popular, with payment of a hapawalu (12-½¢) per day, and food that consisted of fish and poi. By the end of the first year, a crude sugar mill had been set up, 25 acres of sugar cane, 5,000 coffee trees, and 5,000 banana trees had been planted, and 45 taro patches were flourishing.[77:175] [22:244]

Financial results took time, and Ladd and Company became overextended. The discouraged partners decided to either sell or cease their venture. This disturbed the missionaries, who felt that the prime value of the firm was to further Hawaiian free labor, which they considered indispensable to raising up the nation. And this effort should hopefully remain in American hands. Would Ladd and Company stay in business if the scope of their venture was enlarged? A large scale dream developed – the partners would not have to give up *if* they could lease *all* unused lands in the islands, and *if* they could secure a much larger capitalization.

After much discussion and persuasion, the kingdom signed a contract on November 24, 1841 which granted the company the right to use unoccupied and unused lands on a lease basis for 100 years.[77:189] [22:405] Provisions were:

1 They would begin agricultural work within five years (later extended to 10);

2 Each location selected would have 15 acres for a mill site to be chosen within a year (later extended to four years), and 200 adjacent acres for growing crops, primarily sugar cane;

3 The kingdom would plant 50 acres of sugar cane in the vicinity of each mill;

4 The company would grind and process cane belonging to others on shares; and

5 A joint stock company would be formed to provide the necessary capital.

Shrewdly, a supplemental understanding was signed on the same date which stipulated that the contract would be void unless there was recognition of Hawaiian independence by the United States, Great Britain and France. Peter Brinsmade was offered a commission as a Hawaiian diplomatic agent, but strangely declined, on the basis that he already was an American official.

Letters were prepared on November 24, 1841 for Brinsmade to handcarry, addressed to the President of the United States, the Queen of Great Britain, and the King of France. These identical letters proposed that the three countries enter into an agreement acknowledging and guaranteeing kingdom independence; that any differences between the kingdom and one of the countries would be decided by the other two nations; and that all prior agreements secured by visiting warships would be invalidated.[77:190-91] Diplomatically it was a naive attempt, as proven by the reactions of these nations.

Peter A. Brinsmade left Honolulu in December of 1841 after appointing his partner, William Hooper, as United States Deputy Commercial Agent in his absence. The sugar contract and supplemental understanding were kept confidential by all concerned. Brinsmade first went to Washington, where he delivered the king's letter to Secretary of State Daniel Webster. This one interview was the extent of his diplomatic effort. The State Department considered the provisions of the letter not in the best interests of the United States. Brinsmade unsuccessfully tried to secure venture capital, and went on to Europe.

The third attempt for recognition of Hawaiian sovereignty began with the arrival of Sir George Simpson, Governor-in-Chief of the Hudson's Bay Company's Territories in North America. He landed in Honolulu on February 11, 1842. The British Crown had recognized his merit by knighting him the previous year. Many of his voluminous reports back to England were routinely forwarded to the Foreign Office.[104:70] They provided trustworthy information not otherwise available, and this had an influence on British policy, particularly for Northwest America.

Simpson quickly reviewed the company's business of Pelly and Allan, joint agents, and was satisfied with the "moderate profits and quick returns."[111:125n] As far as 1842 business at Honolulu was concerned, he reported that the market was overstocked with goods, there was a continuing demand for company products (timber, salmon, flour, etc.) from the Columbia and Northwest Coast, and that business would increase due to whalers and the potential opening of trade with the Orient. He concluded that Honolulu would become a great entrepot and the Hudson's Bay Company would do well there.[104:90 111:127]

When Simpson talked with Governor Ke-ku-anao'a, he was impressed and reported the governor as being "the most intelligent and important man connected with the government."[34:95] Ke-ku-anao'a's trip to London with the late King Ka-mehameha II had given him a broader perspective than any of the other Hawaiian chiefs and chiefesses whom Sir George met. A far-ranging dialogue for the conduct and future of the kingdom required complete and clear understanding. The governor's knowledge of English was good, but these subjects demanded exact communication. Governor Keku-anao'a asked the trusted Dr. Gerrit P. Judd, who was fluent in Hawaiian, to sit in on the conversations and interpret fine meanings. Simpson found that the doctor had "upright intentions and disinterested motives," [114:96] and also some firm ideas about the direction the Hawaiian kingdom should take.

Sir George Simpson became convinced that Great Britain was not being ably represented by British Consul Richard Charlton ("rather a bustling active man, being very little respected either by natives or foreigners"), and suggested to London that he be pensioned off. [104:92]

During his visit, Sir George talked to many people, and formed the opinion that the king and chiefs were too much under the influence of the American missionaries. However, "to do the missionaries justice…it appears to me they exercise their best judgment for the welfare and prosperity of the country, but in their overzeal they counselled the enactment of some very strange and unusual laws…they have had sufficient influence to get one of their number, a narrow-minded, illiterate American named Richards,* installed as prime minister or principal councillor of the king." [104:91]

He weighed all factors of the apprehension about a French takeover, and concurred that it would be in the best interests of the kingdom and his company that Hawai'i continue to remain independent. This status had to be supported by the maritime powers.

Another concern about Hawai'i disturbed Simpson – disharmony. There were differences and discords between the government and merchants, and between merchants of different nationalities. He found that some merchants and missionaries were barely on speaking terms with one another. [114:156-57] He couldn't judge the Hawaiians as a whole, for he only observed the commoners in the port towns, and wasn't impressed.

Simpson decided to visit the king and premier and discuss the Hawaiian kingdom's future. On March 17, 1842, he, George Pelly and

---

★ Sir George Simpson had not met the Rev. Richards at this time, and later changed his opinion. Hardly illiterate, Rev. Richards had been educated at Williams College and Andover Theological Seminary.

British Consul Charlton left for La-haina, Maui, on the Hudson's Bay Company bark *Cowlitz*. Governor Ke-ku-anao'a had such high regard for Sir George that he ordered the fort to salute the departure, an honor previously granted only to warships. The 72-mile trip bucked the trade winds and took three days, the weather was "close, damp and disagreeable."[114:160] When they went ashore on Sunday, March 20, Sir George Simpson was received with "great civility and attention," no doubt generated by letters from Governor Ke-ku-anao'a to the king and Dr. Judd to Rev. Richards.[111:159 114:165]

During the four and a half days Simpson was at La-haina, he had numerous frank discussions with the Rev. Richards. He changed his sight-unseen opinion and recorded that he "found him to be as shrewd and intelligent as he was pious and humble." Further, in a very English way, "he is a grave, sanctified looking person of fair abilities and although an American, I believe means well."[114:158]

Sir George conferred with King Ka-mehameha III ("good humoured and well-formed, and speaks very tolerable English"), the queen, and other officials.[114:162] He and the Rev. Richards had several three to four-hour discussions at night with Premier Ke-ka-ulu-ohi, who was "very agreeable." Her size impressed Simpson; a woman who was six feet tall, weighed over 300 pounds, and in accordance with old Hawaiian custom, conversed in a reclining position.[114:163]

Finally, Sir George advised the king and his council chiefs that he considered the possibility of Peter A. Brinsmade securing recognition of Hawaiian sovereignty to be very slight. He suggested that the Rev. Richards be sent to Washington, London, and Paris in an official capacity, empowered to negotiate and enter into treaties. He offered to assist. His name, and those of Sir John Henry Pelly and Arthur Colvile, officials of the influential Hudson's Bay Company, should be included in a letter of credence to the British government. Simpson would personally join the Rev. Richards in London and help in any way that he could. In addition, Sir George would provide a letter of credit for 10,000 pounds ($46,000) for the representative's use, with interest at the normal one percent a month.

This complex and rather bold plan was favorably received. Both Rev. Richards and Sir George Simpson were named envoys of the kingdom, along with Chief Timothy Ha-alilio, the king's secretary.[22:412 111:154-56 114:171-72]

Sir George recognized the important role that the Rev. Richards played as the king's counselor. On March 12, he suggested to the king that Dr. Gerrit P. Judd be solicited to replace Rev. Richards in his absence.[22:414n] Judd was trusted by the king and chiefs, was forceful, and had proven in past consultations with Governor Ke-ku-anao'a that he would stand strong for Hawaiian positions.

Dr. Judd was informally queried on April 19, 1842 about joining the government,[22:415] and he arrived in La-haina three days later.[68:111] There were discussions and one interesting result which could hardly have been coincidental. Dr. Judd was a dedicated teetotaler and the king had again become intemperate. La-haina was now a wild town[114:164] after losing the restraining influence of Governor Hoapili, who died on January 3, 1840.[60:374] The king's example only increased the atmosphere of excess and indulgence. Then on April 26, 1842, King Ka-mehameha III and his principal chiefs and chiefesses took the cold-water pledge to abstain from liquor.[68:111 72:181]

A Proclamation was issued by the king and premier on May 10, 1842, with the approbation of the legislature, establishing a National Treasury Board to handle all government finances.[101:107-08] Dr. Gerrit P. Judd, John I'i and Timothy Ha-alilio were named to the Board.[77:232 22:414]

A Resolve of the legislature established a foreign Recorder and Interpreter for the government, to be concerned primarily with business of and with foreigners, May 12, 1842.[101:111] Dr. Judd was appointed to this position on May 15,[77:232 22:414] and his duties included,[69:109] "…we instruct you to aid Governor Ke-ku-anao'a in your official capacity, which relates to all business of importance between foreigners."

Dr. Gerrit P. Judd's resignation and abrupt departure from the Mission to the government did not please his brethren or the American Board back in Boston. No matter how much the overall need was for the islands with the Rev. Richards gone, evangelism and the health of the missionaries were still considered to have the utmost importance.

William Richards and Timothy Ha-alilio, now Ministers Plenipotentiary, left La-haina without announcement on July 18, 1842.[77:192] Their route went by ship to Mazatlan, Mexico, overland through Mexico City to Veracruz, and on to Washington by ship and rail.

Hawaiian concerns about French intentions toward their islands intensified in August of 1842 – word was received that French Admiral Du Petit-Thouars had taken possession of the Marquesas

Islands the previous month.[22:413] Like the Maoris, the Marquesans were brother Polynesians of the Hawaiians.

British Consul Richard Charlton was angered by this development. The French had gotten ahead of his country in claiming the Marquesas. Why hadn't Great Britain taken over the Hawaiian Islands, as he advocated? Some of his business affairs were not doing well. He was insulted by the slights of Sir George Simpson, who had excluded him from conversations with the king at La-haina.[114:171] Word leaked out that the Rev. Richards had departed on a secret mission to London. Consult Charlton resolved to go there himself and stir his government to action. He left Honolulu abruptly on September 26, 1842,[22:420-21] leaving a letter for King Ka-mehameha III:[57:278]

"British Consulate, Woahoo, Sept. 26, 1842.

"Sir: From the insults received from the local authorities of Your Majesty's government, and from the insults offered to my Sovereign, Her most Gracious Majesty, Victoria the First, Queen of the United Kingdom of Great Britain and Ireland, by Matthew Kekuanaoa, Governor of this island; and for other weighty causes affecting the interests of her Majesty's subjects in these islands, I consider it my bounden duty to repair immediately to Great Britain to lay statements before Her Majesty's government and have therefore appointed, by commission, as I am fully authorised to do, Alexander Simpson, Esq., to act as consul until Her Majesty's pleasure be known.

"Your Majesty's government has more than once insulted the British flag, but you must not suppose that it will be passed over in silence. Justice, though tardy, will reach you; and it is you, not your advisers, that will be punished.

"I have the honour to be your Majesty's most obedient humble servant,
RICHARD CHARLTON
Consul"

Alexander Simpson, a contentious estranged cousin of Sir George Simpson, forwarded this letter to the king the next day and presented his commission to Governor Ke-ku-anao'a. He received a curt response in clear Hawaiian writing on September [30:109:59]

"To Alexander Simpson. My respects to you.

"I have received your letter, and that of Richard Charlton, the British Consul, respecting your becoming Vice-Consul for this nation.

"This is my fixed thought, which I now make known to you: it is not proper for you to perform the duties of Consul between this kingdom and the subjects of Great Britain, because you despise the authorities of this kingdom, and you say you are going to make disturbance in the kingdom.

"If you think proper to go to Valparaiso* to complain, then go: and if proper to go quite to Great Britain, then go. Therefore I do not consent for you to work with me. No indeed.

I am with respect,
KEKUANAOA"

Meanwhile, the French corvette *Embuscade* under Captain S. Mallet arrived on August 24, 1842 without firing the customary salute. As expected, the captain made demands, which were blunted when he was advised that Hawaiian envoys were en route to France to consummate a treaty.[77:210 22:419]

Word was received at Honolulu several months later that the French had established a Protectorate over Tahiti. The Tahitians were yet another group of brother Polynesians to the Hawaiians.

Hawai'i settled down to an uneasy calm, a calm like one preceding a storm… But an unexpected storm arose. On February 11, 1843, the British frigate *Carysfort*, commanded by Captain Lord George Paulet, sailed into Honolulu harbor without saluting the kingdom.

---

* The station of H.B.M.'s Naval Forces in the Pacific.

R EV. WILLIAM RICHARDS
and Chief Ha-alilio had left La-haina on July 18, 1842 and arrived in
Washington, D.C. on December 5, 1842.[22:441] Through the good
offices of Massachusetts Representative Caleb Cushing and the American Board, they were quickly introduced to a number of friendly
congressmen and other influential people. The envoys met with
Secretary of State Daniel Webster on December 7, 1842.[22:441] [77:192]
Webster was neither receptive to the treaty request nor interested in
foreign entanglements. Rev. Richards recorded in his journal that
night that his apprehensions had been "considerably awakened by
the coldness." [102]

The envoys talked to more important people, and secured an
informal evening meeting with Daniel Webster at his home on
December 9, 1842.[22:442] The conversation ranged from commerce to
conditions in the Hawaiian Islands. The Secretary asked for a formal
paper on the kingdom's positions and wishes. It was prepared and
delivered to the State Department on the 15th.[77:193] Richard diligently began to draft, to the best of his untutored ability, a proposed treaty.

The kingdom's envoys checked with the State Department on
December 23 and were blandly advised that their letter was being
staffed in the normal manner. Rev. Richards began to understand
that diplomacy was a slow business... He had been unable to secure
an appointment to see the President of the United States. However,
he had accomplished cordial relations with eight senators and 13
members of the House of Representatives.[77:193]

During his discussions with seasoned politicians who were
knowledgeable in how to get things done in Washington, Richards
came up with a good idea. He visited one congressman, who offered
to introduce the envoys to the president, then spread rumors that if

the United States was not prepared to protect their interests in Hawai'i, he would endeavor to place the islands under the formal protection of Great Britain, or have them become part of the British empire.[22:442]

This brought an immediate and great change. The next meeting with Secretary of State Daniel Webster was positive and the envoys were received by President Tyler. The administration's position became established – the United States would not enter into a treaty with the Hawaiian kingdom recognizing sovereignty, but would provide protection. In essence, an extension of the Monroe Doctrine, the 1823 policy of opposition to outside interference in the Americas.

As part of a Message to the Congress on December 31, 1842, President John Tyler sent the following:[60:376]

> "Considering, therefore, that the United States possesses so very large a share of the intercourse with those islands, it is deemed not unfit to make a declaration that their government seeks nevertheless no peculiar advantages, no exclusive control over the Hawaiian government, but is content with its independent existence, and anxiously wishes for its security and prosperity. Its forbearance, in this respect, under the circumstances of the very large intercourse of their citizens with the islands, would justify this government, should events hereafter arise to require it, in making a decided remonstrance against the adoption of an opposite policy by any other Power."

In London, the British Foreign Office had received a letter on January 3, 1843 from their Hawaiian Consul Richard Charlton. It stated that he was coming to England on pressing business, and had appointed Alexander Simpson to act as consul in his absence.[34:130]

On January 23, 1843, Sir John Henry Pelly, Governor of the Hudson's Bay Company, advised the Earl of Aberdeen, British Minister of Foreign Affairs, that the Rev. Richards was on his way to England as an envoy of the Hawaiian kingdom. He enclosed Sir George Simpson's correspondence about the islands, and noted that he was in London and available to provide any further information desired.*

★ American Historical Review xiv (Oct. 1908) pp. 71-73

Richard Charlton arrived in London on February 10, 1843 and deluged the Foreign Office with correspondence.[34:130-55] These included a petition dated September 24, 1842 and signed by 35 British residents who entreated the Foreign Office to receive Charlton's representations "with all confidence and attention." Further, "we are daily liable to be deprived of our property by arbitrary actions prompted by Americans."

Also, a letter from a Committee of British Merchants with three signatures that claimed natives were suffering under tyranny instigated by Americans, there was harsh treatment of British subjects, and losses due to unjust court decisions. They were apprehensive that the islands would become a colony of the United States or taken possession of by the French.

In addition, a lengthy complaint about legal actions, with eight enclosures.

Furthermore, a letter concerning a bankruptcy case, with 35 enclosures. "Justice has been denied us...there is a determination on the part of American residents to deprive us of our property...the king and chiefs forming the government are themselves quite unfit to decide upon any case of importance...it is due to the partiality of this individual (Gerrit P. Judd, a native of one of the New England states) that we attribute the denial to us of our just rights."

One would imagine that these grievances were too petty to concern the Earl of Aberdeen, and certainly contradicted Sir George Simpson's information. Foreign Office interests were worldly and European-oriented, and there was little regard for the Hawaiian islands.

Several dispatches from Alexander Simpson, which he had written 4-½ months earlier, arrived on February 15, 1843. Among them was Governor Ke-ku-anao'a's letter refusing to recognize Simpson as Acting British Consul. This was a matter of significant importance.[34:156] The Foreign Office decided to wait and see what the Hawaiian envoys had to say about this.

Rev. William Richards and Chief Timothy Ha-alilio arrived at Liverpool on February 17, 1843, after a 15-day sail and steam voyage from Boston. They traveled by train to London the next day.[102]

Richards recorded that they started "at 8-¼ and reached this city, 212 miles, at 6 PM, that is 9-¾ hours or about 21.7 miles per hour, including stoppages, and about 26 miles per hour while under way. Excellent cars, 3 classes, our fare 5.11 pounds. Baggage on the same car as we were on. All our carriage 6 persons. Splendid Depot, Iron, many tunnels, smooth heavy rails. Got out but once. Lady not at all. And man read incessantly. Nobody talked."

They called on Sir George Simpson, who was regarded as a co-envoy, at Hudson's Bay House on February 20. No doubt it was a relief to encounter this sympathetic Englishman. They met Sir John Henry Pelly and their reception was cordial and cooperative. A letter was written to the Earl of Aberdeen requesting an appointment. That afternoon they visited with United States Minister Edward Everett and had an amicable discussion. Everything seemed to be going well, particularly without interference from Consul Charlton.

The three envoys and Sir John Henry Pelly called on the Minister of Foreign Affairs on Wednesday afternoon. Their objects were simply stated as: 1) to secure recognition of the sovereign independence of the Hawaiian kingdom; 2) to secure a formal treaty and nullify the 1836 "gunboat diplomacy" agreement between King Kamehameha III and Lord Edward Russell; and 3) to have Richard Charlton replaced as British Consul.[97:7]

When the Earl of Aberdeen learned about their efforts in Washington, he remarked that the United States had denied recognizing Hawaiian kingdom sovereignty because it refused to enter into such a normal treaty. He further stated that from what the Foreign Office knew about Hawai'i, it was dominated politically and commercially by Americans, and thus not its own independent entity. This being the case, the British government would not consider a treaty recognizing Hawaiian sovereignty.[77:197] [134:46] He also informed the envoys that Richard Charlton was in London.

The following week Sir George was able to see Under Secretary Henry U. Addington, and provided recent correspondence from Dr. Judd and George Pelly. In a measure these letters mitigated and rebutted some of Richard Charlton's claims which had apparently formed the basis of the Foreign Minister's position. The envoys were received by Addington on March 6, 1843, addressed the Foreign Minister's adverse position, and provided a copy of the Hawaiian Kingdom Constitution.

Peter A. Brinsmade had arrived from Brussels on February 27, 1843 and reported failures in his diplomatic mission. He had delivered his letters but been unable to secure any important appointment for discussion. He also advised:[96:58]

"You must make up your mind for vexatious hindrances and delays. I have been accustomed to hear loud and strong complaints against the Hawaiian Government for want of a suitable appreciation of the value of time. But I am now sure that all such complaints would be silenced by a little experience in the tardy movements of people in high places in Europe."

Brinsmade was also frustrated that his search for capital to support Ladd and Company had not been fruitful. He urged the Rev. Richards to go on to Paris via Brussels, certain he could arrange an appointment with King Leopold I, known as the "Uncle of Europe" for his many royal family connections. A very influential man, he was in constant contact with the king of France, who was his father-in-law, and close to the queen of England, who was his niece. The three envoys and Brinsmade left London on March 8, 1843 and by ship, stage and train arrived in Brussels two days later.[102]

The envoys were introduced to Count de Hompesch, who not only arranged an appointment with the king, but was involved with the Belgian Company of Colonization with whom Brinsmade was negotiating on behalf of Ladd and Company. Rev. Richards refused to discuss any business matters, although he recorded his first visit to a king on March 13:[102]

"They entered the royal presence, he standing, noble appearance, easy, removed all restraint, free talked with Sir George. Spoke freely of the Sandwich Islands, understood everything in relation to them. Expressed himself decidedly that their independence ought to be acknowledged, that they had been abused, and said he should be happy to extend himself in our favor."

Meanwhile, in London, the Earl of Aberdeen fired Richard Charlton as British Consul to the Hawaiian kingdom on March 9, 1843.[34:173] "Not content however with quitting your post without permission, you addressed to the chief of the Sandwich Islands, when on the point of your departure, a letter so intemperate, so improper, and so ill-judged, that I cannot do less than visit that production with terms of severe censure."

The Hawaiian envoys arrived in Paris on the afternoon of March 15, 1843. There they heard the startling news that French Admiral Du Petit-Thouars had taken possession of Tahiti. Interestingly enough, Rev. William Richards recorded in his journal, "this had a very great tendency to forward our objects."[102] This comment deserves examination.

The considerable rivalry between Great Britain and France for world power and prestige included the Pacific. The French opposed Great Britain taking possession of New Zealand in 1840. Their own acquisition of the Marquesas Islands in 1842 was not of much consequence to the English, as it was "a bit off the beaten track." Establishing a Protectorate over Tahiti was an entirely different matter. British interests there exceeded the French, the Australians considered Tahiti almost a dependency, and the London Missionary Society (Protestant) had gone to Tahiti in 1797 and was dominant there.

Both great powers endeavored to maintain amicable diplomatic relations with each other. The French were aware of British anger about Tahiti and assured them that the rights of Englishmen there would be respected. They also indicated that they had no further acquisition desires in the Pacific – or any intention of interfering with the Kingdom of Hawai'i (mostly controlled by American interests), and presumed that Great Britain would do likewise.[62:19]

Recognition of Hawaiian sovereignty independence thus became a pawn in British-French power politics.

The envoys called on French Foreign Minister Francois Guizot on March 16, 1843:[1:02] "On our entering the room he rose and approached us with great affability – handed us seats in so familiar a manner as to at once remove all restraint, and then said in English, 'Will you please tell me what is the matter?'" He was presented with a Memoranda requesting 1) acknowledgment of Hawaiian independence, 2) nullification of the July 1839 treaty with Captain La Place, and 3) appointment of a new French consul. Guizot assured that he was in favor of Hawaiian independence.[34:175] He promised to give an answer to other specifics in about three weeks.

The Hawaiian envoys returned to London, met with Mr. Addington on March 21, and reported the favorable results of their encounter with M. Guizot. There were more British Foreign Office discussions, mostly with Sir George Simpson.

The Earl of Aberdeen advised the envoys on April 1, 1843:[34:175-76] "I have the honour to inform you…that Her Majesty's Government are willing, and have determined to recognize the independence of the Sandwich Islands under their present sovereign." There were two caveats – equal treatment of Britishers with other foreigners in the islands, and resolvement of grievances.

SUCCESS! But there was much still to do…

Rev. William Richards wrote of Sir George Simpson, who returned to British America on April 3, 1843:[*]

"No zeal, or diligence, or disinterestedness could have excelled that which he has manifested for the last six weeks. He had secured my gratitude and my affection and is worthy of the ever-lasting gratitude of Hawaii."

On the same day, Rev. Richards was advised that a month earlier President Tyler had appointed Mr. George Brown as Commissioner to the Sandwich Islands. The clergyman didn't quite understand the title of "commissioner," and thought it should have been "minister" or "consul." He was not aware of an ambiguous part of Mr. Brown's March 15, 1843 appointment,[108:56-7] which included the following details:

"It is not deemed expedient at this juncture fully to recognize the independence of the islands or the right of their Government to that equality of treatment and consideration which is due and usually allowed to those Governments to which we send and from which we receive diplomatic agents of the ordinary ranks. By this, however, it is not meant to intimate that the islands, so far as regards all other powers, are not entirely independent; on the contrary, this is a fact respecting which no doubt is felt, and the hope that through the agency of the Commissioner that independence might be preserved, has probably, in a great degree, led to the complience by Congress with the recommendation of the President."

However, on March 23, 1843, Secretary of State Daniel Webster did advise American representatives in London and Paris to pass on a clearer policy to those governments:[107:4]

"The course adopted by this Government in regard to the Sandwich Islands has for its sole object the preservation of the independence of those islands and the maintenance by their Government of an entire impartiality in their intercourse with foreign states. The United States desire to exercise no undue influence or control over the government of the islands, nor to obtain from it any grant of exclusive privileges whatever. This was solemnly declared in the President's message to Congress...

"The President would exceedingly regret that suspicion of a

[*] Richards to Anderson, London, April 3, 1843. Letters to the American Board cxxxv, No. 96. Hawaiian Mission Children's Society.

sinister purpose of any kind on the part of the United States should prevent England and France from adopting the same pacific, just, and conservative course towards the government and people of this remote but interesting group of islands."

In early April 1843, the envoys returned to Brussels. Several days were devoted to Rev. Richards and Chief Ha-alilio working with Peter A. Brinsmade and Count de Hompesch on the Ladd and Company venture. It had developed into a three-party agreement – the Hawaiian kingdom, Ladd and Company, and the Belgian Company of Colonization. The "Belgian Contract" was finalized on May 17, 1843. It was complicated,[77:252-53] and obligated the kingdom to free imports and exports, and other commercial matters the same as for all, the control of unused lands, authorization for people to come to Hawai'i subject to acceptance of numbers and quality, profit shares to the king, and so forth. A supplemental agreement stated that the contract could not go into effect until France recognized Hawaiian independence.*

In Paris things did not proceed quite as smoothly. The Hawaiian envoys requested an appointment with M. Guizot on April 13, 1843, but their letter had apparently been misplaced when they checked five days later. Resubmitted on April 18, and again on the 26th, at last they got an appointment for 10 AM on Saturday, April 29. When they arrived shortly before 10 AM by Rev. Richards' watch, the clock in M. Guizot's outer office was at 2-½ minutes after the hour. The Foreign Minister was not available – they could return on Monday, May 1, and please be on time.[102]

They were. M. Guizot repeated that France would recognize Hawaiian independence, as the British intended to do. A new treaty could be negotiated, otherwise the 1839 La Place treaty would remain in force. Two provisions would be required in any new treaty:[22:450-51] 1) France must be on an equal basis with the most-favored nation, and 2) a guarantee that Catholic institutions in Hawai'i would also be treated as equally as Protestant schools and churches. Rev. Richards readily agreed with the first provision, but did not agree with the second. He suggested "religious tolerance" rather than "religious equality," and cited the difficulties with various interpretations of words and

---

* The "Belgian Contract" was not ratified by King Ka-mehameha III or financed by the Belgian Company of Colonization.[77:253] It remained a "South Sea Bubble" dream…

meaning by visiting naval captains. Both sides promised to review the issue, and the meeting was terminated amicably.*

Chief Timothy Ha-alilio wrote home: [109:92] "When we went to Lord Aberdeen he was very grave and angry looking; but he gave us all we wanted: when we went to Monsieur Guizot he was very polite and friendly, but would give us no satisfaction."

The envoys waited and waited, but received no word from M. Guizot, despite several prompting letters.

THEN...on May 31, 1843, they discovered a brief article in *The London Times* dated the day before:

Liverpool May 28. The Sandwich Islands were ceded to the British Crown on the 25th February, and were taken possession of by Lord George Paulet of Her Majesty's ship *Carysfort* next day.

The news must have struck them with the force of cannon fire. All their diligent attempts to be diplomatic and act in the kingdom's best interests seemed to have been in vain.

---

* French Foreign Office *Note sûr les Isles Sandwich et sûr la mission de Mrs. Haalilio and Richards*, April 5, 1843, stated in part: "Our political relations with the Sandwich Islands, as with the Society Islands, are born from the need of protecting the French priests devoted to the service of the Catholic missions in Oceania, against the persecution from which they were suffering at the instigation of the English and American Methodists."

16

THE PAULET AFFAIR

The winds being favorable, the British frigate *Carysfort*, commanded by Captain Lord George Paulet, slowly sailed into Honolulu harbor on February 11, 1843. The captain did not salute the Hawaiian kingdom as was normal naval courtesy.[27]

The warship had arrived off the harbor late the previous afternoon and anchored in the roads. Acting Consul Alexander Simpson went aboard and had a long discussion with Lord George, provided him with documentations, and urged that there be no cannon salute prior to his recognition as Acting Consul.[77:213] Not all of what Simpson had to say was news – Richard Charlton apparently had a meeting with the captain at Mazatlan while en route to England. Lord Paulet's orders clearly stated that he was to support the British representative in the islands and protect the interests of British subjects.

As the *Carysfort* anchored in the harbor, the five American, two British and one French ships there hoisted their colors in respect. The Acting British Consul was saluted with seven guns when he came aboard.[27] French Consul Jules Dudoit and American representative William Hooper came aboard to pay their respects – but were not received as they had not accepted Alexander Simpson as acting British Consul. Doing so was not their prerogative, although it was felt they should have.[34:258] Leading American and British businessmen who also came aboard soon left after a chilly reception. Dr. Gerrit P. Judd presented the compliments of Governor Ke-ku-anao'a, and was advised that Lord Paulet would talk only to the king, and after the acting British Consul was recognized. Following their departure from the *Carysfort*, the American and French ships lowered their colors.[22:428]

It was as if a cold wind had suddenly swept through Honolulu town. Small groups chatted quietly with shaking heads. Such military arrogance could be expected of the French, and people had been apprehensive about a French fleet coming to Hawai'i, but the British being offensive? There must be something terribly wrong...

Lord Paulet sent a brisk letter to Governor Ke-ku-anao'a:

> "Sir: Having arrived at this port in her Britannic Majesty's ship *Carysfort*, under my command, for the purpose of affording protection to British subjects, as likewise to support the position of Her Britannic Majesty's representative here, who has received repeated insults from the Government authorities at these islands, respecting which it is my intention to communicate only with the King in person.
>
> "I require to have immediate information by return of the officer conveying this dispatch whether or not the King (in consequence of my arrival) has been notified that his presence will be required here, and the earliest day on which he may be expected, as otherwise I shall be compelled to proceed to his residence, in the ship under my command, for the purpose of communicating with him.
>
> "I have the honor to be, sir, your most obedient servant,
> GEORGE PAULET,
> Captain"

He received a courteous reply, translated by Dr. Judd:[108:43]

> "Salutations to you, Lord George Paulet, captain of Her Britannic Majesty's ship *Carysfort*.
>
> "I have received your letter by the hand of the officer, and, with respect, inform you that we have not as yet sent for the King, as we were not informed of the business, but, having learned from your communication that you wish him sent for, I will search for a vessel and send.
>
> "He is at Wailuku, on the eastern side of Maui. In case the wind is favorable he may be expected in six days.
>
> "Yours, with respect,
> M. KEKUANAOA"

Soon after this exchange of letters, the U.S. sloop-of-war *Boston* under Captain John C. Long of the East India Squadron, en route from China and Tahiti, anchored in the roads in the late afternoon of February 13, 1843. William Hooper went offshore and brought back the great news that the British war with China (Opium War) was over, and six Chinese ports were now open for foreign trade.

The very American Captain William Paty, Harbormaster, exuber-
ated in his journal that night:[91]

"Hurra! Hurra! Hurra! for the Stars and Stripes. Hurra! for our
gallant Navy, hurra for our glorious country! Oh Ye Yankees who
live at home at ease how little you can imagine the stirring thrill
of joy and pride that agitates the bosom of your countryman,
who, roaming far away in foreign lands, and in the midst of trouble, difficulty and danger, hears the cry of Sail O, and the next
moment sees the Stars and Stripes floating over the brave hearts
and powerful batteries of an American Ship of War. There may be
readers who will smile in derision at this, but I feel assured that
they will not be from among the number of Americans resident
in Honolulu in February 1843."

The winds were adverse the next morning on February 14, and
the *Boston's* log recorded:[21]

"At daylight nine boats from the American Whaling Ships and five
from H.B.M. Ship *Carysfort* came out of the harbor to assist in
towing the Ship in. Sent 700 fms of hawsers ahead to a warping
buoy at the Entrance of the harbor. At 6.30 weighed anchor. Sent
the Boats ahead and commenced warping and towing. At 7 hove
in the hawser. At 7.30 cast off the Boats, and came to in Honolulu
Harbor in 5 fms water. Moored ship. Saluted the American
Consul with 7 guns salute, the French Consul with the same."

By arrangement, on the following day, the *Boston* saluted the Fort
with 21 guns, and this recognition was returned by the soldiers who
manned the king's cannons.

The next few days were very busy for Captain Long. Aside from
receiving welcome visits from many American businessmen,
Governor Ke-ku-anao'a made an official call and was saluted with 13
guns. The captain was concerned about securing provisions for his
ship. Interestingly enough, American representative Hooper had only
a few government stores under his charge: two anchors, five tierces of
vinegar, three barrels of molasses and 70 of whiskey; some fresh pork
and beef which could be salted were available. Fortunately, a vessel
arrived from Valparaiso with a good stock of provisions for sale,
including bread.

A petition from leading American residents was sent to the captain on the 15th:* "We do consider our property and interests in

★ Long, John C. Commanders Letters. The National Archives (RG45).

jeopardy from the trouble state of affairs at this place, and the evidently hostile position assumed towards this Government by the Commander of H.B.M. *Carysfort*, now in this port." Captain Long was requested to remain until the difficulties were settled.

King Ka-mehameha III arrived at Honolulu from Maui on the schooner *Hooikaika* on February 17. As the ship passed the *Boston*, the king was saluted with 21 guns. When he landed, he was saluted by a like number from Honolulu Fort. The king was met by a large number of Hawaiians and foreigners, some 300 uniformed soldiers, and the band also played to express solidarity and support.

Later that afternoon, an officer of the *Carysfort* delivered a brief, curt note to the king from Captain Lord George Paulet, demanding a private interview. The king replied by declining, and stated that any written communication would be given due consideration, and that Dr. Judd would represent the king in any discussions desired.

Lord Paulet replied that night at 10 PM: [34:194]

> "As you have refused me a personal interview, I inclose you the demands which I consider it my duty to make upon your Government, with which I demand a compliance at or before 4 o'clock P.M., tomorrow, otherwise I shall be obliged to take immediate coercive steps to obtain these measures for my countrymen."

At 11 PM Captain Long was awakened to receive a note from Captain Paulet: [34:195]

> "Sir, – I have the honor to notify you, that Her Britannic Majesty's ship *Carysfort*, under my command, will be prepared to make an immediate attack upon this town, at 4 o'clock, P.M. tomorrow (Saturday) in the event of the demands now forwarded by me to the King of these islands, not being complied with by that time.
> I have, &c.,
> GEO. PAULET
> Captain"

Captain Long sent copies of this letter to the American "Consul" and French Consul, and offered "Asylum and protection" aboard the American warship. Lights came on all over town. The king had serious discussions with Premier Ke-ka-ulu-ohi, Governor Ke-ku-anao'a, other high chiefs then in Honolulu, and Dr. Judd.

From the *Carysfort's* log, February 18, 1843: [27] "AM 4. Took off the mooring swivel, laid out the stream anchor to the Eastward and kedge to the Westward. 7. Hove starb^d broadside onto the fort. Down main bulkheads. Got 4 of the port guns over to the Starb^d side employed as most requisite. 8. Crossed Top Gall^t yds. Got boats guns in the boats."

From the *Boston's* log, February 18, 1843:[21] "At 9 beat to Quarters. Shotted the guns. Got a spring on the Starb^d Quarter and cleared the ship for action."

Any pressures by Mr. Hooper or Captain Long to mitigate the British captain's threat to fire on and attack Honolulu have not been discovered in correspondence, journals or official records. It is interesting to note that the *Boston* took this action. She was in position to broadside the *Carysfort's* vulnerable stern.

At 1:30 PM, the *Carysfort's* log recorded that the captain received a communication from the king:[34:96]

"Salutations to the Right Honorable Lord George Paulet, Captain of Her Britannic Majesty's ship *Carysfort*.

"We have received your letter and the demands which accompanied it, and in reply would inform your Lordship that we have commissioned Sir George Simpson and William Richards, as our Ministers Plenipotentiary and Envoys Extraordinary to the Court of Great Britain, with full powers to settle the difficulties which you have presented before us, to assure Her Majesty the Queen, of our uninterrupted affection, and to confer with her Ministers as to the best means of cementing the harmony between us. Some of the demands which you have laid before us, are of a nature calculated seriously to embarrass our feeble Government, by contravening the laws established for the benefit of all. But we shall comply with your demands as it has never been our intention to insult Her Majesty the Queen, or injure any of her estimable subjects; but we must do so under protest, and shall embrace the earliest opportunity of representing our case more fully to Her Britannic Majesty's Government, through our Ministers, trusting in the magnanimity of the Sovereign of the a great nation, whom we have been taught to respect and love, – that we shall there be justified.

"Waiting your further orders, with sentiments of respect,
KAMEHAMEHA III
KEKAULUOHI
"I hereby certify the above to be a faithful translation.
G. P. JUDD
Translator for the Government"

The detailed demands made by Lord Paulet were:[34:194-95]

"1 Removal of an attachment on British Consul Richard Charlton's property. This was the result of a foreigner jury finding Charlton liable for a monetary obligation.

"2 Immediate recognition of Alexander Simpson as Acting British Consul, and Honolulu Fort saluting the British flag with 21 guns.

"3 A guarantee that no British subject would be imprisoned in fetters unless he was accused of a felony.

"4 A new and fair civil trial on the matter of (British) Henry Skinner against (American) Captain John Dominis.

"5 Any jury considering a British subject will be composed of at least half Britisher jurors approved by the British Consul.

"6 Direct communication between the Acting British Consul and King Ka-mehameha III."

On February 18, 1843, the Hawaiian government acquiesced and Honolulu Fort saluted the British flag with 21 guns, which was returned.

The French barque *Jules Simonet* arrived that day from the Marquesas Islands with a rumor that the entire French squadron of warships in the Pacific was coming to Hawai'i in a few months.

Two days later Lord Paulet and Acting British Consul Alexander Simpson met with King Ka-mehameha, his premier and chiefs, and Dr. Judd.[109:83] They were accompanied by Dr. Thomas C.B. Rooke, the kingdom's Health Officer, as interpreter.* Dr. Judd was present as the king's personal interpreter, despite the objections of Simpson, who disliked Judd and his strong relationships with the king. The meeting was brief and formal, and the king visited the *Carysfort* that afternoon.

There were daily meetings for the next several days, which became more and more bitter. Alexander Simpson addressed only the king, and in very abusive and sarcastic language. Demands grew and grew which finally would have destroyed the kingdom.[34:259-62] The Acting British Consul demanded that either Governor Ke-ku-anao'a or Dr. Judd be fired, as one or the other had perpetrated a falsehood

★ Dr. Rooke, a 23-year-old surgeon, had arrived at Honolulu in 1829 on a British whaler. He liked what he saw, stayed, and married Grace Kamaikui, a daughter of John Young who was one of King Ka-mehameha's counselors. They had no children, and adopted a daughter at birth of one of Mrs. Rooke's sisters. The child, Emma, later married King Ka-mehameha IV.

about himself. Ke-ku-anaoʻa later wrote to Ha-alilio that: "The law of our king was broken…we are living in distress."

A meeting on February 24 was canceled while the king and his advisors sought some way to resolve these gross difficulties. Ceding the islands to the French or Americans was ruled out.[34:263] The final decision was to provisionally cede the islands under protest to Great Britain, and trust that the British government would overturn their drastic demands.

At 3 PM on February 25, 1843, Honolulu Fort was filled with people, armed personnel and the band from the *Carysfort*. The king appeared on the second floor lanai with his advisors and the British leaders. He addressed everyone with an oration:[109:86]

> "Where are you, chiefs, people, and commons from my ancestor, and people from foreign lands!
>
> "Hear ye! I make known to you that I am in perplexity by reason of difficulties into which I have been brought without cause; therefore I have given away the life of our land, hear ye! But my rule over you, my people, and your privileges will continue, for I have hope that the life of the land will be restored when my conduct is justified."

A Provisional Cession document was then read by Dr. Judd in Hawaiian and English, stating in part:[34:198] "…with the reservation that it is subject to any arrangement that may have been entered into by the representatives appointed by us to treat with the Government of Her Britannic Majesty…in conference…or subject to the decision which Her Britannic Majesty may pronounce on the receipt of full information from us and from the Right Honorable Lord George Paulet."

Captain Lord George Paulet then proclaimed that:[34:198] 1) The British flag shall be hoisted on all the islands. 2) The king shall govern the Hawaiians, and a Commission appointed to govern foreigners. 3) The present laws will govern the Hawaiians, and form the basis of Commission administration. 4) Present revenues and expenditures may continue, government vessels may be employed for Her Britannic Majesty's service. 5) There shall be no sales, leases or transfers of land. 6) All bona fide engagements of the king shall be executed and performed.

The Hawaiian flag was lowered and the British colors raised, accompanied by the *Carysfort's* band playing "God Save The Queen," and a 21-gun salute from Honolulu Fort was returned by the *Carysfort*. At the end of the ceremony the band played "Isle of Beauty, Fare Thee Well."

🖂

The despondent king returned to Maui. The young high chiefs at the Chiefs Children's School cut off their kingdom buttons, saying:[49:73] "We are no more Hawaiians; our land has been taken from us and we have to submit to English rule."

🖂

Captain Lord George Paulet appointed himself to head the British Commission, and named as members his Second Lieutenant John James Bartholomew Frere and "Major" Duncan Forbes Mackay.* Paulet saw no need for a Hawaiian on the Commission, but did want someone familiar with the islands. Dr. Thomas C.B. Rooke declined and recommended Dr. Gerrit P. Judd. He also declined, and suggested Harbormaster Captain William Paty. The Acting British Consul felt that Paty was not competent enough. The king prevailed upon Dr. Judd to accept, as his deputy. This suited the king because he could count on strength and representation and satisfied Paulet because Judd was in charge of the kingdom finances.

Lord Paulet acted swiftly to resolve the large demands and grievances. Richard Charlton's land was cleared of 23 "squatter" thatched huts. All Hawaiian flags that could be found were destroyed. Kingdom vessels were taken as tenders for the British frigate. No jury trials were permitted because Paulet was the final authority.[7:246]

A "Grand Ball" was held aboard the U.S. sloop-of-war *Boston* on February 27, 1843. Captain William Paty recorded in his journal: "An excellent supper and good liquor were provided, the ladies left at about 2 O'c. and the gentlemen at abut 5 O'c. in the morning."[91]

An intrigue commenced. It was common knowledge that Lord Paulet would send dispatches to London as soon as possible, and that Alexander Simpson would carry them and provide any desired explanations. It was essential that kingdom dispatches also be hand-

---

* Duncan Forbes Mackay was a Britisher visiting in the islands. He had gone to Australia in 1826 as a free settler, and the title "Major" may have been a courtesy as for a while he had been in charge of prisoners at Newcastle. He was not on any British or East India Company military lists.

delivered at the same time to the Hawaiian envoys then in England. The very youthful-looking 23-year-old James F.B. Marshall* was selected as courier for this secret mission. American Captain Charles Brewer advanced the necessary funds, to be reimbursed in firewood, the only source of revenue then at the king's disposal.[120:54]

✉

The first meeting of the British Commission was held on February 28, 1843. Alexander Simpson was appointed secretary because his Acting British Consul status excluded him from being a member of the Commission. Henry Sea† was also appointed secretary. An additional 1% duty was added to the 3% already imposed on goods landed for local consumption to defray the British Commission costs.[109:89] Among other topics covered in following meetings were: Hawaiian vessels had to be re-registered by the British Commission; foreigners were required to present claims for land and structures. Dr. Judd dissented to these and most of the subsequent proceedings. He was overruled or out-voted, and forced into a very difficult position.

During this vulnerable period, Dr. Judd looked around for an absolutely secure place to prepare the secret dispatches for London, and maintain the kingdom's financial records. The Royal Tomb was selected – a coral block building 14 by 18 feet and 10 feet high, with no windows and a heavy door on the makai (south) side. Governor Ke-ku-anao'a had the only key. He admitted Dr. Judd and a confidential clerk after dark, locked the door, and released them before dawn the next morning. Dr. Judd had a lantern and used Kuhina nui Ka-'ahu-manu's large coffin as a desk. They had been close, and he was sure she would have approved. Judd didn't have much home life for five months – during the days he was at his office, and was in the Royal Tomb during the nights.

Lord Paulet wrote a long, well-documented dispatch to the Admiralty in London advising them of the Provisional Cession. Included was:[34:183-85] "The King and the natives appear much pleased

---

★ James F.B. Marshall later became a very successful Honolulu businessman and member of the Hawaiian legislature. He served in the Union Army during the American Civil War, rising to the rank of brigadier general. In his mature years, he served as Treasurer of Hampton Institute, Virginia.

† Englishman Henry Sea came to Hawai'i in 1842 as Sir George Simpson's secretary and stayed. He became Marshal of the Kingdom 1846-49, and in later years was an administrator and auctioneer.

at the change, and the former has expressed to me his satisfaction at the disappointment the French will experience on their arrival here on finding the British flag flying...I am anxiously waiting the arrival of the French squadron, which may be expected here between the 5th and 10th of April...I have no reason to imagine the French Admiral will attempt to make hostilities upon the flag now flying; nevertheless I have thought it advisable to place everything in as proper a state of defence as possible..."

The British Commission schooner *Albert* (formerly the king's *Hooikaika*) sailed at midnight on March 11, 1843 for Mazatlan, Mexico, with Alexander Simpson and James Marshall as passengers. The king had secretly come to Wai-kiki just after dusk and signed all important dispatches to the President of the United States, Queen of England and King of France, and then returned to Maui.[77/217] There was also an extensive, documented letter to the Hawaiian envoys in Europe.

Secrets were almost impossible to keep in Honolulu town – and Paulet soon discovered that the king had signed dispatches, and Marshall had left with them on the same vessel as his own dispatches. The secrecy disturbed him – he would have wanted to speak with the king, and *see* his letters. Paulet became irritated and disagreeable to Dr. Judd. It was all his fault.

Ironically, the Judds' eighth child, Sybil Augusta, was born on March 16, 1843 – under the flag of Great Britain rather than the recently destroyed banners of Ka-mehameha III.

The British Commission schooner *Victoria* (formerly the kingdom's *Pikolia*) sailed on March 17 to deliver Lord Paulet's dispatches to his admiral at Valparaiso. The 5,862-mile voyage would take 87 days. The U.S. sloop-of-war *Boston* also sailed on the 17th. There seemed little that Captain Long could do at Honolulu as the welfare of American residents did not seem threatened.

Lord George Paulet settled down to wait. So did everyone else. It took months to communicate back and forth between Hawai'i and Valparaiso, Washington, London and Paris.

There was a major disturbance in early March. The Governor had apparently not enforced any laws to maintain order among visiting seamen – he had been strictly directed that they were beyond his authority. The sailors, mostly from the *Carysfort*, had a boisterous confrontation with Hawaiians. Order was restored only when the *Carysfort* marines were landed. The following day Governor Ke-ku-anao'a received a directive to enforce an 8 o'clock curfew and authority to restrain unruly foreigners.

The kingdom military units were disbanded, and most joined the new Queen's Native Infantry Brigade. The *Carysfort's* marine lieutenant acted as their Brigade Major, and the longtime Port Captain John Harbottle, an Englishman, was nominally in command under Lord George Paulet. The artillery detachment of 34 men and two infantry companies of 63 each were full-time. Another two infantry companies were maintained as reservists. The *Carysfort's* marines drilled all of them and canes were effective in enforcing discipline.

All sorts of matters came before the British Commission.* William Hooper was recognized as American representative, Captain Jules Dudoit was not recognized as representing France. A British whaleship commanded by an American had a mutiny – what to do with the seamen? Another ship's captain changed and the register and chronometer could not be found. And so on…

Five months of "occupation" were not very pleasant for the British masters. Most Hawaiians and Americans were barely cordial, the French not at all, and there were few British residents to provide a social life. The *Carysfort* had no chaplain aboard, so Lord Paulet officiated at a Church of England service and baptized the white and part-Hawaiian children of a number of Britishers living in the islands. It has been handed down that Paulet had a liaison with a young Hawaiian chiefess and a daughter resulted.

At the April 27, 1843 British Commission meeting, the kingdom's law regarding prostitution and fornication was abolished.[23] The American missionaries rose up in wrath – this was a moral issue, not a political one. The next two meetings were ugly, as Paulet did not like to be questioned. He took out his ire on Dr. Judd. Duncan Forbes Mackay had resigned and returned to Australia. Dr. Judd presented a written Protest which was a bombshell and started a shouting "donnybrook."[49:54-55]

At the May 11, 1843 meeting,[66] Dr. Judd presented his written resignation, "thereby withdrawing King Kamehameha III from all future responsibility in the acts of the British Commission." The king

---

★ The complete British Commission records are in the Archives of Hawaii and are interesting reading.

backed his resignation, refused to appoint another "deputy," and wrote a Protest dated June 24, 1843.[49:55-56] This included "we are oppressed and injured" by the actions of the British Commission. Lord Paulet and Lieutenant Frere "have broken faith with us." The hardening of the Hawaiian position can be attributed to news just received that the United States recognized Hawaiian independence and would oppose any other's interference.

The U.S. frigate *Constellation* under Commodore Lawrence Kearny arrived on July 7, 1843.[22:438] Several days later he presented a Protest to the British Commission and the king, holding them answerable for any adverse impact upon American residents.[2:195] Kamehameha III came to Honolulu on July 25, 1843 to see Commodore Kearny.

Lord George Paulet must have begun to feel beleaguered. Fortunately for him, a large British warship flying a rear admiral's pennant came over the horizon and anchored in the roads on July 26, 1843. Rear Admiral Richard Thomas, Commander-in-Chief of H.B.M.'s Naval Forces in the Pacific Ocean, had arrived.[7:249]

TOP. Rev. William
Richards, 1843. Arrived
Second Company of
American missionaries
April 27, 1823. Left the
Mission to serve the
king as Chaplain,
Interpreter, Teacher of
Political Economy, Law
and the Science of
Government, July 3,
1838. Appointed
Minister Plenipoten-
tiary to the United
States, Great Britain
and France, April 8,
1842. Appointed
Minister of Public
Instruction, April 13,
1846. Died November
7, 1847. (Archives of
Hawaii)

BOTTOM. Chief Ha-alilio, 1843.
He was a punahele (companion)
and private secretary of King
Ka-mehameha III. Appointed
Envoy with the Rev. William
Richards April 8, 1842 to the
United States, Great Britain and
France. Died December 3, 1844
on his way home. (Archives of
Hawaii)

LEFT. Sir George Simpson, 1847. Governor-in-Chief of the Hudson's Bay Company's Territories in North America. King Ka-mehameha III appointed him as a co-Minister Plenipotentiary to the United States, Great Britain and France, April 8, 1842. (Simpson, Sir George. Narrative of a Journey Round the World...1841-42. 2 vols Vol II. London: Henry Colburn, Publisher, 1847)

RIGHT. The Right Honorable Lord George Paulet, about 1867, then an Admiral of the British Navy. (Archives of Hawaii)

Dr. Gerrit P. Judd, 1850. Arrived Third Company of American missionaries March 30, 1828. Left the Mission to serve the king as President of the Treasury Board May 10, 1842, and Recorder and Interpreter May 15, 1842. Appointed Minister of Foreign Affairs November 2, 1843, Minister of the Interior March 20, 1845, and Minister of Finance April 15, 1846 until his resignation September 5, 1853. Died July 12, 1873.

LEFT. Royal Tomb, 1857. Portion enlargement of Hugo Stangenwald's view from the top of Ka-wai-a-haʻo Church looking towards the first ʻIo-lani Palace. (Archives of Hawaii)

BELOW. H.B.M. frigate *Carysfort*, commanded by Captain Lord George Paulet, 1843. Unknown artist. 6th rate, 26 guns, 236 complement. (Archives of Hawaii)

BOTTOM. Govenor Ke-kuanaoʻaʻs Office was located in the two story building to the right at Honolulu Fort. (Portion of Paul Emmert's 1853 painting at the Hawaiian Historical Society.) It was from the balcony that King Ka-mehameha III provisionally ceded the islands to Great Britain February 25, 1843, saying in part: "I have hope that the life of the land will be restored when my conduct is justified."

ADMIRAL RICHARD THOMAS

17

Rear Admiral Richard Thomas' flagship, H.B.M.'s razee* *Dublin* anchored in the roads off Honolulu on July 26, 1843. Salutes were exchanged with British warships already in the harbor. The U.S. frigate *Constellation*, flying the broad emblem of a commodore, was also anchored in the roads and saluted the admiral with 13 guns. The courtesy was returned.

When Captain Lord George Paulet came from shore to report, his reception was brief and chilly. Provisional cession of the Hawaiian islands was not within Paulet's authority or orders. The independent action he had taken was swiftly canceled and led to the tables being turned – amazingly, in favor of the Hawaiians. The only charitable comment the admiral had to say about his conduct was that he must have been partially deranged.[108:58]

Then the *Dublin's* Captain John Jervis Tucker went ashore with the admiral's courteous note to Governor Ke-ku-anao'a:[34:37]

> "It being my desire to obtain the honour of a personal interview with His Majesty King Kamehameha III., for the purpose of conferring with His Majesty on the subject of the provisional cession of his dominions. I have to request that you will be pleased to intimate my wishes to His Majesty, in order that he may appoint the time and place where such interview may be held."

Mr. Sea, Secretary of the British Commission, was requested to announce that the admiral would appreciate no courtesy visits in order to show deference to a first meeting with the king. Gorham D. Gilman recollected:[49:74] "That subtle influence, felt but not seen, by which good news is so often communicated, hardly waiting for spo-

---

★ A razee was a ship of the line cut down to two decks.

ken words, soon ran through the little community at Honolulu, and it was found that a friend indeed had come at a time of need to repair what had been suffered as a grievous wrong."

Admiral Thomas met with King Ka-mehameha III on the morning of July 27, 1843. As a powerful leader in the British navy, he had decided to take matters into his own hands. He was accompanied by his secretary, James Pinhorn, and Dr. Thomas C.B. Rooke as interpreter. The king had Dr. Judd at his side. The admiral was courteous and amiable, and only his sharp blue eyes hinted at a fighter with a well-deserved reputation. He had pondered the Hawaiian situation and was well prepared with lengthy papers. His intention was to restore sovereignty, subject to acceptance of an Agreement, which he presented.

There was another meeting the following morning, and the admiral agreed to a few modifications to his draft. The Articles of Agreement (as dated and signed July 31, 1843) contained: [34:38-40]

"1 British subjects would be protected on a most favored nation basis.

"2 The king would readily grant interviews with any visiting captain of a British warship.

"3 Richard Charlton's property having been restored, there would be no further court action in this case.

"4 No British subject shall be confined in fetters unless riotous or quarrelsome and then only for the security of his person. The British Consul may attend any such proceedings.

"5 A jury sitting in judgement on a British subject shall be composed of one half Britishers approved by the British Consul, and must be disinterested men.

"6 Direct communications between the king and British Consul at all times.

"7 Recognition of an acceptable British Consul.

"8 All British claims and grievances not mentioned in this Agreement shall be adjusted at/by the British government.

"9 The British Consul will be present at major court actions on British subjects.

"10 This Agreement is subject to the approval and ratification or modification by the British government."

Admiral Thomas presented a draft of his formal Declaration, for the sake of information, dated July 31, 1843 and stating in part that he did not accept the Provisional Cession of the Hawaiian Islands to

"Lord George Paulet, as the then and there representative of Her Majesty Queen Victoria," and considered King Ka-mehameha III was to be the legitimate ruler of the islands.[34:40-42]

The restoration ceremony was scheduled for three days later on Monday morning July 31, 1843. The location selected was Kula-o-ka-hu'a* on the plains east of Honolulu town.[49:74]

Governor Ke-ku-anao'a immediately gathered a large number of men who cleared and roped off the area, secured a spare ship's mast and made it into a gigantic flagpole, built and decorated two open-sided thatched structures, gathered rushes and covered the broad dusty path from town to the site. Everyone else was busy collecting flowers and ferns. Criers were sent around town announcing the ceremony and that all were welcome.

Admiral Thomas immediately finalized formal details and all important salutes.[121:58] Junior officers were kept constantly on the go, courteously passing on word of the plans to the American and French representatives, leading businessmen, Commodore Kearny and others. Lord Paulet had no part in the ceremony.[121:50-51] The *Dublin's* sailmaker was busy making large Hawaiian flags to replace those Paulet had ordered to be destroyed.

Flags were also hurriedly made in the town. The Archives of Hawaii (FO&Ex) has a choice note dated July 29 from a leading mercantile firm to King Ka-mehameha III:

> "Allow us to present you with the accompanying Flag for the Glorious 31st coming, and offer you our sincere congratulations on the restoration of your rights, and believe us,
>   Your friends and Servants,
>   Peirce & Brewer"

La Ho'iho'i Ea, Restoration Day, July 31, 1843.[49:74-75 124:65]
[45:166-68 88:187-88 69:123]

The day commenced auspiciously with rain showers drifting from the mountains to the plain. Some 500 men from the three British warships[†] had landed at 8 AM and were thoroughly soaked by

---

* Kula-o-ka-hu'a is now called Thomas Square, and is just south of the Honolulu Academy of Arts.
† H.B.M. sloop-of-war *Hazard*, Commander Charles Bell, had arrived from Tahiti on July 2, 1843.

the time they reached the ceremony site. By 9 AM the weather had cleared to a beautiful sun-filled day. The rain had been beneficial in settling the ever-present dust on the plain. There were decorated buildings all over Honolulu town which emptied of its 8-10,000 people who joyfully sauntered into the appointed area for the ceremony.

Admiral Richard Thomas, his senior officers and Dr. Thomas C.B. Rooke called on Ka-mehameha III at 9:30 AM. The king signed the Articles of Agreement with the admiral and, because the premier was on Maui, she signed later. Then the British admiral and his party proceeded to Kula-o-ka-hu'a in the king's carriage. The colors of Great Britain were flying atop the flagstaff.

King Ka-mehameha III, Dr. Judd, high chiefs and courtiers came to the ceremony site on horseback at 10 AM. The king was escorted by his former troops who had not yet been sworn back into service, the disbanded British Queen's Native Infantry Brigade.

Admiral Thomas greeted the king and respectfully conducted him to the front of the pavilions. At his signal: [69:123] "The English flag officer advanced toward the king...bowed his colors most gracefully, while the splendid Hawaiian standard was unfurled, and, as the breeze caught its ample folds, displaying the dove and olive branch in the center*..."

The three field pieces in the British formation fired a 21-gun salute with all troops at present arms. The British Union Jack was slowly lowered and the Hawaiian Royal Standard raised. Simultaneously, the British colors were lowered from Honolulu Fort, Pu-o-waina (Punchbowl) Battery and the government schooner *Albert* at anchor in the harbor. Hawaiian flags were slowly raised in their places.

In turn, the British warships *Dublin*, *Carysfort* and *Hazard* fired 21-gun salutes in honor of the change of colors. These salutes were answered by Honolulu Fort and Pu-o-waina Battery. The U.S. *Constellation* and ships in the harbor also saluted the Hawaiian flag with 21 guns, which were returned by Honolulu Fort. There was continuous cannon fire and growing clouds of aromatic white smoke which accompanied the prolonged cheers and applause of the assembled spectators.

---

* There were two Hawaiian flags, the royal standard and the national colors.[7:250] The former was a distinctive ensign of the king and had this device emblazoned on the national colors. Another source refers to this device as a crown.[45:168]

The British sailors and marines performed military evolutions for one and a half hours, ending, caustically enough, with the *Carysfort* men forming a final defensive square.

The king and his suite returned to the premier's house, where he pardoned his troops for having been members of the British Queen's Native Infantry Brigade. They swore allegiance to him again and resumed their membership in kingdom organizations.

An impressive ceremony at the overcrowded Ka-wai-a-ha'o Church followed at 1 PM, which the Rev. Lowell Smith opened with a prayer in Hawaiian. The king then made a short address: [45:167]

> "Where are you, common people? The life of these islands has been restored to me as I had hoped it would be. I therefore wish you all to know and acknowledge me as king. The old laws are to be revived and transgressors will be punished. This is my thought, that you acknowledge me king."

King Ka-mehameha III used the words – Ua mau ke ea o ka aina i ka pono – The life of the land is perpetuated in righteousness* – which were adopted as the motto of Hawai'i.

Dr. Gerrit P. Judd then read Admiral Thomas' Declaration in Hawaiian and English. John I'i , as Orator of the Kingdom, spoke with fervor for 20 minutes. He concluded with King Ka-mehameha III's Act of Grace – All adverse actions by anyone during the provisional cession were forgiven, all persons confined as prisoners would be released, and there would be a 10-day holiday. The thanksgiving service was concluded after another prayer by the Rev. Lowell Smith.

The king and his retinue were invited to dine on the *Dublin*. As he passed warships in the harbor and in the roads, he was saluted with 21 guns and manned yards. Admiral Thomas showed him the height of respect – as the king came aboard the *Dublin* his royal standard was hoisted at the mainmast, and the admiral's broad color taken to the frigate *Carysfort* for as long as the king was on the warship.

Dr. Gerrit P. Judd finalized a long letter to Rev. William Richards, dated August 1:† "Tis Done! The swoon is passed away! The Hawaiian

---

* This is the translation in Revised Laws of Hawaii, 1959, Sec. 5–9. With due respect for legal interpretation, authorities differ in the motto translation of "in" or "by" righteousness. As examples, five favor "in" (Bushnell, Gilman, I'i, Pukui and Taylor), and five favor "by" (Alexander, Dutton, Kame'eleihiwa, Kuykendall and Thrum). The author prefers the translation "by" as it seems more meaningful to connote initiative to attain the end result of pono.

† Judd to Richards, Honolulu, August 1, 1843, Accounts of Hawaii (FO&Ex) British Commission Documents.

Flag is Restored and people once more enjoy their freedom under the mild dominion of Kamehameha III." Dr. Judd had worked hard day and night for 155 days of difficult relationships and[138:64] "broke down completely; was attacked with fever and opthalmia, losing the sight of one eye."

During the continuing celebrations, the king hosted a great aha'aina (feast) at his retreat of Luakaha (Place of Relaxation) in verdant upper Nu'u-anu Valley on August 3, 1843.[45:168-60 63:164-65]

Governor Ke-ku-anao'a and his officials had been in a frenzy of activity – only several days to plan, levy, assemble, prepare and construct over 100 imu (underground ovens), then assemble rocks for cooking, secure cooks and servers, decorations, and all the rest. The immense quantity of food included:[63:165]

Two hundred seventy-one hogs, 482 large calabashes of poi, 602 chickens, 3 whole oxen, two barrels of salt pork, two barrels of biscuit, 3,125 salt fish, 1,820 fresh fish, 12 barrels of luau leaves and cabbage, four barrels of onions, 80 bunches of bananas, 55 pineapples, 10 barrels of potatoes, 55 ducks, 82 turkeys, 2,245 coconuts, 4,000 heads of taro, 180 squid; oranges, limes, grapes and various fruits.

There were invitations for prominent people, and town criers invited the rest of an estimated 10,000 guests. The royal party led the way from Honolulu town escorted by the king's troops. They were followed by 1,000 horsewomen, 2,500 horsemen, and a walking throng of happy, chattering people.

The aha'aina was served on three lengthy rows of ti leaves spread in the open glade. At a head table, the king took his place in the center with Admiral Thomas on his right and Commodore Kearny on his left. All sat on the ground, with plates and cutlery provided for those at the head table who desired them. The royal standard was above the king, and flanked by British, French and American colors.

The H.M.S. *Dublin* band provided the initial entertainment. This was followed by such Hawaiian warrior skills as warding off javelins, boxing and wrestling; then numerous chants and songs and dancing groups accompanied by drums, calabashes and nose flutes.

The royal party left the festivities several hours later and adjourned to the king's nearby house. There some missionary wives sang the "Restoration Anthem," with lyrics by missionary Edwin O. Hall set to the music of "God Save the Queen" and similar "My County 'Tis of Thee."[45:168-69]

"Hail to our rightful King!
We joyful honors bring
This day to thee.
Long live your Majesty
Long reign this dynasty
And for posterity
The sceptre be.

"Hail to the worthy name!
Worthy this country's fame
Thomas the brave!
Long shall thy virtues be
Shrined in our memory
Who came to set us free
· Quick o'er the wave.

"Praise to our heavenly King!
To thee our thanks we bring
Worthy of all.
Lord we thine honors raise!
Loud is our song of praise!
Shine on our future days
Sovereign of all."

That evening the U.S. frigate *United States*, flagship of Commodore Thomas ap Catesby Jones, Commander of the United States Pacific Squadron, came to anchor in the roads. The following morning, on August 4, the U.S. sloop-of-war *Cyane* under Commander Stribling also arrived — bringing the news of the initial successes of the Hawaiian envoys in Europe.

There were more cannon salutes as senior naval officers visited each other, consuls made official calls, and there was a crescendo of cannon fire from all the warships when the king visited.

Admiral Thomas was busy writing dispatches to the Admiralty at London, to Pacific British consuls, and to his headquarters at Valparaiso. He had the difficult task of commanding his squadron from this unexpected and relatively remote location. Courteously he advised all that the sloop-of-war *Hazard* would leave for Mexico on August 7 and take any and all dispatches and letters to be forwarded on from there.

The assembled warships gradually departed. H.B.M.'s frigate *Carysfort* was becalmed for two days and unable to get out of the harbor as scheduled — which no doubt infuriated Captain Lord George Paulet.

The king graciously made Mauna Kilika available for the admiral's use. It was a two-story plastered building with a pleasant verandah all around it, and located on the shore near Honolulu Fort's Sally Port.[13:22] Its large flagstaff flew the admiral's emblem. He settled down to a long wait for advice from London. It was always chancy for a naval officer to make major diplomatic decisions which his government might or might not approve.

ADMIRAL RICHARD THOMAS remained in Hawai'i for seven months and was active, out and about most of the time. One resident observed that, "He speaks to everybody and looks at everything and knows more about matters and things in the vicinity *now* than some who have been here ten years."[*] He was easily approached and, when necessary, interpreters were readily available. The admiral was immensely popular and adulated as a hero.

Hawaiian society was similar to British society with its aristocracy and commoners. He sadly became aware that Hawaiians were rapidly declining in numbers and surmised the reasons for this adverse trend – a collective lack of immunity to diseases, and infertility.

He was especially interested in the Chiefs' Children's School, which was ably led by Mr. and Mrs. Amos Cooke under the trusteeship of Dr. Gerrit P. Judd.[98:25] There were only 15 students – descended from Ka-mehameha's conquering chiefs and chiefesses. He was not aware of it, but five would become sovereigns – Alexander Liholiho (King Ka-mehameha IV), Lot Ka-mehameha (King Ka-mehameha V), William Luna-lilo (King Luna-lilo), David Ka-la-kaua (King Ka-la-kaua), and Lydia Makaeha (Queen Lili u-o-ka-lani). There was one especially enjoyable occasion when he had them all to a western lunch at Mauna Kilika.[98:262]

Governor Ke-ku-anao'a was the natural father of four students (no question about his fertility), and had adopted a girl who was also a student. The many adoptions bewildered the admiral – 12 of the 15 had foster parents. The students sometimes came with "30 attendants

[*] Armstrong to Anderson, Honolulu, November 7, 1843. Hawaiian Mission Children's Society (? File).

who loll about the gate or play ball till school is out, and then follow
the little fellows or carry them in their arms to their home
again." [88:27-28]

Honolulu became seasonally busy with whalers – 383, almost all
of them Americans, came to Hawai'i in 1843.[87:225] Some 37 merchantmen visited or passed through, and imports far exceeded the
small exports of sugar, molasses, hides, salt, coffee, etc. There was brisk
business servicing, supplying and provisioning ships. The seamen,
especially from the whalers, were a rough bunch and eagerly sought
shore excitement and enjoyment. Governor Ke-ku-anao'a had his
hands full maintaining law and order, but was able to do so with the
assistance of a tough group of policemen.

United States Commissioner George Brown arrived in Honolulu on
October 16, 1843. He felt the importance of his official position had
been demeaned when the vagaries of available transportation routed
him from Washington to Panama, and on to Honolulu by way of
Tahiti in the British brig *Catherine*.[116:13] Fortunately, the U.S. sloop-
of-war *Cyane* under Commander Stribling was in port, and the commissioner was mollified when he could be taken to La-haina, Maui,
for his official call on the king.

But the commissioner got off to a bad start after the official greet-
ings, interpreted by Dr. Judd, when he began a tirade about the evils
of intemperance.[116:13] [115:90] Brown was to prove to be tactless, irascible
and domineering. He inquired what government official he should
work with other than the king and premier. The reply was, Dr. Gerrit
P. Judd. But his title was Interpreter? Judd quickly became appointed
Secretary of State for Foreign Affairs on November 1, 1843.[77:234]

As Commissioner Brown saw it, his major concern was to safeguard and enhance the preponderant American commerce in the
islands. His March 15, 1843 appointment and instructions couldn't help
but indicate a lack of respect for the Hawaiian kingdom – the United
States did not recognize it as an independent nation.* Brown felt he
was sort of a quasi-guardian of the kingdom, would be consulted on all
important matters, and his judgment deferred to by authorities.[77:235n]

H.B.M. ketch *Basilisk* came to Honolulu harbor the morning of
December 19, 1843, with a load of welcome dispatches for Admiral

★ Webster to Brown, Washington, March 15, 1843.[108] (p. 124)

Thomas. Among those was Admiralty No. 57 (July 29, 1843), which announced the forthcoming appointment of General William Miller* as British Consul-General to the Sandwich, Society, Friendly and other islands in the Pacific, and advised the admiral to have a ship standing by for him at Mazatlan to convey him to Honolulu. Copies of Admiralty No. 80 and 83 (September 30, 1843) advised that the new Consul-General would restore sovereignty after resolution of grievances.

Unbeknownst in Hawai'i, British and French joint recognition of Hawaiian independence was signed on November 28, 1843:[34:43-44]

> "Her Majesty the Queen of the United Kingdom of Great Britain and Ireland, and His Majesty the King of the French, taking into consideration the existence in the Sandwich Islands of a Government capable of providing for the regularity of its relations with foreign nations, have thought it right to engage reciprocally to consider the Sandwich Islands as an Independent State, and never take possession, either directly, or under the title of Protectorate, or under any other form, of any part of the territory of which they are composed."

The French frigate *Boussole*, commanded by Captain Vrignaud, arrived on December 23, 1843 and stayed for 11 days. He knew that the admiral had restored sovereignty, and pressed him for the reasons Lord Paulet had treated French Consul Dudoit as he did. The admiral calmly responded that all information had been forwarded to the British Admiralty for consideration.

The British sloop-of-war *Hazard* arrived in Hawai'i on February 3, 1844, with the new British Consul-General. Honolulu Fort appropriately saluted General Miller with 13 guns as he disembarked. The new British consul was accompanied by his secretary, Robert Crichton Wyllie,† who had joined him in Mexico.

---

* General William Miller, 48, was appointed to this position on August 16, 1843. He had been a British Army officer who became a mercenary general fighting with distinction in the Chilean and Peruvian wars for independence.

† Forty-six-year-old bachelor Robert C. Wyllie was a Scot, a medical doctor who didn't care to practice. He became a merchant in Chile and returned to London a wealthy man. Wyllie shortly became acting consul and joined the Hawaiian kingdom as Minister of Foreign Affairs in 1845. He has been described as impulsive, puckish, given to intrigue and on occasion ridiculously long-winded.[68:129] His handwritten records in the Archives of Hawaii are a terrible scribble. He served the kingdom ably and with integrity and loyalty until his death 20 years later. He was so highly regarded that he was buried in the Royal Mausoleum.

General Miller conferred at length with Admiral Thomas, who was pleased that his restoration of Hawaiian sovereignty was in accord with Foreign Office policy. The consul-general was pleased that the admiral's action had created a great aura of goodwill for the British among both Hawaiians and western residents.

His appointment instructions included:[88:84] "The Sandwich Islands are scarcely more than nominally governed by a native sovereign and native chiefs. Citizens of the United States are in fact the virtual rulers, and directors of the Government. We have no right to entertain jealousy...our policy ought to be to seek to conciliate the real rulers of the Islands...simply by observing towards them a proper courtesy of demeanour, and by giving them fair credit for the good which they do."

The British Foreign Office viewpoint was concerned with western matters, and recognized the paramount American interests in Hawai'i. The king and premier devoted most of their attention to the majority of Hawaiians, and generally left contacts and considerations about westerners to the trusted and loyal Dr. Gerrit P. Judd and Governor Ke-ku-anao'a. The foreign impact on Hawai'i's people mainly had to do with education and religion, with their attendant ethics and social evolution.

Miller had many lengthy discussions with Dr. Judd. He had carried dispatches from Rev. Richards so there was common ground on most subjects. Dr. Judd indicated that grievances settled in London would be ratified by the kingdom.

When the new consul-general presented his credentials to the king on February 10 at La-haina, he also gave him a Convention for Britisher rights which had to be signed by the king and premier before Miller could ratify the restoration of sovereignty. It was practically a copy of the French 1839 La Place Convention. Dr. Judd demurred at some of the articles, but there were no concessions – the Convention was signed two days later.

At the conclusion of the official business, Admiral Thomas announced that he was leaving Hawai'i. The king sincerely responded:* "While residing with us on shore, your polite, courteous and gentlemanly conduct to me, my officers and people, has gained the esteem of all, and I cannot hear the tidings of your departure without much sorrow. The name of Admiral Thomas will rank prominently in

★ The Friend (Extra), February 20, 1844, p. 21

the history of our Islands, and will be remembered by me and my successors with the respect and gratitude due to a benefactor."

United States Commissioner Brown was astonished that the kingdom had entered into such an agreement without his prior knowledge and consultation. He criticized the Convention and protested the potential harm that might come to Americans, for whom he demanded the same rights and privileges as British subjects had been granted. Dr. Judd blandly replied that the kingdom was severely disappointed that the United States had not seen fit to enter into a treaty guaranteeing Hawaiian independence. Despite this, in practice it was the kingdom's policy that Americans should enjoy the same treatment as other foreigners.

One of the many farewell parties for Admiral Thomas was given by Dr. and Mrs. Gerrit P. Judd. It was a "cold water" catered dinner for 14 served resplendently with linen, porcelain, crystal and silver borrowed from Governor Ke-ku-anao‘a. The menu was extensive;[69:126] soup, mullet, curry and rice, roast beef, mutton, boned turkey, ham, duck, chicken, hot and cold salads, lobster, game, omelets, patties, puddings, pies, almond pastry, fruit, nuts and raisins, and crackers and cheese. The admiral's secretary, James Pinhorn, said he had cramps in his stomach since cold water always had that effect upon him, and ate nothing after the soup during the three-hour dinner.

H.B.M's razee *Dublin* parted the cable of her best bower in the roads on February 26, 1844, and had to sail off and on the harbor. Hawaiian divers were fortunately able to secure the anchor, as a similar large one was not available in the Pacific. Admiral Thomas finally departed from Honolulu on March 4, 1844[121:145 148] and was genuinely missed.

The some 600 resident westerners, mostly Americans, felt that Hawai‘i was a frontier similar to the American frontier which was expanding westward to California. They considered the kingdom weak – had not the islands just been occupied by the British, and had not there been a lack of resistance to the French warship belligerence? They accepted customs and harbor fees as a reasonable expense of doing business, supplying 1844's 490 whalers, 42 traders and 14 national ships; imports of $350,000 and exports of $169,000. Their efforts provided most of the funds for the kingdom's some $60,000 in revenues.[87:225 230]

Of course, they found some laws and regulations burdensome, but that was normal anywhere. A major irritation was that westerners did not feel right about being apprehended and judged by "natives." Fortunately, there was a system now of jury selection which made this almost fair.

These issues were a major cause of disharmony and difficulty for Dr. Gerrit P. Judd, who had been charged by the king to deal with westerners. He came up with the idea that the best way to assure the permanency and tranquillity of all in the kingdom was to "unite the foreign with the native element as subjects and officers of the government."[69:244] Judd took the lead and swore allegiance to the Hawaiian kingdom and renounced his American citizenship on March 9, 1844:*

"The undersigned, a native citizen of the United States formerly resident in the State of New York, being duly sworn on the Holy Evangelists, upon his Oath, declares that he will support the Constitution and Laws of the Hawaiian Islands, and bear true allegiance to His Majesty Kamehameha III the King, hereby renouncing all allegiance to every other Government and particularly to that of the United States.

G. P. JUDD

Subscribed and sworn to this 9th March A.D. 1844 before me.

M. KEKUANAOA"

John Ricord became a naturalized subject of the king on this same day, and was appointed Attorney General. This 32-year-old American lawyer, who had wended his way to Hawai'i, was of great assistance to Dr. Judd – a layman in legal matters and burdened with a heavy load of duties and responsibilities.[77:236] Ricord served as attorney general for three years and was characterized as:[77:237] "He had certain tempermental defects which stirred up most bitter hostility in those with whom he came into conflict and this was one of the factors which served to keep the whole community in a ferment during this period; he seemed at times to be possessed by sheer lust of battle."

Some of the almost 100,000 Hawaiians were averse to naturalizations,† and the introduction of foreigners into their government other

---

* Naturalization Book C, March 9, 1844, Archives of Hawaii.
† About 350 foreigners became naturalized subjects of the king within two years.[7:256n]

than advisors in minor roles. They wanted to be ruled by their own chiefs in their own islands as in the past. David Malo, a graduate of the Mission Seminary at La-haina and a member of the legislative lower house, was particularly vociferous on this point.[7:256] No matter that Ka-mehameha had established a precedent by appointing the trusted Englishman John Young to be governor of his home island of Hawai'i.

The 1845 legislature addressed this subject and concluded that: 1) It was impossible to avoid intercourse with foreigners and other nations; 2) It was necessary for the kingdom to have the services of some foreigners; and 3) Those selected foreigners must be naturalized subjects to assure loyalty to King Ka-mehameha III.[77:259]

British Consul-General Miller left Honolulu for Tahiti in July 1844, his primary task in Hawai'i being accomplished. He appointed his secretary, Robert C. Wyllie, to be Pro-Consul in Hawai'i during his absence.[90] (When Miller arrived in Tahiti to aid the resident British in their struggles with the French masters, the British flag was not permitted to fly over the consulate. He remained in Papeete for eight difficult months.[24:153])

Due to the western pressures on kingdom affairs, King Ka-mehameha III moved his court to Honolulu from La-haina in early February 1845.[77:257] This shift had much more than simply a geographical significance. Historically, in Hawai'i a ruler was bound to his land by a powerful spiritual connection.

Governor Ke-ku-anao'a had just completed a fine house at Pohukaina for his young daughter, Kuhina nui Victoria Ka-mamalu. The king admired it, being the most imposing structure in Honolulu, so of course the governor gave it to him. It became known as Hale Ali'i (House of the Chief), and in later years as 'Io-lani Palace (Palace of the Bird of Heaven).

The building was designed and constructed by an unknown master carpenter and resembled the Seven Oaks plantation house in Westwago, Louisiana.[93] James J. Jarves described it just before it was given to the king (The Polynesian, November 9, 1844):

> "The flight of stone steps leading to the hall, is just completed. Underneath the building is a deep cellar and outside of that, below the spacious verandah, the floor of which is raised six feet from the ground, are extensive accommodations for the guards and household servants. The main hall occupies the entire depth of the house, but is disfigured at one end by an enclosed flight of

stairs leading to the upper rooms. On either side of the hall are lofty and spacious apartments of larger size, with broad and high windows reaching to the floor, and so constructed that they can be thrown entirely up, and given free access to the verandah, which entirely circles the house. The verandah is of great width, supported by ranges of stone columns of the same material as the body of the house, and affords a fine promenade. ...The view from the upper story is very fine. It commands an extensive prospect, not only of the town, but the mountains and vallies and seaward. It is divided into two rooms, and is, we believe, designed for smoking and lounging during the heat of the day. ...The whole house from its massive walls and deep verandah, must necessarily be very cool, in the hottest weather."

The king and his court were now installed in the grand style of westerners rather than the semi-outdoor living arrangements which their ancestors had used for more than a thousand years.

There were many people changes in the mid-1800s:

— Rev. William Richards returned to the islands on March 23, 1845, after being an envoy extraordinary in the United States and Europe for two and a half years. Chief Ha-alilio died at sea en route home.

— General Miller returned from Tahiti a few days later and resumed his post as Consul-General to the Hawaiian kingdom.

— The Executive Ministry of the kingdom was organized and appointed in April 1846.[7:340] John Young II became Minister of the Interior; Dr. Gerrit P. Judd, Minister of Finance; Rev. William Richards, Minister of Public Instruction; John Ricord, Attorney General; and Robert C. Wyllie joined the kingdom as Minister of Foreign Affairs. A balance between Hawaiian and non-Hawaiian leadership was endeavored by forming a Privy Council composed of the ministers, island governors and any others the king might appoint.

— Premier Ke-ka-ulu-ohi died on June 7, 1845, during an influenza epidemic, and was replaced by John Young II (Keoni Ana).[7:255] He continued to also function as Minister of the Interior.

— Governor Ke-ku-anao'a married his fourth wife, Kalolo, on August 24, 1845. He followed the ali'i custom, as exemplified by Kamehameha, by taking a young chiefess "to warm his old age."[70:208] By this time the governor was 51, she was "a very pretty girl of about 15."[14:192] But like so many who had only a short life span, Kalolo died four years later, without issue.

There was now a ministerial government of the kingdom composed of mostly non-Hawaiians – they were largely concerned with
western affairs, but still provided leadership for the entire Hawaiian
kingdom. The king and premier gave minimal direction and guidance, and the strong incumbents began to jockey for position and
power. As one observer broadly put it:[90:25] "their temperments were
all so crotchety and obstinate that none could give way to the other,
each believing his own plans to be the only ones worth following."

It took strong men in government to deal with Honolulu's
strong entrepreneurs and their nations' aggressive representatives. To
stand for a position of kingdom policy or law was often challenged.

United States Commissioner George Brown was especially
difficult to deal with. It finally got to a point where all official intercourse with him was suspended and the king requested that he be
removed and replaced.[7:247] [262] Among other things, he charged Dr.
Judd with misconduct in office and for being heavy-handed. Judd
was exonerated in an impeachment proceeding.[68:137-38]

Such a result surprised few because Dr. Gerrit P. Judd was more
equal than his peers in the government. Fluent in Hawaiian, he was
invariably at the king's side and had his well-earned trust for loyalty
and holding to positions favorable to the kingdom. He was obstinate.
He knew power and its uses. There was his way and the wrong way.
He knew best, and was hard to get along with for those who dis-
agreed with him. In addition, Dr. Judd had little use for non-
Hawaiian residents who did not become naturalized subjects of the
king, and the government was usually deaf to any of their
requests.[37:128-29] Regardless of how difficult Dr. Judd may have been
to some people, Gavin Daws concluded (1968):[37:128] "Of all the white
men in the Hawaiian government no one did more for the chiefs
than Gerrit Judd."

MAHELE
(LAND DIVISION)

O N AN ISLAND, LAND IS LIFE AND POWER.
Like everything else in Hawai'i, this truism had its evolution.

In the past, land was held in common, and each island ruler allocated portions of his island to his high chiefs. They in turn suballocated use and control to lesser chiefs. When an island ruler died, his designated or conquering successor reallocated the island. Some ali'i families grew almost as large as clans and became powerful – providing they were on the right side of a successor's reallocation.[72:51] [39:6] Over several generations, some astute ali'i families had what amounted to fiefdoms.

A commoner "lived under the shade of" and worked on permitted farming plots in an ahupua'a (land area) with lowland taro patch irrigation controlled by the chief.[141:77] [55:88] Those granted such use had the customary privilege of going onto their chief's other land, with permission, to gather poles and thatch for housing, firewood and underground oven stones for cooking, materials for making tools and implements, edible fruits and nuts, wauke for making kapa (bark cloth), olona for making cord, and so forth. This included shoreline foodstuffs and fishing.[3:80] [4:89] [95] Each chief took a portion of a man's labor and what he produced, and it was estimated that a commoner retained only a third of his efforts.[77:270] No one could go into another ahupua'a and take anything without permission of its konohiki (landlord) chief.[141:80] He possessed the land.

When Ka-mehameha conquered most of the islands in 1795, he allocated the captured lands and people to his chiefs, usually spread about to preclude power bases. He gave large amounts of land to the four Kona chiefs who had so faithfully supported him. These were granted in perpetuity, and allowed for descent.[72:52] [58] After

Ka-mehameha died in 1819, his designated successor, Liholiho, continued his land allocations.[141:77]

Lord Byron, who brought back Liholiho's remains from England in 1825, recommended to the council that lands held by the chiefs should not be reallocated, and should descend to their children.[39:8] Ali'i awards of land continued and descent was recognized. When Kuhina nui Ka-'ahu-manu died in 1832, another precedent was established. Her extensive lands devolved to Kina'u, the designated successor kuhina nui (premier).[72:120]

The 1839 Declaration of Rights had a provision which endeavored to preclude caprice when dealing with those on the land[77:160] "Protection is hereby secured to the persons of all the people, together with their lands, building lots, and all their property, where they conform to the laws of the kingdom, and nothing whatsoever shall be taken from any individual except by express permission of the laws."

The revised laws of 1842 further stated:[132:18] "No man living on a farm whose name is recorded by his landlord, shall without cause desert the land of his landlord. Nor shall the landlord causelessly dispossess his tenant." This was probably indicative of harsh treatment of tenants by a chief. In 1892, it was stated that the oppressive severity of konohiki (landlords) in dealing with the cultivators of the soil was notorious. As a consequence, a large number of dispossessed and homeless commoners were wandering about the country.[39:6] [11]

Section v of the 1840 constitution read:[132:3] "Kamehameha I was the founder of the kingdom, and to him belonged all the land from one end of the Islands to the other, though it was not his own private property. It belonged to the chiefs and people, in common, of whom Kamehameha I was the head, and had the management of the landed property." Jon C. Chinen, an authority on Hawaiian land matters, concluded in 1961:[31:3] "This was the first acknowledgement by the sovereign that his people had some form of ownership in the land, aside from an interest in the products of the soil. It was this acknowledgement that led to the award of lands in fee simple to the people of the islands and eventually the abolishment of the ancient land system within the islands."

The revised laws of 1842 contained two other sections of interest:[132:21 28] Anyone could fish anywhere beyond the reef (thus abolishing konohiki chief rights to this area); and one-third of any inherited lands would revert to the king.

Land tenure was an important concern to the westerners, who were used to fee simple ownership. Land use in Hawai'i was at the pleasure of the ruler, either verbal or written, and could not normally be transferred or bequeathed. In Ka-mehameha's time, when a westerner died, the land he was occupying reverted back to the ruler.[72:59] A westerner naturally asked, what about structures and improvements when I no longer need the property or die? The obscure answer seems to have been considered on a case-by-case basis.

In 1825 Prime Minister Ka-lani-moku allowed John Wilkinson to farm land in Manoa Valley and "he could have it until the ground was wanted by themselves."[82:43] Ten years later, King Ka-mehameha III granted a 50-year lease to Ladd and Company to grow crops on 1,000 acres on the island of Kaua'i.[77:175] (The so-called Belgian Contract would have greatly increased the years and acreage, but this did not come about.)

An aberration to common land policy occurred in 1845, when the British imposed settlement of the Charlton Land Case. His over 200 year lease was deemed leasehold ownership.[77:246]

A significant factor in land concerns was that the influential missionaries were seeking for some way commoners could evolve from serf-like labor to free labor. This in furtherance of their basic goal "of raising up the whole people to an elevated state of christian civilization."[59:27]

The time was ripe for drastic updating and changing land policies from feudal to private property principles. In 1892 Sanford B. Dole concluded about King Ka-mehameha III:[39:8] "The landed reforms of that reign were the results of causes which had been long and powerfully at work." Ralph S. Kuykendall took a slightly different approach toward the land issue in 1938:[77:284] "The feudal conception was breaking down or giving way before the new ideas introduced from the outside world."

By the mid-1800s, the king and chiefs became convinced that their land system was imperfect and had been fragmented – there were too many exceptions. This was a hindrance to their further progress in evolving to world civilization. Each chief could see that more permanent possession of his land would be a personal benefit,[39:8] [77:270] even though their authority and power over the commoners could diminish.[77:274-75] The present system was also causing many bothersome disputes with foreign residents.[7:256] These were invariably resolved by stating that land possession by them should continue to those holding verbal or written leases.[77:275] We gave our word.

There were many pro and con discussions among the chiefs, mostly behind the scenes, to seek the best possible solution. A small group of legislative lower house members were against the whole idea of change, especially allowing westerners to own land in the islands. These men thought in terms of Hawai'i for the Hawaiians.[72:193-94] They had secured some petitions from commoners but those were brushed aside. The chiefs opted for a basic land change to fee simple ownership.[72:185]

Two initial experiments of selling land to Hawaiian commoners were authorized by the 1845 and 1846 legislatures.[77:283] Land at Maka-wao, Maui, was put up for sale in parcels of 5-10 acres at $1 an acre. The king charged the Rev. Jonathan S. Green with publicizing, explaining and advising, and administering sales. His diligent efforts resulted in the sale of almost 100 parcels, 900 acres in all being sold. John I'i was the agent for selling land in Manoa Valley back of Honolulu town. Some 30 parcels of 1-10 acres were sold.

A law was passed by the 1845 legislature which established a Board of Commissioners to Quiet Land Titles.[132:137] Commonly known as the Land Commission, it was created:[31:8] "For the investigation and final ascertainment or rejection of all claims of private individuals, whether natives or foreigners, to any landed property acquired anterior to the passage of the Act."

The Commission could grant a Land Commission Award similar to today's title search, but had the authority of a judicial court action.[31:13] Aliens could initially secure only lease awards – it was not until 1850 that they were permitted fee simple titles.[31:11-12] Any awardee must secure a survey at his own expense.

A Royal Patent of ownership in lease or fee simple could be obtained by awardees from the Minister of the Interior. Fee simple required payment of a commutation, usually one-third of the unimproved value of the land.[77:280]

The initial Land Commission was chaired by the Rev. William Richards, with members Zorobabela Kaauwai, James Young Kanehoa and John Ricord, the Attorney General. It was established for two years and extended until 1855.[77:279] The commission developed Principles to be Used When Considering Awards; these were approved by the Legislative Council in October of 1846.[77:281] The preface to these principles suggested that three basic classes of persons each had one-third vested rights in all Hawaiian lands: 1) Government (King), 2) Landlords (Chiefs), and 3) Tenants (Commoners).[132:142] It took about a year of more discussions before there was agreement about the concept of partition between the king and chiefs. This led to the so-called Great Mahele (division)* when all land was formally portioned out.

The Mahele began with the December 18, 1847 Privy Council authorization:[39:17] "The king should retain his private lands as his individual property, to descend to his heirs and successors; the remainder of the landed property to be divided equally between the government, the chiefs and the common people." A committee was appointed to determine portions of land.[39:17] [77:287] Those given this responsibility were Dr. Gerrit P. Judd (chairman), Mataio Ke-ku-anao'a, Ioane Pi'ikoi and John Young II (Keoni Ana, Premier).

The committee met for 40 days – from January 27 to March 7, 1848 – 245 chiefs appeared and each arrived at an acceptable division between himself and the crown and the government.[87:132] The king signed the agreement of each division. It was a remarkable accomplishment by all concerned.

The division was amazingly amicable. There were many tangible and intangible factors which became generally acceptable. Among them was a rule-of-thumb starting point that if an ali'i held three lands, he could retain one (33%); if two lands, he could retain one (50%), and so on.[77:286] In actuality, high ali'i with many lands retained an average of 38%, high ali'i with lesser lands retained 47%; ali'i of lower status with many lands retained 27%; those with lesser lands retained 53%.[72:229] [268] Chiefs followed the procedural route of the Land Commission for title, and the Minister of the Interior for Royal Patent upon payment of commutation in cash or land.[31:20-21]

The Mahele was completed on March 8, 1848.[31:25] The king divided his lands and those that had reverted from the chiefs into two parts: 1) Crown lands (about one million acres) "for me and for my heirs and successors forever as my property exclusively," and 2) Government lands (about a million and a half acres) "to my chiefs and people forever." The Ali'i received over a million and a half acres.[31:25] [31]

Three years later, the kingdom found it necessary to pass an Act which established that when land became fee simple, tenants (commoners) continued to have the same customary privileges of gathering materials, etc. for their own use from the ahupua'a in which they lived.[32:356]

---

* It should be appreciated that these land processes were vastly complicated and difficult to summarize and simplify. For further reading on details from different perspectives, see Ralph S. Kuykendall's "The Hawaiian Kingdom 1778-1854" (1938) and Lilikala Kame'eleihiwa's "Native Land and Foreign Desires" (1992).

Fee simple ownership of land was available to commoners who farmed, lived on and occupied it. They were called kuleana.[77:292] When the people heard about this innovation, they sought advice. The trusted missionaries advocated with enthusiasm. Their landlord konohiki chiefs usually discouraged the idea.[141:84]

Except for Honolulu, La-haina and Hilo houselots, awards were free of any commutation.[31:29] Most of the property filed on was valuable taro land. Quite often the parcels considered were those under cultivation; fallow lands were objected to by konohiki. Thus, average taro lands were often about three acres, too small for family subsistence.[72:295] Required land surveys, which were poor, and other costs were usually $6-12 per kuleana, a big expense for potential landholders.[81:425-26]

Some who considered the idea filed but failed to appear before the Land Commission.[31:31] Its final report on March 31, 1855 stated that there had been 13,514 claims and 9,337 awards of kuleana lands totaling less than 30,000 acres.[77:293-94] (Another source states 14,195 claims and 8,421 awards.[72:295])

Those who received kuleana awards found that they were no longer considered "tenants" of the ahupua'a. They possessed land within the geographic confines of the ahupua'a, carved from a chief's land award. They no longer had to pay labor taxes to the ahupua'a's chief, but they no longer had the customary permission to secure necessary materials from elsewhere on the chief's awarded ahupua'a. In most cases, if they voluntarily continued the labor taxes and other prerequisites of the chief, the traditional privileges could continue. What was the benefit of fee simple ownership of a kuleana?[55] [77:289] [87:132-33] However, it can be roughly estimated that some 40% of maka'ainana adult males received kuleana.

The Mahele land distribution by 1855 was:[*72:136]

CHIEFS LANDS	1,619,000 acres
GOVERNMENT LANDS	1,495,000
CROWN LANDS	984,000
KULEANA	28,600
	4,126,000 acres

This had brought enormous and permanent changes which would continue to influence all levels of life in the islands.

---

* It was estimated 38 years later in 1893 that only 10% of lands conveyed to Hawaiians remained in their hands. Westerners controlled the larger parcels, Chinese the kuleana. (Blount interview with Loeberstein, April 11, 1893.)

CHANGE

THERE WERE LIGHT MOMENTS IN HAWAIʻI
because King Ka-mehameha III and his Queen Kalama loved parties.
For several years now he had been intemperate and wine regularly
appeared at his public dinners.[68:156] The exuberant Lieutenant Henry
A. Wise, USN, of the frigate *Independence* described an official reception at Hale Aliʻi in September 1848:[140:333-34]

> "From the opposite side of the terrace appeared the regal cortege
> – brilliant in embroidery, gold lace, nodding plumes, and swords
> at their sides. On they came, two abreast – foremost the King,
> with the Minister of Finance (*ed*: Dr. Judd), then a brace of
> Chamberlains, followed by the high chiefs and officers of State,
> and the procession closed by the two young princes, Alexander
> and Lot.
>
> "In a few moments, his Excellency the Minister of Foreign
> Relations (*ed*: Robert Wyllie) imparted august intelligence of all
> being prepared for our reception. Forming in line – the Admiral
> leading under pilotage of Mr. Wyllie – we entered the saloon, and
> approached the throne. The King was standing, and the courtiers
> ranged on either side. Our Admiral backed his topsails, and let go
> an anchor on the Lonely One's port beam. We were then
> telegraphed by name – shotahead – hove-to abreast of his
> Majesty – exchanged signals – filled away, and took position by
> order of sailing on the starboard bow!
>
> "His Excellency the Minister of Finance – who, by the way, was
> not an ill-looking nobleman – in full Court costume, and a field-
> marshal's chapeau tucked under his arm, announced to the
> Admiral that his Majesty would deign to lend a willing ear to any
> observations upon religion, war, politics, or any other topics most
> agreeable. Whereupon, the Admiral having a few remarks all ready
> prepared in his pocket, proceeded to dilate on the happiness he

felt in being thus honored – spoke of the extraordinary beauty of the islands – touched upon usefulness of missionaries, and ended by expressing solicitude for his Majesty's welfare and dynasty.

"This speech was immediately translated by the courtly Judd, who, with admirable foresight, had provided himself beforehand with a copy. Thereupon he handed the King a reply, who began in much the same strain as the Admiral, and concluded by hinting that he hoped his dynasty *would* last a long time!

"The business being now happily arranged, his Majesty and the Admiral became seated, and the rest of us were permitted to mingle freely with the Kanaka Court.

"Kammehamma, and his native attendants, had handsome, agreeable faces, and were extremely well made. The Premier, John Young, a half-breed, would be recognized for an elegant person in any part of the world. Two were of just and colossal proportions – one the High Chief Parkee (*ed*: Paki), the greatest Chamberlain probably in the world, for he weighs nearly four hundred pounds. I forget the precise number of chairs he crushes annually, but it something enormous, and he is the terror of all housekeepers."

Gold was discovered at Sutter's Mill near Sacramento, California, in January of 1848. This started the California Gold Rush, which became particularly strong in 1849. It had its impact upon Hawai'i, where some people called it the Yellow Fever.[98:313] In those sailing ship days, San Francisco was about three weeks away from Honolulu.

News of the gold discovery arrived in Hawai'i on June 17, 1848 and caused an uproar. By August, at least 125 westerners had left for the gold fields, and an equal number by November 1848.[69:175] Many Hawaiians joined them.

Laura Judd recorded:[69:175]

"Provisions are high in California. Sugar, butter, ham, coffee, potatoes sell at a dollar a pound in the mines and woolen blankets from fifty to a hundred dollars apiece. There are already twenty-seven vessels running between the islands and the coast. Old blankets, cloaks, pea-jackets, etc., are shipped; our market is likely to be stripped of eatables and we may be reduced to fish and poi."

High prices were a great stimulant to Hawaiian agriculture. The major crops exported were potatoes, sugar and coffee. Exports in lesser amounts were fruits and vegetables, dried pork, fish, barreled beef, and other staples.

Potatoes were in special demand from 1849 to 1851. Kula, Maui, was noted for growing them and Hawaiians humorously called the area Kalifonia.[77:321] Parcels of land were offered in fee simple to Hawaiians. During these three years, the barrels of exports were:[87:155] White (Irish) potatoes – 900, 52,000 and 43,900; sweet potatoes – 300, 9,600 and 56,700.

Sugar and molasses were beginning to be produced from a few small plantations. There was no centrifugal process for separating molasses at that time and it was drained imperfectly from boxes or barrels. Nevertheless, exports for the same time period were impressive:[122:37] Sugar (pounds) – 653,820, 750,238 and 31,030; molasses (gallons) – 41,235, 129,432 and 43,742. Coffee was grown even more sparsely. But it was in high demand and exports for 1849–51 were, in pounds:[123:51] 28,231, 28,428 and 27,190.

This activity decreased generally in 1851 due to a drought in the islands and competition for the new large market in California. Oregon farmers in particular found that white potatoes grew well there and were much closer to the market.[77:321-22 324]

Something quite unexpected happened in Hawai'i during the rainy winter of 1849, as Laura Judd recorded:[69:191]

"Multitudes from California poured in upon us for food and shelter, from their own inclement regions; and they were accused of bringing their climate with them. All the hotels, boarding-houses, and untenanted buildings became full. Food grew scarce. Prices ran up exorbitantly high, and still the tide of immigration poured in. Flour was thirty dollars per barrel! California gold was scattered about with reckless hands, but no alchemist's skill could change it to bread. Kalo (*ed*: taro), that nutritious substantial vegetable (thanks to the toil of the kanaka) did not fail.

"Spring came, the rain ceased, and the tide of humanity set back to the *El Dorado*, leaving the evil of high prices and increased wages for all kinds of labor, but binding us with the strong cords of reciprocal interests and mutual dependence."

A great anecdote has been handed down about Governor Ke-ku-anao'a during this time of high prices. A calabash of poi which formerly sold for 25¢ was now selling for 75¢. Complaints soon reached the governor, who considered it pure speculation which must be stopped. "So the next day, taking his cane, he walked out to the poi

market, where the calabashes were all ranged in a row, and the specula-
tors in the 'staff of life' were assembled and hawking their wares as
eagerly and noisily as brokers in a modern stock exchange. His
Excellency watched them a little while, when, walking up to the first
calabash, he asked the price. 'Ekolu hapaha' (75 cts) said the owner, and
the Governor drew up his cane and smashed in the container, scatter-
ing its contents, here and there. Passing on to the second calabash, he
made the same inquiry and received the same answer, when it and its
contents were scattered in the same manner. The next seller wisely
dropped his price to 50 cts, and the Governor spared his lot, and found
no one else above that figure. The price of poi suddenly collapsed, and
no further complaints were heard of the combination of poi dealers." *

The 1849 statistics on exports revealed similarly inflated
prices: [30:384] potatoes (barrel), white (Irish) $3., sweet $1.50; sugar
(pound) 5¢; molasses (gallon) 25¢; coffee (pound) 10¢; beef (barrel) $12.

All of this increased economic activity added another incentive for
more Hawaiians to leave serf-like labor and become free labor craftsmen such as carpenters, coopers, blacksmiths, shoemakers, and so on.
They also had a well-deserved reputation for being excellent seamen.
It was estimated that some 4,000 were annually afloat. [30:396] This sudden increase in free labor was very pleasing to the missionaries.

By now the American missionaries had been in the islands for three
decades. During this time, 82 came with 66 wives, and 36 left (with-
drew, released, sickened, died), which amounted to an attrition of
44%[85] In 1849, there were 48 missionaries (28 clergymen and 20 lay-
men) on 21 mission stations.

What had they accomplished? At the risk of oversimplification,
three areas can be summed up. 1) Evangelism had resulted in 22,831
Christian church members in good standing by 1849, over a quarter
of the population. [106:42] Twice as many more attended teachings and
services but had not been admitted as church members. 2) In the
field of education and literacy, the kingdom now operated a common
system of 437 schools with 13,261 students.† [77:357] The missionaries
deserve great credit for providing the written language, and promoting
and educating Hawaiians to a level of literacy at least equal to that in

---

*   *Pacific Commercial Advertiser,* April 16, 1863.
†   The average annual wage of teachers was $33.42. [77:357]

the United States. 3) Moral codes had changed, evolving closer to the social norms of the western world and civilized societies.

The missionaries were very concerned about the decline of the Hawaiian population. Their 1849 church records revealed that there had been 1,418 births to church members and 7,568 deaths.[30:406] Twenty chiefs had a total of only 19 children.[30:397] The year 1849 was coined "The Year of Death" as some 10,000 or more Hawaiians died from epidemics of measles, diarrhea, whooping cough, and influenza.[30:396-97] [105:37] It was estimated that the mortality rate of the Hawaiian people could result in the extinction of the race in 100 years.[30:392] There was little the missionaries could do about this – they found it very depressing – and could only pray more fervently and labor harder for the salvation of their flock.

Evolution in Hawai'i was not only Hawaiian. The islands had become virtually christianized and the nature of religious work also went through essential changes.[11:108] In 1848 the Boston-based American Board of Commissioners for Foreign Missions altered the Hawaiian Mission status from "foreign" to "home."[77:341] The American missionaries thus evolved to become pastors of their own congregations. Each church was supposed to become self-supporting as soon as this was practical, and Boston funds continued but on a basis of decreasing aid.

The Board urged acceleration of the program to provide a "Native Ministry" to make sure that Hawaiians were included in this high office.[77:337] The goal had not been easy to establish, as imbuing Christian leadership meant overcoming generations of authority held only by chiefs. Selecting and training candidates was often difficult. There were nine Hawaiian Licensed Preachers in 1848; James Kekela was ordained on December 21, 1849 and became pastor of the church at Ka-huku, O'ahu.[77:339] Each new minister was carefully recorded as a hope for the future.

The American Board established measures to reduce attrition of experienced missionaries who could speak Hawaiian. They encouraged them and their families to stay in the islands and become Hawaiian subjects.[11:109] Fifteen did so in 1849.[77:340] The Board granted mission station property of houses, lands, herds, etc., to those who chose to remain. The kingdom concurred, and gave them fee simple titles to the lands.

In 1850 the government further supported this effort by authorizing those who had been in the islands for eight years to purchase up to 560 acres of land at 50¢ an acre less than the market price.[87:94n] Other than taro patches, agricultural land was then valued at $1-5 an acre. The provision offered a form of help to the pastor.

In effect, non-clergymen missionaries were given notice that their devoted services would no longer be needed. The Assistant Superintendent of Secular Affairs and a teacher left the mission in 1851 and started a business firm in Honolulu. They took over the mission common merchandise stock at cost, and agreed to sell to the missionaries at cost plus five percent (later raised to 10 percent).[113:311] Soon they expanded and sold to the local market and engaged in commission business. The firm, Castle and Cooke, prospered throughout the years and continues to the present day.

The Hawaiian Evangelical Association was formed a few years later to coordinate activities, license preachers and ministers, and serve as an ecclesiastical court.

Robert Elwes, an observant artist, wended his way around the world. He visited Hawai'i when aboard H.B.M. frigate *Amphitrite*, commanded by Captain Rodney Eden, which arrived on May 22, 1849:*

"The appearance of the island of Oahu is sterile and barren. The mountains, many of which are evidently extinct volcanoes, are furrowed from top to bottom with deep-cut watercourses; but no trees are visible. As we approached, everything looked burnt up and desolate, and it was not till we were close to shore that we saw little valleys running up into the mountains, dotted with some straggling cocoanut trees, and from the midst of which peered a few huts. But Honolulu itself looks quite a town, and boasts of stone houses, churches and stores, while a fort, surmounted by cannon, guards the entrance of the harbour.[40:180-81]

"Honolulu has a population of about five thousand natives and four hundred foreigners, viz: two hundred and fifty Americans, one hundred English, and forty Chinese. It is laid out with streets on a regular plan, but there are large spaces between the houses, and it is more like a straggling village than a town. The foreigners have good houses, sometimes of stone, sometimes of adobie or unburnt bricks, but the natives live generally in grass huts, built

---

* Every once in a while one runs across an obscure book with marvelous descriptions that should be shared. Herewith a relatively unknown eyewitness view of Hawai'i at the time.

after their original pattern. They are, however, really very good houses, far superior to those of most other savage nations. They look outside like square hayricks, long in the roof, which slopes down to the ground without any eaves. Inside they are good and commodious. They are very suitable for a volcanic country, as no earthquake could injure them. The floor is covered with mats — one end, set apart for a couch, having six mats laid over each other, the finest at the top.[40:182-83]

"Some of the streets are planted with hibiscus trees, which, with their large yellow flowers, have a pretty effect. There are four churches in Honolulu — two native, one Protestant, and one Catholic. The three former are under the superintendence and guidance of the American missionaries, the last under those of France. There are two hotels, one kept by a Scot, the other by a Frenchman. Each boasts a billiard-table, a fragment of civilization that I did not expect to find in the Sandwich Islands. The King, who is a very good player, and fond of the game, also had a billiard-table. So many Americans being here, the town, of course, could not exist without a bowling-alley. The whole number of licenses held now, by the Report of the Minister of the Interior for the year ending March 31, 1848, is as follows:

Wholesale goods, wares, &c.	23
Retail ditto, ditto	84
Wholesale spirituous liquors	8
Retail	13
Hotels	6
Victualling houses	26
Billiard-tables	6
Bowling-alleys	19
Auctioneers	3
Hawkers and pedlers	71
Newspapers	2 [40:184]

"The production of the islands are kalo, or taro, as it is sometimes called, sugar-cane, bananas, arrow-root, potatoes, yams, sweet potatoes, and all sorts of tropical vegetables and fruits. Taro, or Kalo (Arum esculentum) is the principal food of the native. It is grown in patches in shallow ponds, surrounded by low banks, placed one below the other, so that they can be irrigated at pleasure. Many seem to have the water always in them, and are stocked with fish; and it is said that this is the best plan, as nothing is required but to clear the weeds out. The leaf of the plant is something like the English dock, but larger, and it has a large tuberous root. This is beaten into a paste of the consistency of hasty-pudding, called poe (*ed*: poi), and is always eaten from a calabash with the fore-finger – the natives, from long practice, being able to take up a good mouthful with that alone. They stir the finger two or three times round in the mess, then take it out with a dexterous twist, and put it into the mouth. A spoon seems never to be used with poe; and even when it is ladled from one vessel to another, they resort to the hand. Poe is not bad when fresh; but the natives generally keep it, and seem to prefer it a little sour. The plant requires one year to come to maturity; and it is said that an acre of kalo land will furnish food for twenty persons.[40:186]

(At Kai-lua, Hawaii) "We generally sat down about sixteen to dinner, the King sitting at the head of the table. I on his right hand, the Prince on his left. Our dinners were partly in the native style, comprising a good many dishes of different sorts of fish, some cooked, some dried, and some raw; pork dressed in several ways, and what in Hawaii is considered a great delicacy, a large dish of dog. This was dressed in the native way, wrapped in leaves, and put in the ground with a fire over it, and then served up in a large calabash. I generally ate some of it, and found it very good. It was fat, and tasted something like pork. The dogs, bred for the purpose, are fed on nothing but poe, potatoes, cocoa-nut and vegetable substances; so there is no reason that they should not be good.[40:198]

"Fish is also a great article of food, and the natives have extensive fish-ponds of salt-water, fenced round with coral rocks and well-stocked. The sweet potatoe (Ipomaea batatas) grows well here, and the common potatoe flourishes on the hills. Some of the natives have made a great deal of money by growing the latter, as potatoes are in great request by the whale-ships. In Maui, Kaui, and Hawaii, there are several large sugar estates belonging to Americans and Chinese, and they seem to do well. The natives prefer a more idle mode of earning their living, and many keep horses and breed them. Thus by letting a horse to a foreigner for a few weeks, they get enough to support it and themselves for the rest of the year; or they keep a mare and breed a foal from her every year, which brings a good price, enabling its master to live almost in idleness, and ride his own horse."[40:187]

And so in this era of continuing change, one visitor found much of interest and much to admire.

Rear Admiral Richard Thomas, 1837.
Portrait by Godwin Williams. When
Admiral Thomas died in England, 1857,
King Ka-mehameha IV ordered 15 days of
official mourning in the Hawaiian kingdom.
(Courtesy of Christie's, London, 1976)

Hale Aliʻi (House of the Chief), and in later years
known as ʻIo-lani Palace (Palace of the Bird of
Heaven). Built in 1845 by Governor Ke-ku-anaoʻa and
given to King Ka-mehameha III. It was used as royal
palace by Kings Ka-mehameha III, IV, V, Luna-lilo and
Ka-la-kaua, with living quarters adjacent. The palace
was razed in 1879 and replaced with the present ʻIo-lani
Palace on the same site. (Archives of Hawaii)

RIGHT. Robert
Crichton Wyllie, 1847.
Daguerreotype.
(Archives of Hawaii)

BELOW. John Young II
(Keoni Ana). Governor
of Maui, Minister
of the Interior and
Premier 1845–1855.
(Archives of Hawaii)

Honolulu, 1853. Portion of center view drawn and published as a lithograph by Paul Emmert. Fort Street diagonally lower right to left center terminating at Honolulu Fort, where the Hawaiian flag is flying. (Baker, Ray J. Honolulu in 1853. Honolulu: 1950)

Queen Street, Honolulu, 1857. Watercolor by George H. Burgess painted from atop the Hale Mahoe building at the foot of Queen and Ka-'ahu-manu streets looking towards Diamond Head. Left front is the Hudson's Bay Company building. Right is the town-side wall of Honolulu Fort. The large building just beyond the fort wall is the Court House built in 1851. (A similar watercolor from the same location was made in 1856.) (Archives of Hawaii)

TURMOIL

BY 1849 THE NEW FRENCH CONSUL Guillaume Patrice Dillon had been in the islands for a year – like most representatives of his country, a stubborn nationalist – and his relations with Minister of Foreign Affairs Robert C. Wyllie were bitter and antagonistic.[57:313-15] On August 12 the French frigate *Poursuivante* under Rear Admiral Legoarant de Tromelin arrived in Honolulu, then the following day the French steam corvette *Gassendi* under Commander Faucon came to anchor. The time was ripe for another episode of gunboat diplomacy.

The French consul and the rear admiral presented 10 Demands to the Hawaiian government on August 22:[7:266]

"1 The complete and loyal adoption of the treaty of March 26, 1846.

2 The reduction of the duty on French brandy to fifty percent, ad valorem.

3 The subjection of Catholic schools to the direction of the chief of the French Mission, and to special inspectors not Protestants, and a treatment rigorously equal granted to the two worships and their schools.

4 The use of the French language in all business intercourse between French citizens and the Hawaiian Government.

5 The withdrawal of the (alleged) exception, by which French whalers, which imported wine and spirits, were affected, and the abrogation of a regulation which obliged vessels laden with liquors to pay the custom-house officers placed on board to superintend their loading and unloading.

6 The return of all duties collected by virtue of the regulation the withdrawal of which was demanded by the fifth article.

7 The return of a fine of twenty-five dollars paid by the whale ship *General Teste*, besides an indemnity of sixty dollars for the time that she was detained in port.

8 The punishment of certain school-boys, whose impious conduct (in church) had occasioned complaint.
9 The removal of the governor Hawaii for allowing the domicile
   of a priest to be violated (by police officers, who entered it to
   make an arrest), or the order that the governor make reparation
   to that missionary.
10 The payment to a French hotel keeper of the damages committed in his house by sailors from H.B.M.’s ship *Amphitrite*.”

This concluded with a requirement for a satisfactory response
within three days or the existing treaty would be canceled and the
rear admiral would “employ the means at his disposal to obtain a
complete reparation.”[7:267]

When two days passed with no reply, the rear admiral had circu-
lars posted about Honolulu, announcing that he would attack the
town on the following day.[37:133]

This time, the king and council advised the rear admiral at noon
on the third day, August 25, that they could not accede to the
demands. But there would be no resistance made to his force.[7:267]
The French consul lowered his flag and took his family and possessions to the *Gassendi*.[37:133] [69:186] Preparations for war were made on
the French ships. The United States naval vessel *Glyn* was then in the
harbor – she had springs on her cables and was in position to engage
the French warships if they opened fire on the town.[37:134]

That afternoon, two hundred French sailors and marines with
scaling ladders and two field-pieces landed without opposition.[7:268]
When they entered Honolulu Fort through the open gates, the only
person there was Governor Ke-ku-anao‘a. Based on minor clues, one
can imagine an almost Gilbert and Sullivan dialogue that must have
gone something like this:[42:20-21] [113:295]

> *Where are your soldiers?*
>   *They have all been sent to the country.*
> *Where are their arms?*
>   *Each man has taken his gun with him.*
> *I require you to surrender this fort and all munitions of war.*
>   *You have got everything already, there is nothing left*
>   *to surrender.*

Governor Ke-ku-anao‘a refused to lower the Hawaiian flag and
left. The flag remained flying during the days of “occupation” which
followed.

The French took possession of the nearby government buildings and seized the king's yacht *Kamehameha*. Vessels flying the Hawaiian flag were detained.[77:393] For 10 days they destroyed and plundered – other than Honolulu town. All prisoners were released. The 70 cannons were thrown off the fort walls, spiked, the trunnions broken off, and their carriages demolished. The magazine was broken into and tons of powder were dumped into the harbor. All weapons and military equipment were destroyed.[7:268 15:48]

Doors and windows and furniture in the cells of the fort were smashed, along with other entire structures. French graffiti covered the walls of buildings. Governor Ke-ku-anao'a's house was wrecked. His large collection of calabashes, feather cloaks, royal heirlooms that had belonged to Kina'u and others were either demolished or stolen.[69:186] The French destruction became known as "the war of the calabashes."[42:21]

On August 28, there were some fruitless discussions. The French squadron finally sailed on September 5, 1849, taking their consul and the king's yacht with them.[77:394-5] For some mysterious reason the *Kamehameha* would not move when the sails were set, but finally did when a line was removed which attached her keel to the shore.[42:22]

Laura Judd ironically recorded in her journal:[69:189-90]

"In order to appreciate the necessity of this manifestation of French prowess, one must know the magnitude of French interests in these islands. Aside from the priests and their missions, there were twelve French subjects, one of whom is a merchant, who transacts about one-thousandth part of the commercial business of the place. One cargo of French merchandise has been imported and one French ship-of-war has visited the islands during the last five years. French schooners have occasionally brought freight for English and American merchants, and there are a few whalers in the Pacific who touch now and then at this port."

Dr. Gerrit P. Judd was appointed Special Commissioner and Plenipotentiary Extraordinary to the United States, Great Britain and France on September 10, 1849, with basic instructions to protest Rear Admiral de Tromelin's actions and damages, and to secure better treaties.[77:395 1:ix] He left Honolulu on September 11, 1849, accompanied by Heir Apparent Prince Alexander, who was 15, and his 18-year-old brother Prince Lot.[77:395-96]

Four months later, on January 23, 1850 in London, they saw

British Foreign Secretary Lord Palmerston, who seemed indifferent to French activities in Hawai'i. Great Britain had more pressing concerns with France.[77:396] After some negotiations, a new treaty was eventually signed in Honolulu on July 1, 1852.[77:381]

French Minister of Foreign Affairs General de la Hotte held to the present treaty and refused to accept the Hawaiian kingdom's claim of $100,060 for Rear Admiral de Tromelin's damages in Hawai'i and taking the king's yacht.[37:134]

Dr. Judd and the princes had cordial meetings with United States Secretary of State John M. Clayton in June of 1850. James J. Jarves, Hawaiian diplomatic envoy, had successfully negotiated an earlier treaty between the kingdom and the United States which was signed on December 20, 1849.[77:380] [1:x] Officials promised to do what they could to promote a settlement of French-Hawaiian difficulties. Secretary Clayton stated that if any country took Hawai'i by force, the United States would intervene militarily and restore the islands to the king.[77:398]

This was no doubt reassuring but did not provide restitution for the arrogant destruction that had taken place. The Hawaiian party visited Dr. Judd's family in various parts of New England for several weeks, then returned to Honolulu on September 8, 1850.[77:398-99]

One incident during this trip that lasted a year has been singled out and embellished out of all proportion. A train conductor in Washington tried to put Prince Alexander out of a car because of his color.[9:xii] In his own words:[1:108]

> "...a man came to me and told me to get out of the carriage rather unceremoniously, saying that I was in the wrong carriage. I immediately asked him what he meant. He continued his request, finally he came around by the door and I went out to meet him. Just as he was coming in, somebody whispered a word in his ears – by this time I came up to him, and asked him his reasons for telling me to get out of the carriage. He then told me to keep my seat. ...I found he was the conductor and probably (had) taken me for somebody's servant. Just because I had a darker skin that he had. Confounded fool. ...Here I must state that I am disappointed at the Americans. They have no manners, no politeness, not even common civilities, to a Stranger."

NOTE: The year of travel away from the islands to the centers of western world maritime powers broadened the young princes. They were especially impressed with how they were treated and what they saw in England.[77:399] They also had a pleasant visit with Admiral Richard Thomas.[7:269] But they were not impressed with American democracy, in comparison to the English monarchy, which in later years as sovereigns contributed to their anti-annexation and anti-missionary attitudes.[1:xiv]

☒

Tranquillity was hard to come by in Honolulu. A new French Consul and Commissioner, Emile Perrin, arrived on the French naval corvette *Serieuse* under Commander Coshier on December 13, 1850.[77:399] The corvette did not exchange salutes with Honolulu Fort.[6:2] It wasn't long before Consul Perrin presented the previous French 10 Demands. Negotiations were thorny. The kingdom was very apprehensive about the apparently unfriendly French warship in the harbor. Fortunately, the United States warship *Vandalia*, commanded by Captain Gardner, arrived on February 16, 1851, and was greatly welcomed. The captain agreed to extend his planned stay.

British Consul-General Miller was asked if his government would accept a Protectorate over Hawai'i. He reluctantly declined, as the Great Britain-France Convention of November 28, 1843 precluded any such action.[77:401] United States Commissioner Luther Severance accepted a deed dated March 10, 1851, to be acted upon in case of emergency, and subject to United States government approval:[6:2] [15]

"We, KAMEHAMEHA III., by the Grace of God, of the Hawaiian Islands, King.

"By and with the advice and consent of Our Kuhina Nui and Council of native Chiefs, finding our relations with France so oppressive to Our Kingdom, so inconsistent with its rights, as an independent state, and so obstructive of all Our endeavors to administer the Government of Our Islands with equal justice to all nations and equal independence of all foreign control, and despairing of equity and justice from France;

"Hereby proclaim as Our Royal will and pleasure that all Our islands, and all Our rights as a sovereign over them, are from the date hereof, placed under the Protection and Safeguard of the United States of America, until some arrangements can be made to place Our said relations with France upon a footing compatible with our rights as an independent sovereign, under the laws of nations, and compatible with Our treaty engagements with other foreign nations; or if such arrangements should be found impracticable, then it is Our wish and pleasure that the protection aforesaid under the United States of America be perpetual.

"And We further proclaimed as aforesaid, that from the date of the publication hereof, the flag of the United States of America shall be hoisted above the national ensign on all Our forts and places and vessels navigating with Hawaiian registers.

"Signed by the King and Kuhina Nui, March 10, 1851."

When French Consul Perrin was advised of this document, he modified his demands to a point where a Joint Declaration was signed with the kingdom on March 25, 1851.[6:3] [15-17] The French warship left five days later, the American warship on April 3, and French Consul Perrin returned to France for consultations in May.[77:404]

Americans were rapidly migrating westward in the mid-1840s. "Manifest Destiny" became a popular and accepted expression.[77:383] Texas was annexed in 1845. The following year, the Northwest Territory was acquired by settlement and treaty with Great Britain. As a consequence of the Mexican War during 1846-48, lands north of the Rio Grande were ceded to the United States. The 1849 Gold Rush added impetus to migration, and California became the 31st State in 1850. The sudden increase in the population in the gold fields was quite beyond the control of what little law and order capabilities existed, and there was a large number of unruly and violent men.

Some of this lawless activity spilled over into Hawai'i in the form of threats. There were initially only rumors of armed and dangerous men – who had their sights set on the islands – and alarmingly scant information about them. Their aim seemed to have been to topple the kingdom, form a new government led by themselves, and hope for adding the islands to the United States.[77:385] At the time there were about 100 policemen and 75 guards of the prison cells in Honolulu Fort.[89:10] The Hawaiian military was negligible following the recent French sack of the fort.

One "filibuster" scare occurred in San Francisco when newspapers there reported in October 1851 that 150 "restless young bloods" were about to sail for Honolulu to "revolutionize the government of his Kanaka Majesty."[37:137]

Twenty-five "filibusters" arrived on the clipper ship *Game Cock* on November 15, 1851.[37:137] [89:27] The leader, Sam Brannon, sought an interview with the king who was at La-haina, Maui. He was not received. These men were unwelcome not only to the government but also to the whalers in harbor. En route to Hawai'i, the filibusters had rifled the mail sacks and thrown the contents overboard. This included many letters addressed to whalemen in Honolulu.[6:4] No reinforcements arrived, conditions were unfavorable and military ardor faded. The troublemakers quietly left the islands.

🖾

The 1852 whaling season was very successful, and as usual many whalers gathered in Honolulu for refitting, provisioning, stores, watering and recreation.[37:138] [130:62] There were 124 whale ships and 23 merchantmen in the harbor on November 8, 1852. An additional 26 whalers arrived during the following week.[130:62] The ships were moored and anchored in such long lines that it was said one could walk from one vessel to another from the waterfront almost to the entrance of the harbor.[89:35] [28:22]

Some 3,000 seamen came ashore looking for relaxation after arduous months at sea. Among them was Henry Burns of the whale ship *Emerald*. He was arrested for drunkenness and disorderly conduct and locked in a cell ("crazy drunk") with 8-10 other malefactors.[89:36] Riotous protests followed, as bricks were torn up from the cell floor and hurled against the door. Jailer George Sherman called for the drunks to stop – they didn't – and he entered the dark cell, was rushed, and lashed back with his club. Burns was hit on the head and felled. The next morning he was found dead.[130:63]

Word rapidly got around the ships, and excited seamen poured ashore and derided "the cowardly police and the wretched kanaka government."[130:63] A lynch mob soon formed at the gates of Honolulu Fort. They were closed, and Marshal William C. Parke summoned all of his men.[37:138]

A Coroner's Jury was quickly assembled on November 9, composed of five resident westerners and five shipmasters. Julius A. Anthon, foreman, reported:[130:63] "We believe the blow was not given with malice aforethought, but rather from cowardice in quelling the disturbance which caused his visit to the cell where Burns and others were confined." The jailer, George Sherman, was arrested for his own protection and charged with manslaughter.

Marshal Parke was about to take 75 men and disperse the crowd that had heard this news, when he received orders from Governor Keku-anao'a to remain within the fort and, if attacked, to fire. Two field-pieces loaded with grape and canister were trained on the gate.[89:38] The crowd dispersed but belligerent sailors roamed the town.

Henry Burns was buried in the Nu'u-anu Cemetery on November 10. The graveside service was attended by several thousand seamen.[130:64] The sailors then took over the town, menacing and pillaging, and whipping their emotions into a frenzy.[89:38] Businesses were closed and stores barricaded. Small groups of seamen roamed the streets and entered private houses where they made themselves at home. Dr. Edward Hoffman was able to simmer down a gang who came to his house by playing popular music on the piano and providing ale.[130:65]

That evening when an arrested seaman at the Station House at the foot of Nu'u-anu Street was freed, the building was ravaged and set on fire. Even greater excitement followed as the flames ignited a nearby vessel.[130:64] Many willing hands put it out, for if the fire had spread in the crowded harbor, the results of all the sailors' arduous labor at sea would have gone up in smoke.

Then a crowd of unruly seamen set out in the dark to attack the homes of Minister of Public Instruction Richard Armstrong and Minister of Finance Dr. Gerrit P. Judd. They couldn't find Armstrong, and when they got to Dr. Judd's house in Nu'u-anu they were repulsed at pistol point.[37:139] Somebody had obviously directed the seamen to single out these two government officials.

The following morning, on November 11, a meeting of leading westerner residents was called at the marshal's office. This resulted in 200 men volunteering to patrol the streets in small detachments.[130:65] The next day the governor issued a write of Martial Law, and police and hundreds of both Hawaiian and non-Hawaiian volunteers* cleared the streets and arrested 50 seamen who resisted. The riot was over, and authorities regained control of Honolulu town.[37:139] [89:43] The final point of conclusion came when the jailer, George Sherman, was convicted of a minor degree of manslaughter and "banished" to the island of Hawai'i.[130:67]

Several Organic Acts passed by the legislature had rendered the Constitution of 1840 "out of date" and inadequate. Three commissioners were appointed by the king in 1851 to draft a new constitution

---

* The militia infantry company 1st Hawaiian Guard, composed of non-Hawaiians, and the 1st Hawaiian Cavalry, composed of Hawaiians. These two units were the first formal components of Hawaii National Guard heritage.[135:14-15] In the past, every able-bodied male was considered to be a militiaman.

by the following year: Dr. Gerrit P. Judd; for the nobles, Judge John I'i; for the representatives, and Chief Justice of the Superior Court William L. Lee.[77:266] The finished document was presented to the 1852 Legislature.

Princes Alexander and Lot thought it was unsuitable and didn't like the American political philosophy.[5:52] British background Minister of Foreign Affairs Robert C. Wyllie stated:[78:16] "I entertain much doubt…of giving the right of suffrage to all men, irrespective of any property qualification, or of any proof that they have paid their taxes, or hold any stake in the country." The king is said to have remarked:[77:267] "It gave to the people a power which they were not prepared to use judiciously."

The draft was considerably amended by the 1852 Legislature, approved and signed by the king to go into effect on December 6, 1852. King Ka-mehameha III promulgated the new Constitution on this date at a ceremony in Ka-wai-a-ha'o Church. He stated, in part:[89:46] "Adhere to this constitution one and all. It is not with us now as in former times, when the chiefs alone governed as they pleased, and the people had no voice. We are now reckoned among the enlightened nations, and we must follow their example, and conduct our affairs by a constitution and laws."

Thus another change had come about which moved the island kingdom further from its ancient past and toward a future that included a more sophisticated, modern form of government. In another act that pointed toward the future, Prince Alexander Liholiho was formally proclaimed heir to the crown on April 7, 1853.[77:415]

The American clipper ship *Charles Mallory* arrived off the harbor on February 10, 1853, flying the yellow flag of pestilence on the foremast.[89:49] One crew member was ill with smallpox, then prevalent at the last port they visited, San Francisco.[7:275] The vessel was ordered anchored off Wai-kiki, the crew brought ashore and quarantined near Diamond Head, and the sick man isolated in a thatched house on a small islet in the harbor. As the ill man recovered, and none of the other crew members fell sick after three weeks' quarantine, they were released and the ship left. All bedding, the men's clothing and the ill man's isolation house were burned.[89:50] This time the islands seemed to have been spared.

Then, two months later, on May 15, 1853, a Hawaiian woman and girl were diagnosed as having smallpox, and another girl at the same location on Mauna Kea Street was convalescing from the same disease. It was suspected they had been infected by clothing sold at an auction which had been brought by the brig *Zoe*[125:97] or that had been brought by a San Francisco merchant ship captain to these women for washing.[89:57]

A guard was placed on the house and the ill women were moved to a government building on Queen Street to be used as an Isolation Hospital. Several other cases were found in the same area and taken to this location. Soon the disease had spread throughout the town, and yellow flags were found everywhere. As Thomas G. Thrum put it:[127:86-87] "...the piteous wail of bereaved ones in the neighborhood, day after day, told the sad story of its steady progress...the frequency of the 'death cart' on the streets to receive bodies, many of whom simply wrapped in mats, called for heroic work by a force of employees of the health authorities to prevent secret interments on the premises." Forced labor by men who had recovered from smallpox buried the dead.[89:55]

The king appointed Commissioners of Health on May 16, 1853, three men empowered to take actions to control and stop the epidemic:[77:412] [89:52] The chairman, Dr. Thomas C.B. Rooke, worked with Dr. Gerrit P. Judd and Marshal William C. Parke. Medical knowledge about how to treat smallpox and handle an epidemic, other than isolation, was imperfect. Different doctors had different methods, but none were known to be infallible. When Dr. Judd discovered that vaccines on hand from America and England had often lost their potency, he tried unsuccessfully to infect a cow to secure cowpox vaccine.[68:203] The epidemic was at its height between July and August 1853.★

★ The commissioners reported at a later date that there had been 6,405 cases of smallpox and 2,485 deaths. Another report doubled these figures, probably due to illness and death not under the purview of the commission.[77:412] The main epidemic was on Oʻahu, the other islands isolated themselves as best as they could and had few cases. Gradually the crisis ended by October 1853. Census data reveals a decrease of population in four years, much of which can be attributed to this epidemic:[105:43 74]

	HAWAIIAN	PART-HAWAIIAN	NON-HAWAIIAN	TOTAL
JAN. 1850	82,035	558	1,572	84,165
DEC. 1853	70,036	983	2,119	73,138
	-11,999	+425	+547	-11,027

A public meeting was called on July 18, 1853 to consider what further could be done about the smallpox epidemic to assure that the port would be safe for the fall visit of whaleships.[77:413] Dr. Wesley Newcomb led the discussion, then a committee was formed to report to another public meeting on the following day.[72:48] They did, and recommended:[51:49] 1) secure houses for more hospitals, 2) free mandatory vaccination program, 3) administrative divisions and reporting, 4) vehicles to transport the sick to hospitals, the dead to burying grounds, and have provisions for their burial, 5) interpreters for the doctors, 6) houses and property to be destroyed because of the pestilence, and owners compensated, and 7) all dogs should be killed and buried.

In the midst of the epidemic, Dr. George A. Lathrop, a recent arrival from California, introduced a political resolution. It condemned Rev. Richard Armstrong, Minister of Public Instruction, and Dr. Gerrit P. Judd, Minister of Finance. They were the two members of the king's cabinet who had been missionaries and stood for their high moral values. The meeting was adjourned without action.

At the third meeting on July 20, 1853, a resolution by Dr. Lathrop was adopted, which read in part:[15:439]

"Resolved, That the Ministers of Finance and Public Instruction, members of his majesty's present cabinet, are not so fortunate as to have either the confidence or esteem of this meeting, nor, as we believe, of any considerable portion of his majesty's native subjects, or of foreign resident citizens throughout his kingdom, and that their retention in office is in direct opposition to the wishes and interests of a very large majority of the natives and citizens of the Sandwich Islands.

"Resolved, That these same ministers, having the command of the principal channels of influence, viz., treasure, education, and the almost absolute control of government patronage, have most wickedly neglected their duty in not using the means within their control to protect the people from the pestilence which is now depopulating the islands. That, instead of devoting themselves to the public good, they have ever sought their own aggrandizement, regardless alike of the high duties devolving upon them, or of the evils necessarily following their malfeasance in office."

A petition was prepared by J.D. Blair asking for their dismissal from office. This document was eventually signed by 260 "foreigners" and 12,220 "natives."[15:440-43] Later study of these names found that

189 "foreigners" were not subjects of the king, and that the numbers of "natives" (11,500 in another report) were suspect as most signed with an illiterate X.[37:142] Judge John I'i chaired yet another public meeting on July 25 at Ka-wai-a-ha'o Church with Governor Ke-ku-anao'a as secretary. Attendees were mostly Hawaiians. A counter petition was signed by some 3,000 expressing confidence in Armstrong and Judd, and deploring the false and scandalous charges.[37:142 77:414]

There were strong undercurrents in the divided privy council. On the one hand the public meeting resolutions smacked of filibustering and annexation efforts; on the other hand they were a frontal attack on the power of Dr. Gerrit P. Judd. The time when he was always at the king's side had begun to wane as the government became more formalized. There were now a number of power bases. Active antagonism and dislike had grown between Dr. Judd and Mr. Wyllie to a point where they were hardly civil. There had been half-truths, intrigues and downright lies. The king appreciated Dr. Judd's strength and loyal guidance, yet one may be sure he was irked at times by his advisor's dominance.[68:210]

To summarize a complicated situation, there were several months of deliberations, mostly "behind the scenes." The king requested all of his ministers to resign on September 3, 1853. They did, and all were reappointed two days later except for Dr. Judd.[27:415] Those who had vigorously fought for his ouster organized a torch light parade on the evening of September 10, complete with band, banners and cannon fire, which ended at Hale Ali'i.[37:441] A bitter pill for the doctor who had devoted 11 years of loyalty to the Hawaiian crown.* His spirit of deep hurt and depression must have lifted somewhat when he heard that Governor Ke-ku-anao'a had loudly stated: "If he had not assisted them the government would have been lost or gone."[72:192]

---

* Dr. Judd stayed in Honolulu as a physician, businessman, and general advisor for the remaining 20 years of his life.

THE POLITICAL TURMOIL CONTINUED. Nineteen respectable Honolulu businessmen presented a memorial to the cabinet and king on August 22, 1853, which favored annexation to the United States.[68:208] The British and French representatives met with the king and privy council on September 1, 1853 and protested any such consideration as being unconstitutional and not in accord with treaties with their countries.[6:6] Revs. Ephraim W. Clark and Peter J. Gulick publicly wrote on September 10, 1853:[6:5-6]

> "The Protestant missionaries at the Islands had never engaged in any scheme of annexation. It has been their cherished wish that the government may remain independent under the present Constitution and rulers. Whatever may have been done by merchants, planters and others, the Protestant clergymen at the Islands have neither advised nor signed any memorial to the King touching annexation."

The dream of annexation flourished among those who would benefit the most – three-quarters of business was in the hands of Americans, and the main markets were on the Pacific Coast of the United States. The decrease in the number of Hawaiians – especially their leaders, the chiefs – was very unsettling.

The king appeared to favor annexation as a way of getting out from under vexing international concerns. The princes were against any consideration of the idea. The cabinet's new strong man, Robert C. Wyllie, was ambivalent about annexation, except in an emergency. The remainder of the cabinet accepted it as a good course of action. The Hawaiian population was not consulted, and probably would not have understood the question.

In February of 1854, Mr. Wyllie was instructed to secretly negotiate a treaty of annexation with newly arrived United States
Commissioner David L. Greig. The Hawaiian position was:[6:9]
1) Hawaiian subjects would have all rights of American citizens,
2) admission as a state, 3) liberal support of schools, and 4) due com-
pensation to the king and chiefs. Every proposition had to be
reviewed by the privy council and Heir Designate Prince Alexander
Liholiho. The latter procrastinated as long as he could, and the negotiations were stretched out.[6:9-10]

The draft was not finalized until November–December 1854.
The final impetus was the strong rumor of a large group of filibusters
coming from California.[6:13]

·But then…King Ka-mehameha III became ill. His end was sudden and unexpected for a robust man of only 41.

Amos S. Cooke recorded in his journal on December 15,
1854:[99:430] "The king died this forenoon at 11¾ O'clk, had been sick
with inflamed lungs for about a week." This was announced to the
people by 41 minute guns being fired from the Punchbowl Battery,
the number of shots acknowledging his age. All Hawaiians soon
began wailing at the loss of their beneficent king.[128:59]

The funeral was the most impressive procession ever held in
Honolulu. It was delayed until January 10, 1855, due to great preparations and the weather. *The Polynesian* of January 13, 1855 reported:

"…at five o'clock on the morning of the 10th a signal gun was
fired from Punch Bowl Hill, which was a notice for the natives
to spread grass in all the streets through which the procession was
to pass, as the recent heavy rains had otherwise rendered the
streets impassible. In a short time the streets were covered with a
thick layer of grass, which made walking easy.

"Long before ten o'clock the natives began to gather in and
around the Palace, and at the same time the different orders, military companies, and marines from the men-of-war took their
assigned positions in the procession.

"At eleven o'clock religious services were held in the Palace,
conducted by the Rev. R. Armstrong Minister of Public
Instruction. After these were concluded, the coffin was placed
upon the car, which was heavily draped in black, having a large
black kahili at each corner. A canopy surmounted by a gilt crown
was elevated over the coffin, which was partially enveloped by
rich feather cloaks of rare workmanship. The coffin was surrounded by kahilis and other insignia of royalty in the Hawaiian Islands.

"At ten minutes of twelve A.M., the procession moved from the Palace under the direction of the Grand Marshal, His Excellency M. Kekuanaoa, Governor of Oahu.

"Through the energetic and efficient management of Mr. Parke, Marshal of the Hawaiian Kingdom, the divisions of the procession assumed their respective positions with little or no delay, and proceeded through the carpeted streets, whose sides were lined by a dense throng of spectators, while the many eligible positions on the line of march were occupied by the families of foreign residents who had assembled to witness the most imposing spectacle which ever transpired on the Hawaiian Islands.

"The Hawaiian Cavalry, uniformed in blue trimmed with red, and with chargers decked in black, formed an appropriate escort to the sable pageant. They were followed by a body of physicians and clergymen, both native and foreign; and following these were the members of the Hawaiian Chapter of Masons, in full regalia, while the Lodge of Odd Fellows, arrayed in the appropriate badges of the order came next, – the two orders presenting an attractive feature in the procession.

"The scholars of the Royal School, followed by the President and students of Oahu College, and the native and charity schools came next; all these bodies were appropriately dressed in black. The Artillery followed these with their uniforms of blue trimmed with red, their caps also being bound with red. Their cannon, enshrouded with black, seemed to have vowed to speak no more. The cannon carriages were draped in black, and every piece was decorated with four black wands surmounted by black ostrich feathers. The company did credit to themselves and their officers.

"The band of Native Hawaiians, consisting of fifteen pieces, with their drums muffled, preceded the first divisions of Hawaiian Infantry. Then came the Purveyor, household servants, and Physician of the late King.

"After this body, and preceding the funeral car, was led the black charger of his late Majesty, whose vacant saddle and empty trappings spoke feelingly of their absent lord and master.

"The car was drawn by a large company of Hawaiians, who were preceded by two large yellow kahilis, and the late King's standard draped in black.

"On each side at the foot, and at the head of the car, were carried two large green kahilis; and on the two sides were also sixteen smaller kahilis of various sizes and color.

"From the four corners of the car rose four pillars covered with black canopy, which was raised in the centre to a point upon which rested a crown. The floor of the car was covered with the ancient cloak, or quilt, of Kamehameha I., and on this rested the coffin of his Majesty Kamehameha III., which was covered with crimson velvet and decorated with armorial paintings.

"At the head of the coffin was a silver plate bearing this inscription: –

KAMEHAMEHA III.
Hanauia 17 Maraki 1813.
Make 15 Dekemaba 1854.
Ke 29 Makahiki Kona.
Noho Alii Ana.

"At the foot, and in front of the coffin, was the Royal Crown, covered with crape and resting on a velvet cushion, from the four corners of which hung handsome tassels, while over the coffin itself was thrown the feather cloak of Kamehameha I. Surrounding the car were the High Chiefs, both male and female.

"Her Majesty the Queen, her Royal Highness the Princess Victoria, and Prince Kamehameha followed in a carriage, the horses being lead by two footmen. In the next carriage came his Majesty Kamehameha IV., and John Young the Premier, their horses being led in the same manner as the previous carriage.

"The Hon. William L. Lee, Chancellor of the Kingdom, accompanied by the Cabinet of the late King, the Privy Council, and Ladies of the Court, occupied the next position, and were followed by Representatives of Foreign Nations, supported by officers of the various ships of war now in port. The judges and other Government officers were also in this section of the procession.

"The second division of Hawaiian Infantry, flanked by the Hawaiian Guard, – a body of foreign residents called into military existence by their attachment to the late King and their desire to preserve the peace of the Kingdom from lawless violence, and now uniting in this, the last earthly testimonial of respect and affection, – was followed by a body of marines from the different war-ships in port. They were led by the marines of the English ship "Trincomalee," her captain being the senior officer in port. Their uniforms of white and red contrasted pleasantly with the costume of the French marines of the ship "Eurydice," as these latter were black trimmed with white, and also of the marines of the American ship "St. Mary," her men wearing a uniform of blue and white, trimmed with red.

"Next in the line came the fire companies, and they were followed by a dense throng of Hawaiians, eight and ten deep. Among this number were the young and old, strong and weak, the infant of days, and the decrepit of years; all had come to pay their last tribute of respect and affection to the King, who bound the past to the present, and was, as it were, a part of former generations. A third division of Hawaiian Infantry brought up the rear and ended the procession.

"The procession moved from the Palace down King Street to Nuuanu, then up Nuuanu to Beretania Street. Here there had assembled a dense throng of people who, when they saw the riderless horse preceding the car that held the remains of the late King, could contain themselves no longer, but burst forth in a low, suppressed wail. The procession then proceeded with no other incident along Beretania Street to Punch Bowl Street, down Punch Bowl Street to King Street and the sepulchre. Again did the natives yield to ancient customs, and a long low wail arose from the thousands congregated here.

"Except these, nor indeed in this trace of former customs, was there anything during the day inconsistent with the utmost order and decorum.

"The procession entering the cemetery, the funeral car was drawn through the division of Hawaiian Infantry and Household Troops to the door of the sepulchre. This was followed by the High Chiefs, the Queen and her suite, the King and his suite.

"The Infantry then formed a hollow square about the sepulchre, and the remainder of the procession passed on without, the Hawaiian Guard and Foreign Marines being stationed a short space to the north and east of the tomb.

"The door of the tomb being opened, his Excellency the Rev. R. Armstrong, his Majesty's Minister of Public Instruction, offered a short and appropriate prayer, after which the Royal mourners left the cemetery.

"The troops then fired three volleys, and the High Chiefs removed the coffin of the King from the car and placed it in the centre of the tomb. This building is of stone, nicely carpeted, and contains nine coffins of adult members and three children of the Royal line. These are placed on koa frames at the northern side of the room, the entrance being on the south.

"For a few minutes the populace were permitted to look into the tomb, then the door was closed, and this was the last of the King so beloved by all his people.

"At ten minutes past two P.M., his Majesty Kamehameha IV. returned to the Palace, the Royal Standard was raised, the guns ceased firing, the bell of the stone church ceased its tolling and the procession was dismissed as it had formed."

It was estimated that there were 5,000 people in the procession and it took 45 minutes to pass a given point.

One phrase in the preceding report that catches the eye is that King Ka-mehameha III "bound the past to the present." An apt way of expressing a 29½-year reign, which stretched from the time of Ka-'ahu-manu to the constitutional Hawaiian Kingdom. William D. Alexander, respected historian, summed Ka-mehameha III in 1891:[7:279]

> "His memory will ever be dear to his people for his unselfish patriotism, for the liberal constitution which he granted them, and for the gift of the right to hold lands in fee simple. His reign will also be memorable for the unexpected progress made by the nation, and for its wonderful preservation from the many perils which beset it. While there were grave faults in his character, there were also noble traits. He loved his country and his people. He was true and steadfast in friendship. Duplicity and intrigue were foreign to his nature. He always chose men of tried integrity for responsible offices, and never betrayed secrets of state, even in his most unguarded moments."

The first order of business when Prince Alexander Liholiho ascended the throne as Ka-mehameha IV on January 11, 1855 was to terminate negotiations for annexation to the United States. It also appears that annexation would not have been acceptable to the American president and congress.[2:14] The effort was premature...its time had not come. And yet by now Hawai'i had truly joined the world and any return to the ways of the past was impossible.

RIGHT. Governor
Ke-ku-anao'a, at a
later unknown date.
(Archives of Hawaii)

BELOW. The Royal Family, 1852. Portrait by Chase. A strange title as the king
and queen had no surviving children and the younger people were the natural
issue of Ke-ku-anao'a and Kina'u. The younger were the only living grand-
children of Ka-mehameha, the king was their uncle, one had been adopted at
birth by the king and was heir designate (Alexander), the other two were heirs
presumptive to the throne and all were known by western royal titles. L to R:
Princess Victoria Ka-mamalu (14) (hereditary kuhina nui), Prince Lot Kapu-
aiwa (22) (to be King Ka-mehameha v), King Ka-mehameha III (39), Prince
Alexander Liholiho (18) (to be King Ka-mehameha IV), and Queen Kalama
(35). (Bishop Museum)

Funeral of His late Majesty Ka-mehameha III. Honolulu, January 10, 1855. Drawn and lithographed by Paul Emmert. (Series fastened on cloth, Honolulu Academy of Arts, Gift of Mrs. H. D. Penhallow, 1927 [5852])

Governor Ke-ku-anaoʻa, Grand Marshal / 1st Hawaiian Cavalry

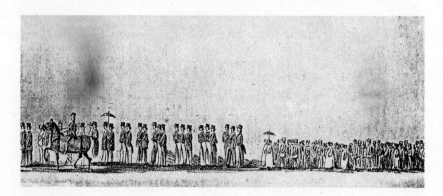

Masonic Order / schools

Sovereign's standard / kahili / catafalque

Chamberlain Abner Paki (1st carriage) Her Majesty Queen Dowager,
Her Highness Princess Victoria Ka-mamalu, His Highness Prince Lot Ka-
mehameha / Royal Standard (2nd carriage) His Majesty Ka-mehameha IV,
His Excellency Keoni Ana.

199

Funeral of His late
Majesty Ka-mehameha
III. Honolulu, January
10, 1855. Drawn and
lithographed by Paul
Emmert. (Series fas-
tened on cloth,
Honolulu Academy
of Arts, Gift of Mrs. H.
D. Penhallow, 1927
[5852])

Diplomatic Corps / Marshal W.C. Parke / Ladies of the Court

Hawaiian women

Artillerymen

Civil Officers / 1st Hawaiian Guard

EPILOGUE

HINDSIGHT CAN CONCLUDE that there were a number of significant impacts which generated the rapid Hawaiian evolution from Polynesian feudalism to a stage where the islands joined the western world's civilization.

Early contacts with westerners, commencing with Captain Cook in 1778, startled the long-isolated Hawaiians. They knew from their traditions that people like themselves lived on islands far across the sea to the south, from where their ancestors had come. These white men were different, and came from some large place elsewhere far over the horizon where there were many more people than Hawaiians. These visitors had such marvelous large ships and things, especially iron tools. Hawaiian coveted western goods as rarities and improvements over what they had.

At first the chiefs cautiously accepted these white men with interest, curiosity and esteem. Although communications were difficult, this contact had a tremendous impact on Hawaiian beliefs, ideas and thinking. Ruling chiefs tolerated the westerners who did not know and did not venerate Hawaiian gods or comply with the kapu (forbidden). And they came to no psychic harm! Something was very wrong! Were not the Hawaiian gods and kapu for all men, as their lore stated?

The ali'i, chiefs and chiefesses, who had imposed their will and way over the previous Polynesian inhabitants, held fast to the veneration of their gods and compliance with the kapu system – despite the noncomplying white men. However, serious and surreptitious questioning began, heretical and soul searching. Why was the Hawaiian way of life applicable only to them? And...other ways of life seemed to provide a better standard of living and possessions for these other people!

When Ka-mehameha the Conqueror died in 1819, these fester-
ing questions came to a head. It took tremendous and apprehensive
courage for his successor ruler, regent and high chiefs to overthrow
their generations-old belief in their false gods and abolish the inter-
twining kapu. Abruptly there were two voids:

– RELIGIOUS. Formal veneration of the gods at the temples
ceased, images were destroyed, and Hawaiian spiritual beliefs began
to wither.

– SECULAR. The kapu, disciplines which had been uniformly
enforced, became fragmented and administered by various chiefs as
they saw fit.

Chaos ensued. Add to this the estimated halving of population
from 300,000 at the time of Captain Cook to Ka-mehameha's death,
due primarily to intruded diseases – and one finds considerable
depression and bewilderment among the people.

The American Protestant missionaries arrived four months after
the overthrow of the Hawaiian religion – most fortunate timing.
They were initially accepted on a year's trial basis, proved themselves
concerned only with the welfare of Hawaiians, and were permitted
to remain.

They were successful with their original emphasis on evangelizing
Hawaiian leaders. Three decades later over a quarter of the people
were church members, and twice as many more attended their
Christian teachings and services.

One must recognize that it took great effort, time and concentration to become fluent in Hawaiian – so the missionaries could
preach adequately. A great tribute must be paid to them for reducing
spoken Hawaiian to written words. They printed numerous lessons
and texts, a dictionary, and eventually translated and printed the
Bible. With the impetus provided by Queen Regent Ka-'ahu-manu,
the adult population was taught to read and write their own language. Hawaiians became as literate as Americans in remarkably few
years. A magnificent accomplishment.

The missionaries were trusted by Hawaiian leaders and became
influential advisors and interpreters, most useful in dealing with
white men. They also became very unpopular with entrepreneur
traders, mostly fellow Americans, because they deplored the exploita-
tion of Hawaiian chiefs who coveted almost any foreign goods no
matter how frivolous.

The Hawaiian Islands were a convenient stopping place for ships in the northern Pacific Ocean. First came the fur traders who bought pelts in the northwest and took them to China for lucrative sales. Sandalwood was discovered in the islands which was also in high demand in China. The chiefs were paid for the fragrant wood with western and oriental goods. They were not good trade-balance managers and most fell into constant debt to the traders. When sandalwood was depleted, many transient whaleships, mostly American, began to come to the islands twice a year.

Hawai'i provided these visiting ships with water, food, firewood…and recreation. The establishment of a western mercantile class and local craftsmen capable of ship repair began mainly at the good harbor of Honolulu. Some white men started to farm when they could obtain land leases. The major impact of these visiting ships was that Hawaiians began to "grow and gather" for sale to foreigners, as well as continuing self-subsistence and supporting their chiefs by paying taxes in the form of food and labor. Commoners, who lived under serf-like conditions, began to leave the land and perform "free labor" as workmen for ships. This influx brought both good and evil, and established a western-style economy within the Hawaiian agrarian society.

The Puritan moral code of the missionaries was slowly accepted by the chiefs, and the commoners followed. Dress became less scanty and clothed the entire body. Marriage was formalized, and having multiple husbands and wives was deplored. Incest to improve a bloodline was absolutely forbidden. Yesteryear's hysteria and sacrifices upon the death of a high chief were replaced with a solemn Christian service and public burial. Fornication and "sleeping around" were discouraged. Drinking and drunkenness were looked upon with scorn. The abolishment of the kapu had already favorably changed family life: men and women could now eat together, and women could enjoy food that had been forbidden.

When Ka-mehameha died in 1819, he was succeeded by Liholiho, his designated son of the highest lineage, with Dowager Queen Ka-'ahu-manu as Regent with co-ruler powers. The ali'i became restless in the absence of a strong hand, and the government was only able to continue with shrewd concessions.

Liholiho was in England on a quixotic visit to his brother sovereign when he died in 1824. His younger brother, Kau-i-ke-aouli, became ruler as Kamehameha III the following year, with the strong

Ka-'ahu-manu continuing as Regent co-ruler. When she passed away in 1832, the king began to make his own way with continuing difficulties from his divided chiefs.

Rev. William Richards joined the government in 1838 as advisor and teacher. Due to his efforts, a Declaration of Rights was proclaimed the following year and a Constitutional Monarchy was promulgated in 1840. The feudal rule of the islands under Ka-mehameha the Conqueror had evolved. For the first time all Hawaiians had a say in their government.

A major difficulty for the fledgling kingdom was that British, French and American consuls loudly demanded favorable treatment of their subjects or citizens in the islands. They were backed up with "gunboat diplomacy" by their visiting warships. It was decided to send Rev. Richards and the king's secretary to Washington, London and Paris in 1842 to secure recognition of the Hawaiian kingdom's independence. Missionary Dr. Gerrit P. Judd joined the government and became a strong advisor. The envoys were eventually successful, despite the complications of a five-month occupation by a British frigate and provisional cession of the islands to Great Britain in 1843.

Land was power on an island, as commoners worked the land for the chief who was allocated control of that area by the island's high chief. The Great Mahele, the land division of 1847–1855, assigned 1.6 million acres to the chiefs, 1.5 million acres to the kingdom, almost 1 million acres to the crown, and some 30,000 acres to commoners. It is debatable whether the commoners were properly advised by the chiefs, as the award of a parcel of land relinquished control of the recipient from the landlord chief of the area. However this may be, it was done and there was fee simple ownership of land.

What of Ke-ku-anao'a, whom we have traced through these evolving events? His Hawaiian Gazette obituary some years later read: "He has in his own person seen this transition between two of the extreme phases of human life – and has done himself honor in all the situations in which he has been placed..."

In final summation, did the Hawaiians join the world? Yes, indeed. Their leaders were able to control their own destiny in this great evolution. There were lots of pressures. Yes, there were some good strong men and advisors, but final decisions were made by the Hawaiian rulers. History speaks for itself...

ભ PAU ઇ

Appendix 1

KE-KU-ANAO'A GENEOLOGY

Male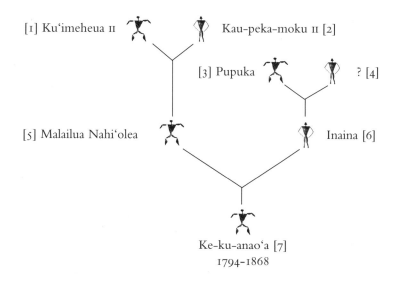

Female

[1] Ku'imeheua II   Kau-peka-moku II [2]

[3] Pupuka   ? [4]

[5] Malailua Nahi'olea   Inaina [6]

Ke-ku-anao'a [7]
1794-1868

[1]   Cousin of Ke-kau-like, ruler of Maui. (Kamakau. *Tales and Traditions...* p.16. Fornander. II p.223n.)

[2]   Ali'i family I of Hilo, Hawai'i. She had two other sons by different husbands: Ka'i-ana (descended from Keawe, ruler of Hawai'i) and Na-makeha' (descended from Maui ruler.) (Fornander. II pp.222, 223n. Miller. *"Ka'iana..."* HJH Vol 22 [1985]. Barrere. *The King's Mahele...* p.352.)

[3]   Prominent O'ahu Chief. (Fornander. II p.223n. Kame'eleihiwa. *Native Lands...* p.266.)

[4]   ? Family of Kahus of Ka-mehameha I, lived at Keokea, Honaunau, Hawai'i ? (*PC Advertiser* Nov. 28, 1868 Obituary.)

[5]   Warrior chief with Ka-mehameha who defected en route O'ahu and killed at Battle of Nu'uanu April–May 1795. (Fornander. II p.348. Ii. *Fragments...* p.146)

[6]   Son Ke-ku-anao'a born on visit to Hilo, Hawai'i Jan. 9, 1794. (Fornander. II p.223n. Ii. *Fragments...* p.146)

[7]   Governor of O'ahu. Father of Kings Ka-mehameha IV and V.

KE-KU-ANAO'A
WIVES & ISSUE

Appendix 2

1 Ka-lehua. "wife since the time of Ka-mehameha." Issue: son Pa'a-lua. (Kamakau. *Ruling Chiefs* 347)

2 Kauahi. Daughter of Mailou. She was his wife when he went to England in 1823. (Barrere. *King's Mahele* 352)

3 Pauahi. Daughter of Pauli Ka-'o-lei-o-ku, first-born son of Ka-mehameha. (Kame'eleihiwa. *Native Land* 231) Married November 28, 1825. Died June 17, 1826. Issue: (Princess) Ruth Ke-eli-kulani. (Ii. *Fragments* 147)

4 Kina'u. Daughter of Ka-mehameha. (Kame'eleihiwa. *Native Land* 101) Married September 19, 1827. (Ii. *Fragments* 150) Died April 4, 1839. (Kamakau. *Ruling Chiefs* 348) Issue:
   1 David Ka-mehameha (1828-1835)
   2 Moses Ke-ku-aiwa (1829-1848)
   3 Lot Kapu-aiwa (Ka-mehameha v) (1830-1872)
   4 Alexander Liholiho (Ka-mehameha iv) (1834-1863)
   5 Victoria Ka-mamalu (1838-1866)

5 Ka-lolo. "A very pretty girl of about 15." Married August 24, 1845. She died December 29, 1849. (Barrere. *King's Mahele* 192)

208

KINA'U RELATIONSHIPS

Male
Female

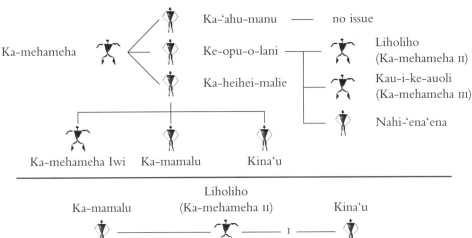

Ka-mehameha

Ka-'ahu-manu —— no issue

Ke-opu-o-lani —— Liholiho (Ka-mehameha II)

Ka-heihei-malie —— Kau-i-ke-auoli (Ka-mehameha III)

Nahi-'ena'ena

Ka-mehameha Iwi   Ka-mamalu   Kina'u

Ka-mamalu   Liholiho (Ka-mehameha II)   Kina'u

—— I ——

no issue   no issue

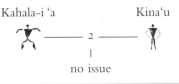

Kahala-i 'a   Kina'u

—— 2 ——

no issue

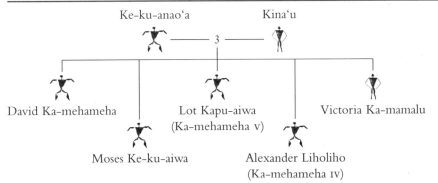

Ke-ku-anao'a   Kina'u

—— 3 ——

David Ka-mehameha   Lot Kapu-aiwa (Ka-mehameha V)   Victoria Ka-mamalu

Moses Ke-ku-aiwa   Alexander Liholiho (Ka-mehameha IV)

BIBLIOGRAPHY

1 ADLER, JACOB (ED.) *The Journal of Prince Alexander Liholiho...* Honolulu: The University of Hawaii Press, 1967

2 ALDEN, CARROLL S. *Lawrence Kearny: Sailor Diplomat.* Princeton: Princeton University Press, 1936

3 ALEXANDER, JAMES M. *Mission Life in Hawaii, Memoir of Rev. William P. Alexander.* Oakland: Pacific Press, 1888

4 ALEXANDER, MARY C. *William Patterson Alexander...* Honolulu: 1934

5 ALEXANDER, WILLIAM D. *"A Sketch of the Constitutional History of the Hawaiian Kingdom."* The Hawaiian Annual (1894)

6 ALEXANDER, WILLIAM D. *"An Account of the Uncompleted Treaty of Annexation..."* Hawaiian Historical Society Papers No. 9 (1897)

7 ALEXANDER, WILLIAM D. *A Brief History of the Hawaiian People.* 2nd edn NY: American Book Co., 1899

8 ALEXANDER, WILLIAM D. *"The Story of Cleopatra's Barge."* Hawaiian Historical Society Papers No. 13 (1906)

9 ALEXANDER, WILLIAM D. *"Overthrow of the Ancient Tabu System in the Hawaiian Islands."* 25th Annual Report of the Hawaiian Historical Society (1917)

10 ALLEN, GWENFREAD E. *"Kaahumanu, A Study."* The Friend, June 1915

11 ANDERSON, REV. RUFUS. *The Hawaiian Islands...* Boston: Gould & Lincoln, 1864

12 ARAGO, JACQUES. *Narrative of a Voyage Round the World... 1817–1820.* London: Treuttel & Wertz, 1823

13 BAKER, RAY J. *Honolulu in 1853.* Honolulu; Ray J. Baker, 1950

14 BARRERE, DOROTHY B. *The King's Mahele...* Ms Honolulu: 1994

15 (BATES, GEORGE W.) *A Haole. Sandwich Island Notes.* NY: Harper & Brothers, 1854

16 BELCHER, SIR EDWARD. *Narrative of a Voyage...* 2 vols Vol 1 London: Henry Colburn, 1843

17 BINGHAM, HIRAM. *A Residence of Twenty-one Years in the Sandwich Islands...* NY: Sherman Converse, 1847

18 BISHOP, SERENO E. *Reminiscences of Old Hawaii.* Honolulu: Hawaiian Gazette Co., Ltd., 1916

19 BLOXAM, ANDREW. *Diary of...* (BPB Mus Sp Pub 10) Honolulu: Published by the Museum, 1925

20 BOOTHBY, H.E. *"Up From Idoltry."* Hawaiian Almanac and Annual 1920

21 U.S. SLOOP OF WAR BOSTON LOG. National Archives (RG 24)

22 BRADLEY, HAROLD W. *The American Frontier in Hawaii...* Stanford: University Press, 1942

23 BRITISH COMMISSION MINUTE BOOK. Archives of Hawaii

24 BROOKES, JEAN I. *International Rivalry in the Pacific Islands 1800–1875.* Berkeley: University of California Press, 1941

25 BRYAN, W.D. *Natural History of Hawaii.* Honolulu: The Hawaiian Gazette Co., Ltd., 1915

26 CARTER, SYBIL A. *Kaahumanu, A Memorial.* Ph Honolulu: R. Grieve, 1893

27 H.M.S. CARYSFORT LOG. British Public Record Office (Adm 51/3714)

28 CASTLE, W.R. *"Centennial Reminiscences."* 28th Annual Report of the Hawaiian Historical Society (1919)

29 CHAMBERLAIN, LEVI. *Journal...* Ms Hawaiian Mission Children's Society

30 CHEEVER, REV. HENRY T. *The Island World of the Pacific.* NY: Harper & Brothers, 1851

31 CHINEN, JON J. *The Great Mahele...* Ph Honolulu: The University Press of Hawaii, 1958

32 THE CIVIL CODE of the Hawaiian Islands 1859

33 CLARK, T. BLAKE. *"Honolulu's Streets."* Hawaiian Historical Society Papers No. 20 (1939)

34 CORRESPONDENCE RELATIVE TO THE SANDWICH ISLANDS. Gov't Pub London: Foreign Office, 1843–44

35 CUMMINGS, C.F. GORDON. *Fire Fountains...* 2 vols Vol I London: William Blackwood & Sons, 1885

36 DAWS, GAVIN. *"The High Chief Boki..."* The Journal of the Polynesian Society, Vol 75 No. 1 (March 1966)

37 DAWS, GAVIN. *Shoal of Time...* NY: The Macmillan Co., 1968

38 DIBBLE, SHELDON. *History of the Sandwich Islands.* Lahainaluna: Press of the Mission Seminary, 1843

39 DOLE, SANFORD B. *"Evolution of Land Tenures."* Hawaiian Historical Society Papers No. 3 (1892)

40 ELWES, ROBERT. *Sketcher's Tour Round the World.* 2nd edn London: Hurst & Blackett, 1854

41 EMERSON, N.B. *"The Honolulu Fort."* 8th Annual Report of the Hawaiian Historical Society (1960)

42 EMERSON, OLIVER P. *Pioneer Days in Hawaii.* NY: Doubleday, Doran & Co., 1928

43 FORNANDER, ABRAHAM. *An Account of the Polynesian Race...* 3 vols Vol III London: Trubner & Co., 1880

44 FRANKENSTEIN, ALFRED. *The Royal Visitors.* Ph Portland: Oregon Historical Society, 1963

45 FREAR, MARY D. *Lowell and Abigail.* New Haven: 1934

46 FREYCINET, CAPT. LOUIS. *Account of a Voyage Around the World in the French ship l'Uranie.* (Translation of the portion relating to the Hawaiian Islands is in the Archives of Hawaii.)

47 GAST, ROSS H. *Don Francisco de Paula Marin.* Honolulu: The University Press of Hawaii, 1973

48 GAST, ROSS H. *Contentious Consul, A Biography of John Coffin Jones.* Los Angeles: Dawson's Book Store, 1976

49 GILMAN. G.D. *"Restoration Day: A Recollection."* Hawaiian Almanac and Annual 1893

50 (GRAHAM, MARIA) *Capt. The Right Hon. Lord Byron. Voyage of H.M.S. Blonde to the Sandwich Islands in the Years 1824–1825.* London: John Murray, 1826

51 GREER, RICHARD A. *"Oahu's Ordeal..."* Hawaii Historical Review. Honolulu: Hawaiian Historical Society, 1969

52 GREER, RICHARD A. *"Honolulu in 1838."* The Hawaiian Journal of History, Vol XI (1977)

53 HALFORD, DR. FRANCIS J. *9 Doctors and God.* Honolulu: University of Hawaii, 1954

54 HANDY, E.S.C. *"Government and Society" "Religion and Education." Ancient Hawaiian Civilization.* Honolulu: Kamehameha Schools, 1933

55 HAWAIIAN REPORTS II OF THE SUPREME COURT *(Oni vs Meek)* 1858. Honolulu: Government Press, 1866

56 "HISTORY OF HAWAII, Written by Scholars of the High School and Corrected by One of the Instructors." The Hawaiian Spectator, Vol 2 No. 2 (1839)

57 HOPKINS, MANLEY. *Hawaii, the Past, Present and Future of its Island Kingdom.* London: Longman, Green, Longman & Roberts, 1862

58 II, JOHN PAPA. *Fragments of Hawaiian History.* Bishop Museum Press, 1959

59 INSTRUCTIONS OF THE PRUDENTIAL COMMITTEE OF THE AMERICAN BOARD OF COMMISSIONERS FOR FOREIGN MISSIONS TO THE SANDWICH ISLANDS. Lahainaluna: Press of the Mission Seminary, 1838

60 JARVES, JAMES J. *History of the Hawaiian or Sandwich Islands.* Boston: Tappan & Denney, 1843

61 (JOERGER, PAULINE K. ED) *Robert Dampier. To the Sandwich Islands on H.M.S. Blonde.* Honolulu: The University Press of Hawaii, 1971

62 JOHNSON, DONALD D. *"Powers in the Pacific: Tahiti and Hawaii, 1825–1850."* 66th Annual Report of the Hawaiian Historical Society (1958)

63 JOHNSTONE, ARTHUR. *"Storied Nuuanu."* The Hawaiian Annual 1908

64 JUDD, BERNICE. *"William Richards' Report to the Sandwich Islands Mission on His First Year in Government Service 1838–39."* 51st Annual Report of the Hawaiian Historical Society (1943)

65 JUDD, BERNICE. *Voyages to Hawaii Before 1860.* (Revised from 1929 edn) Honolulu: University Press of Hawaii, 1974

66 JUDD, DR. GERRIT P. *Journal* (time of 1843 Paulet Affair) Typescript in Archives of Hawaii

67 JUDD, DR. GERRIT P. *Journals 1830–32.* Fragments IV, 1928

68 JUDD, GERRIT P. IV. *Dr. Judd, Hawaii's Friend.* Honolulu: University of Hawaii Press, 1960

69 JUDD, LAURA FISH. *Honolulu, Sketches of Life...* NY: Anson D.F. Randolph & Co., 1880

70 KAMAKAU, SAMUEL M. *Ruling Chiefs of Hawaii.* Honolulu: Kamehameha Schools Press, 1961

71 KAMAKAU, SAMUEL M. *Ka Po'e Kahiko, The People of Old.* (BPB Mus Sp Pub 51) Honolulu: Bishop Museum Press, 1964

72 KAME'ELEIHIWA, LILIKALA. *Native Land and Foreign Desires...* Honolulu: Bishop Museum Press, 1992

73 KELLY, ANTOINETTE. *Liholiho, His Life and Reign.* Ms 1924 University of Hawaii Library, Hawaiian

74 KING, PAULINE (ED.) *Journal of Stephen Reynolds.* Honolulu: Ku Pa'a Inc., 1989

75 VON KOTZEBUE, CAPT. OTTO. *Voyage of Discovery in the South Seas.* London: Sir Richard Phillips & Co., 1821

76 KUYKENDALL, RALPH S. *"Historical Notes."* 40th Annual Report of the Hawaiian Historical Society (1932)

77 KUYKENDALL, RALPH S. *The Hawaiian Kingdom 1778–1854...* Honolulu: University of Hawaii, 1938

78 KUYKENDALL, RALPH S. *"Constitutions of the Hawaiian Kingdom."* Hawaiian Historical Society Papers No. 21 (1940)

79 LEE, W.S. *The Islands.* NY: Holt, Rinehart & Winston, 1966

80 LYDGATE, JOHN M. *"Ka-umu-alii, the Last King of Kauai."* 24th Annual Report of the Hawaiian Historical Society (1915)

81 LYONS, C.J. *"Land Matters in Hawaii."* 52nd Cong 2nd Sess House of Representatives Ex Doc 47 (1893)

82 MACRAE, JAMES. *With Lord Byron at the Sandwich Islands in 1825.* Ph Honolulu: William F. Wilson, 1922

83 MALO, DAVID. *Hawaiian Antiquities.* (BPB Mus Sp Pub 2) 2nd edn Honolulu: Museum, 1951

84 MILLER, DAVID G. *"Ka'iana the Once Famous Prince of Kaua'i."* The Hawaiian Journal of History, Vol 22 (1988)

85 MISSIONARY ALBUM. Honolulu: Hawaiian Mission Children's Society, 1969

86 MONTGOMERY, JAMES (Comp) *Journal of Voyages and Travel by Rev. Daniel Tyerman and George Bennet Esq.* 2 vols Vol I London: Frederick Westley & A.B. Davis, 1831

87 MORGAN, THEODORE. *Hawaii, A Century of Economic Change 1778–1876.* Cambridge: Harvard University Press, 1948

88 MORRELL, WILLIAM P. *Britain in the Pacific Islands.* Oxford: Clarendon Press, 1960

89 PARKE, WILLIAM C. *Personal Reminiscences…* Cambridge: Printed at the University Press, 1891

90 PASKE-SMITH, M. *"Early British Consuls in Hawaii."* Mid-Pacific Magazine Oct–Dec 1936

91 PATY, CAPTAIN WILLIAM. *Journal.* Archives of Hawaii

92 PAULDING, LT. HIRAM. *Journal of a Cruise of the United States Dolphin…* Honolulu: University of Hawaii Press, 1970

93 PETERSON, CHARLES E. *"The Iolani Palaces and the Barracks."* Journal of the Society of Architectural Historians, May 1963

94 PIERCE, RICHARD A. *Russia's Hawaiian Adventure 1815–1817.* Berkeley: University of California Press, 1965

95 PLEADWELL, FRANK L. *The voyage to England of King Liholiho and Queen Kamamalu.* Essay read at the 71st Meeting of the Social Science Association (June 2, 1952)

96 *Report of the Proceedings and Evidence in the Arbitration Between the King and Government of the Hawaiian Islands and Messrs. Ladd & Co.* Honolulu: Government Press, 1846

97 *Report of the Minister of Foreign Relations, Hawaiian Kingdom, 1855.* Archives of Hawaii

98 RICHARDS, MARY A. *The Hawaiian Chiefs' Children's School.* Rutland: Charles E. Tuttle Co., 1970

99 RICHARDS, MARY A. *Amos Starr Cooke and Juliette Montague Cooke.* 2nd edn Honolulu: The Daughters of Hawaii, 1987

100 (RICHARDS, REV. WILLIAM) *Memoir of Keopuolani, Late Queen of the Sandwich Islands.* Boston: Crocker & Brewster, 1825

101 (RICHARDS, REV. WILLIAM) *Translation of the Constitution and Laws of the Hawaiian Islands Established in the Reign of Kamehameha III.* Lahainaluna: 1842 (Reprint by Ted Adameck, 1994)

102 RICHARDS, REV. WILLIAM. *Journal (1843–44)* Ms Archives of Hawaii

103 SAHLINS, MARSHALL. *Anahulu…* 2 vols Vol I Chicago: The University of Chicago Press, 1992

104 SCHAEFER, JOSEPH. *"Letters of Sir George Simpson 1841–1843."* The American Historical Review, Vol XIV. London: The Macmillan Co., 1909

105 SCHMITT, ROBERT C. *Demographic Statistics of Hawaii 1778–1965.* Honolulu: University of Hawaii Press, 1968

106 SCHMITT, ROBERT C. *"Religious Statistics of Hawaii 1825–1972."* The Hawaiian Journal of History, Vol XI (1973)

107 *Senate Executive Documents 52nd Cong 2nd Sess No. 57*

108 *Senate Executive Documents 52nd Cong 2nd Sess No. 77*

109 SIMPSON, ALEXANDER. *The Sandwich Islands…* London: Smith, Elder & Co., 1843

110 SIMPSON, SIR GEORGE. *Narrative of a Journey Round the World.* 2 vols Vol II London: Henry Colburn, 1847

III   SIMPSON, SIR GEORGE. *London Correspondence Inward From...1841–1842.* London:The Hudson's Bay Record Society, 1973

112   SINCLAIR, MARJORIE. *Nahi'ena'ena...* Honolulu:The University of Hawaii Press, 1976

113   SMITH, BRADFORD. *Yankees in Paradise.* Philadelphia:J.B. Lippincott Co., 1956

114   SPAULDING, THOMAS M. *"Early Years of the Hawaiian Legislature."* 38th Annual Report of the Hawaiian Historical Society (1930)

115   STEEGMULLER, FRANCIS. *The Two Lives of James Jackson Jarves.* New Haven: Yale University Press, 1951

116   STEVENS, SYLVESTER K. *American Expansion of Hawaii 1842–1898.* Harrisburg:Archives Publishing Co., 1945

117   STEWART, REV. CHARLES S. *A Residence in the Sandwich Islands.* 5th edn Boston:Weeks, Jordan & Co., 1839

118   STEWART, REV. CHARLES S. *A Visit to the South Seas...* 2 vols Vol II NY: John P. Haven, 1831

119   STOKES, J.F.G. *"New Bases for Hawaiian Chronology."* 41st Annual Report of the Hawaiian Historical Society (1932)

120   SULLIVAN, JOSEPHINE. *A History of C. Brewer & Co...* Boston:Walton, 1926

121   THOMAS, REAR ADMIRAL RICHARD. *Journal of the Proceedings of...* 1st April 1843 to 26 November 1845. British Public Record Office (Adm 50/229)

122   THRUM, THOMAS G. *"Notes on the History of the Sugar Industry..."* Hawaiian Almanac and Annual for 1875

123   THRUM, THOMAS G. *"Notes on the History of Coffee Culture..."* Hawaiian Almanac and Annual for 1876

124   THRUM, THOMAS G. *"History of the Provisional Cession of the Hawaiian Islands and Their Restoration."* Hawaiian Almanac and Annual 1893

125   THRUM, THOMAS G. *"Hawaiian Epidemics."* Hawaiian Annual 1897

126   THRUM, THOMAS G. *"An Historical Residence."* The Hawaiian Almanac and Annual 1897

127   THRUM, THOMAS G. *"Honolulu Sixty Years Ago."* The Hawaiian Annual 1914

128   THRUM, THOMAS G. *"Honolulu Sixty Years Ago."* The Hawaiian Annual 1915

129   THRUM, THOMAS G. *"Centennial Chronology of the Hawaiian Mission."* 28th Annual Report of the Hawaiian Historical Society (1919)

130   THRUM, THOMAS G. *"When Sailors Ruled the Town."* Hawaiian Almanac and Annual 1921

131   THRUM, THOMAS G. *"Heiaus (Temples) of Hawaii Nei."* 32nd Annual Report of the Hawaiian Historical Society (1923)

132   THURSTON, LORRIN A. *The Fundamental Law of Hawaii.* Honolulu:The Hawaiian Gazette Co., 1904

133 THURSTON, LUCY. *Life and Times of...* Ann Arbor: S.C. Andrews, 1882

134 WALSH, CRAIG W. *The Forgotten Chapter.* Ms 1970 University of Hawaii Library, Hawaiian

135 WARFIELD, CHARLES L. *History of the Hawaii National Guard...*Master's Thesis, 1935 University of Hawaii

136 WESTERVELT, W.D. *"Hawaiian Printed Laws Before the Constitution."* 16th Annual Report of the Hawaiian Historical Society (1909)

137 WESTERVELT, W.D. *"The First Twenty One Years of Education in the Hawaiian Islands."* 19th Annual Report of the Hawaiian Historical Society (1912)

138 WIGHT, ELIZABETH L. *The Memoirs of Elizabeth Kinau Wilder.* Honolulu: Paradise of the Pacific Press, 1909

139 WILKES, CHARLES. *Narrative of the United States Exploring Expedition...* 5 vols Vols III & IV Philadelphia: Lea and Blanchard, 1845

140 WISE, HENRY A. *Los Gringos...* London: Richard Bentley, 1849

141 WISE, JOHN H. *"The History of Land Ownership in Hawaii."* Ancient Hawaiian Civilization. Honolulu: The Kamehameha Schools, 1933

142 YZENDOORN, FR. REGINALD. *History of the Catholic Mission in the Hawaiian Islands.* Honolulu: Honolulu Star-Bulletin, 1927

INDEX